THE ULTIMATE ULTIMATUM

Terry Zufelt

THE ULTIMATE ULTIMATUM

Our Final Destination Depends on the Choice We Make

iUniverse, Inc.
Bloomington

The Ultimate Ultimatum
Our Final Destination Depends on the Choice We Make

iUniverse books may be ordered through booksellers or by contacting:

iUniverse
1663 Liberty Drive
Bloomington, IN 47403
www.iuniverse.com
1-800-Authors (1-800-288-4677)

ISBN: 978-1-4759-7270-2 (sc)
ISBN: 978-1-4759-7272-6 (hc)
ISBN: 978-1-4759-7271-9 (ebk)

Library of Congress Control Number: 2013901368

Printed in the United States of America

iUniverse rev. date: 02/21/2013

CONTENTS

ACKNOWLEGEMENT

When Kelli and I were struggling to have children (we have three wonderful girls) and we had become quite desperate to have a child I prayed to God. I prayed that I would do something to honor who He is and how awesome He is if He would give us a child. I thought maybe I would carve a cross at the entrance to our drive way or something symbolic like that. Upon the completion of the Ultimate Ultimatum I prayed: God I was not capable of writing this book, thank you! May it honor who You are and how great You are. If the Ultimate Ultimatum steers one person towards the light it will have been worth it!

Your servant, Terry

INTRODUCTION

The Mission

The Gates of Hell will Not Prevail! The Gates of Hell will Not Prevail! The first twenty-nine years of my life I did not hear those words a single time. But for the last sixteen years, those words have been my rallying call while on my journey.

I am not so far removed from the days when I was locked behind the gates of hell that I cannot recall the torture I experienced. I know if I look hard enough over my shoulder I will be able to see the fence that kept me captive for so many years.

I managed to escape and I have found myself on an awesome journey. After escaping from hell I found this small gate and after entering through the gate I found myself on this narrow road. I am running down this road putting as much distance as I can between hell and myself. I do not have a clear picture of what is ahead of me but I know the destination, Jesus! I know hell is behind me but the road in front of me is relatively unknown.

The further away I get from Satan's domain the less I see of the bars of hell. The shadows are not able to cast as far. I am gaining confidence with every step forward. I do not ever want to go back. I want to get as far away as I can from Satan's prison.

The road I am traveling on goes up, down, and has exits and on-ramps. My life didn't instantly become perfect when I entered through the gate but life did become easier and now my life has meaning.

I still face trials and tribulations but these trials and tribulations are followed by periods of growth. As I overcome these trials and tribulations, the road becomes straighter and even narrower. The narrower the road becomes the more I am able to keep my eyes fixed on the prize, Jesus. I know God will not give me more than I can handle.

I know I am not alone on this journey. In fact, there are many people on a journey similar to mine. The journey is different for every one of us but the direction and goal is the same. We are heading towards Jesus so we can experience eternal life with our heavenly Father.

The further I get down the road the more I realize that there are people who need to be rescued from hell. I begin to ask myself if I have a responsibility to help rescue some of these people who are still being held captive. Something within me quickly affirms that I do have a role.

Who are these others who need rescued? They may be people I have never met or people I know and love.

I do not get to choose who I get to rescue. God has already chosen these people. Maybe it will be a family member or a complete stranger. God may choose a Muslim or even an Atheist. God is not a respecter of people. This means He does not show partiality. My part requires action and obedience.

There will be missed opportunities to rescue souls. Rescue missions are not easy. If they were, everybody would be in the heavenly kingdom and the enemy would have no prisoners of war.

There are the missions where I get scared. I lack confidence and or wisdom to complete the mission. Other times I change the mission God had for me. I think to myself, "not that one this one." What does it matter as long as I am on a mission? God will not mind if I seek to compromise. Not true! A mission without God's vision fails.

Some missions I get so close. Other missions I never get started, I abort before I begin.

There are missions where casualties occur. During my attempt to rescue someone I go the wrong direction or down a path that was booby-trapped. It is my fault people stumble and are recaptured. I ask the Lord for forgiveness while anticipating my next opportunity for a chance at success.

There are missions when everything is going according to plan. The rescue is close to complete, but the enemy counter-attacks and manages to grab the prisoner again. They were so close but a little stumble, a little trip along the path, and they fell back into the hands of the enemy.

I may be wounded in my attempt to rescue someone, but I refuse to be captured. I know what hell is. The training I am receiving that comes from reading the Word and praying to God has rewarded me with wisdom. I understand who I am. I am a child of the Most High God.

There are times when the mission is completed. The rescue is successful and the persons are free. They are in the light looking for the opportunities God has for them but the relentless often-subtle attacks from the enemy begin to weigh on them. They are wounded in battle and lack the strength to continue. Unfortunately, they are captured again. I can hear the black gates close behind them. These are the cases where I am left to wonder why, what went wrong, how could this happen?

There are people who do not want to be rescued. These are the tough ones. I ask myself why? Why do they not want to be rescued? They believe life is good. They are content now but why are they choosing eternal hell? Do they not know hell is forever?

Then there are the times when everything lines up. God's plan, His wisdom, our faith, our boldness, no fear, and souls are saved never to be imprisoned again. They see the light and begin to run towards it. They know in their heart of hearts they never have to live in hell again. They realize they never have to go back behind the steel dark bars of hell.

They realize they have gained compassion for those who are still lost and they know there is more to their journey. They have been commissioned to go on their own rescue mission. They seek tirelessly for God's wisdom so they can become equipped for their new mission.

The Ultimate Ultimatum is about my testimony and what I have discovered while on my journey. God kept encouraging me to put my journey on paper. I did not have to ask why, I knew the answer. God has given me a testimony to inspire those who are looking to be rescued or those who are looking to rescue others.

I am excited to share my journey with you. Sharing my journey is not something I ever imagined I would do but when God encourages us to do something we should not lean on our own understanding but be obedient. God has truly brought me out of the miry clay and put my feet upon the Rock. I will trust the Holy Spirit to take me through this new journey.

So many of us are satisfied with just wondering through life. We fail to focus and reach for the "Promised Land." The Israelites had to walk around the desert for forty years before they entered the land God had promised them. God had promised them a land through their ancestor Abraham. It was a land of bountifulness. Grapes so big they had to carry them on poles. Their disobedience and lack of faith kept them from receiving the good things God had in store for them.

Instead of trusting God, the Israelites decided they knew best. They complained and became rebellious. As a result of their rebellion, they had to wander through the desert for forty years, enduring tough times. In fact, if we look at the story in Exodus more closely, we learn that nobody from the original generation under twenty years of age, except for Caleb and Joshua, were allowed into the Promised Land. Joshua and Caleb were the only two who trusted God. If God said it was to be their land then that was all the assurance they needed.

Like the Israelites I did my fair share of wondering in the desert. God took me through the Red Sea and I am doing my best to lean on Him. I know I cannot walk through this life without His presence in my life. None of us can.

The Lord gave me a wonderful vision before I started writing the Ultimate Ultimatum. The vision was very clear. There were bars casting shadows over a beautiful green field that had a road right down the middle. It was bright outside, a perfect summer day, but pitch dark behind the bars. There were no gates in the vision just steel bars.

I was lost and spent many years behind his bars, inside his prison. I had no understanding of God, Jesus, or the Bible. I thought I was living a good life. I was sowing lots of seed. But it was not good seed. I was living in the world and the devil probably thought we would be partners for eternity. I was all flesh and executing the devil's game plan to perfection while taking people down with me.

The bars that held me hostage were thick, tall, and black. No light seemed to be able to penetrate this area. It was as dark as a full lunar eclipse. I did not even realize where I was until I escaped. I was on earth but in hell. Alcatraz would have been a vacation compared to this place.

Alcatraz of course was the island that served as the infamous maximum-security prison for notorious Mafia criminals and high-risk convicts. Before 1934, Alcatraz was controlled by the U.S. military, but in that year it shifted to the Department of Justice, which had found itself ill-equipped to deal with the violent criminals who emerged after the Great Depression.

Alcatraz Island is located one mile from shore and surrounded by the frigid water of the San Francisco Bay. The legendary myths of man-eating sharks in the bay are just that-myths.

A leading security expert was commissioned to design a six hundred-cell prison that would be escape proof. Security measures included installation of bars that were unbendable. Tunnels were cemented to eliminate possible escape routes. A ratio of one guard to every three prisoners was maintained at Alcatraz prison. Alcatraz proved the perfect solution for incarcerating the most violent criminals the Justice Department had ever dealt with.

Even with all of its security measures there were still inmates who attempted to escape but with little success. In June of 1962 three Americans came up missing from Alcatraz but there is no proof or evidence that would substantiate that their escape was successful because they were never seen or heard from again.

You may recall the movie "Escape from Alcatraz" that Clint Eastwood starred. After six months of chipping away at vents Eastwood finds himself outside the prison walls and on his raft made from prison rain coats. Not a true story but made for a good movie.

Fortunately, many people have escaped from the grasp of hell. Escaping from hell will not be a picnic because its forces are real but there is a much greater power offering us the opportunity to escape. It is a power so great it is almost unimaginable. A power great enough to create a universe that is so vast we are still discovering what it consists of daily and I am positive long after we are all gone these new discoveries will continue.

If it has been a while since you have slept out under the stars on a clear night I would highly recommend you make it a priority. There is a feeling of serenity that exists when you look up and ponder at that great big sky. God's creation is so amazing!

It is hard to fathom, but if you snap your fingers, the speed of light will have traveled around the earth seven times while you are hearing that snap. God is so powerful He created the earth and universe in just six days.

The prophet Jeremiah wrote, "But God made the earth by his power; he founded the world by his wisdom and stretched out the heavens by his understanding" (Jeremiah 10:12 NIV). This is why I say God's power is almost unimaginable. It is unimaginable but yet very real. God's power is real! It is this power we must believe in to escape the power of darkness.

As a wildland firefighter I have some vivid memories from days on wildfire's when the fire kicked our butt well into the next morning. I would like to say we never get our butts kicked but we do.

Nobody enjoys losing battles but the reality is battles are going to be lost when you are a professional wildland firefighter and you fight fire summer after summer. It is also reality the devil is going to win some battles. We need to possess the ability to pick ourselves up and move forward after we lose a battle.

I recall those early morning hours between 4:00 a.m. and 6:00 a.m. when we would start gathering for the day's operation. While our eyes were still burning from the smoke that cut our visibility to a few feet and with the snot crust to the side of our face this would usually be our first opportunity to grab a breath, look back, and see the devastation created by the wrath of the fire.

This was usually the time when the beast (fire) would lie down if it was going to, as if it were resting, preparing for the battle that was going to take place hours from now. Just like the previous battle we were fully expecting the next battle to go well into the night.

It was during these times when I knew we needed help. We needed something to grab on to, something that could refocus our attention and give us hope. I needed a rally call for the troops. What would that rally call be? Finally, when we needed it most the sun would begin to peak from the horizon to the East. You could watch the sun as it began to push the darkness out.

I have been fortunate to be able to watch this phenomenon occur many times. The darkness has no choice but to concede to the light as it begins to advance. Darkness is powerless over the light. Darkness must surrender to the light of the sun.

God's kingdom operates the same way. If we have God in our lives darkness has no choice but to surrender to the power of the light. God offers this light. He gives hope to those who accept Him and His ways. 2 Samuel says the Lord turns my darkness into light. God's word encourages us to walk in the light. He wants us basking in the light. Just as the *sun* creates light that gives us hope to stand and fight the good fight the *Son* gives the same hope to all who call on His glorious name. The name above all names. There is power in his name.

Every day the sunrises bringing with it the reminder of what the Son did for us. The sun brings light into our dark world. The light from the Son brings hope we desperately need and we should realize every day is new. Today is a new day! We will do battle again and this time we will be victorious. Yesterday was yesterday our focus needs to be in the present. We should begin to get that pep in our step and our eyes should be focused again. Today is the day the Lord has made and the Son is on our side, we will rejoice and be glad.

It is in 1 Samuel where we find the story of the young shepherd boy David, who slays the Philistine giant, Goliath. David was the youngest of Jesse's son's but he was the one God chose to replace Saul as the King over all Israel.

The Israelites were in a war against the Philistines, enemies of God. The Israelites had established camp on one side of the valley and the Philistines on the other side. They had been at a standstill for awhile with no movement favoring either side.

Goliath who was very powerful and stood over nine feet tall would go down to the bottom of the valley every day and challenge the whole Israelite army to send someone down to fight him. It was a winner takes all challenge. Not a single Israelite would take him up on his challenge. They were all afraid of this giant.

David the shepherd boy was instructed by his father to take some supplies up to his brothers who had joined King Saul's army and he was to report back to his father how the battle was going. David was present that day when Goliath came out and made his usual challenge. Upon hearing the Philistine shout his daily challenge David inquired of some of the men what the challenge was all about.

David was a boy after God's heart. He was angry someone would defy the army of the living God. A few Israelite soldiers told David of the challenge and David immediately said he would face Goliath. He had no doubt God would deliver this uncircumcised Philistine into his hands.

David was taken to King Saul who was not exactly thrilled the person who had finally stepped up was a boy who was not even full grown but nonetheless he gave David his blessing. David's weapon of choice was his slingshot and five smooth rocks although he would only need one. He might have grabbed five so he could kill some other Philistine's.

Using a rock was symbolic because throughout the Bible Jesus is referred to as the Rock. David trusted the Rock to be his weapon of choice. David was brave, bold, and confident while standing on the battlefield across from Goliath. He completely trusted God would deliver Goliath into his hands and he was correct.

The Israelites and Philistines who were watching probably didn't think David stood a chance to defeat Goliath. They likely thought David had a death wish. But David knew his God. David knew the power of the light. He knew he would see the sun rise again. In David's heart he knew God was good and evil would not prevail.

"David said to the Philistine, 'You come against me with sword and spear and javelin, but I come against you in the name of the LORD Almighty, the God of the armies of Israel, whom you have defied. This day the LORD will hand you over to me, and I'll strike you down and cut off your head. Today I will give the carcasses of the Philistine army to the birds of the air and the beasts of the earth, and the whole world will know that there is a God in Israel. All those gathered here will know that it is not by sword or spear that the LORD saves; for the battle is the LORD's, and he will give all of you into our hands'" (1 Samuel 17:45-47 NIV).

David ran at Goliath while pulling a rock from his bag. He slung the rock and hit Goliath right in the forehead killing him instantly. David did what he said he would do and he cut Goliath's head off by using the giant's own sword.

The story of David and Goliath has been passed from generation to generation. David and Goliath is a classic story of good triumphing over evil. Good and evil have fought from the beginning of time. It is very rare somebody actually roots for the powers of darkness. It is not in our DNA to root for or to like evil.

The movie Star Wars and all of its sequels were popular because they pitted good against evil. People wanted to see Darth Vader and his empire defeated by Luke Skywalker and the forces of light. We couldn't get enough of these epic movie adventures of good versus evil. After six movies Star Wars films have totaled approximately $4.3 billion, making it the third highest grossing film series ever.

Many people have not found the light. They have not been able to escape from the clutches of hell. I imagine each story is different but somehow I escaped. I remember being behind the bars and what it was like but I do not know how I escaped. Did I scale the fence, or did I gain some kind of super strength and bend the bars? Maybe it was as simple as Jesus taking some keys and unlocking the gate. Perhaps someone was fighting spiritually for me. Our struggles are not against flesh and blood, but against the rulers and against the authorities and powers of this dark world we live in and against the spiritual forces of evil in the heavenly realms.

I was miserable, trapped, and felt helpless. I was in prison and Satan was my warden. I had never experienced the light that comes from knowing the Son. I had lived in constant darkness. Then one day I was on the outside of the bars searching for direction. I can still recall thinking to myself I am free! My eyes hurt and it took a little time to get them adjusted so I could see. I started walking away from the darkness and into the light.

There was a sense of urgency to get as far away as possible from the darkness. There was still something happening. There were powers from behind the bars that were trying to call me back, tempting me, and trying to persuade me things weren't so bad. The anguish coming from behind the bars was very real. Hell is real.

The devil takes it personally when someone leaves his dark world and begins a journey towards the light. Misery likes company and the devil takes pleasure in misery.

In front of me was a beautiful horizon, the sun was setting, symbolic perhaps, and I began to wonder if this could be the end of an old way and the beginning to a new way. Out with the old in with the new!

There was a feeling of peace and tranquility in this new world. The feeling was so strong. I could feel something or someone rooting for me, yelling do not look back keep coming. Two worlds were colliding for one soul. I had a decision to make and the decision could only be made by me. Neither side physically grabbed me. It was my will. Did I like where I just came from or did I want to roll the dice for something better?

The prison bars seemed to grow taller as I got further away. The shadows from the fence kept casting further and further as if it were stalking me. I could sense the power from behind the fence was fading. It was dissipating as I got further away. What was happening? Is escaping even possible? This horizon I see in front of me where does it go? How do I know when the sunrises it will be any better? How do I know this is not a dream? I quickly realized it wasn't a dream because there are no dreams in hell only nightmares. Will I be alone on this journey? There are so many questions and not any answers.

I remember thinking out loud what are you doing? You don't like change. How true I don't like change. Maybe that is why I lived behind those prison bars for so long. I fought the idea of change and I casted the idea of escaping from my mind many times because change can be scary. In fact, not many of us like change. Change is unknown and we are scared of the unknown.

We need to understand a lifestyle change is living a completely new or different way of life than what we have become accustomed to. For example, if you have never read the Bible or have never gone to church, then one day you start doing both of these things and start living a biblical life that would be a lifestyle change.

If you exchange a life style that did not include Jesus for a life style where Jesus was the focus of your existence you would experience a life style change. Jesus is better than any rewards program you will ever sign up for.

Not all changes equate to a lifestyle change. If you decide things aren't going well in your marriage and you decide to get a divorce and remarry someone else you have changed your spouse but not your lifestyle.

Maybe we should look at it from the viewpoint that we are exchanging an old lifestyle for a new lifestyle. We exchange things all the time. We exchange clothes that don't fit for clothes that do. If we don't like one thing we often exchange it for something we do like. If we purchase something and it doesn't work we take it back and exchange it for one that does work. We can look at our lives in the same manner.

We can exchange our old lifestyle that is not working anymore for a new lifestyle. President Obama won the 2008 presidential election with a simple theme that he kept driving home and that theme was 'change'.

It won him the election and it can win us the peace of mind knowing we have a place in heaven and our name has been written in the Book of Life. It is imperative that we believe that it is possible to exchange a lifestyle that is guarantying us a life in hell for a lifestyle that will guarantee us eternal life in heaven.

Jesus tells us the enemy comes to steal, kill, and destroy but he came to give us an abundant life. He has a better deal for anyone who is willing to walk a life with him as Commander and Chief. Jesus' store is always open 24/7 365. Jesus is more than willing to exchange an old life style for a new life style. What is the cost? One Lamb already paid in full. Jesus paid the price and we receive the gift if we accept it.

I am still walking towards that horizon with the setting sun. The sun setting is a daily reminder that every day will be new. The sun makes its journey and then rises the next morning. The whole process is a message from God reminding us that new beginnings are possible daily in His kingdom.

I no longer feel that pulling to go back into the darkness. I know that world still exists and that there are many people still locked behind the gate. My desire and my purpose are to help them. Charles Spurgeon who was known as the Prince of Pastors went as far to say if you didn't want to help others become saved you were not saved yourself. I believe he was correct in his thinking.

We need to reach others for Jesus. Jesus offers mercy. Another word for mercy is clemency. We receive forgiveness for our sins. Forgiveness from whatever it is we want to leave behind and hope that comes with starting over.

I am not so far removed from the gates of hell that I don't remember what it was like. I know how the devil operates. I know if the devil is bold enough to tempt Jesus Christ, the King of Kings and Lord of Lords, than who am I that he would not try everything in his arsenal to bring me back into his world? I need no more motivation then that. I keep my eyes forward and continue to resist the devil not wanting to lose the momentum I have gained.

We all have a choice to make. God gave us the ability to make choices. We can choose to live in hell or we can choose to try something new. We can choose to wonder about our salvation or we can know for certain our destination when we pass from this life to the next. The road is going to be unknown but that is one of the exciting things. We all have a little adventure in us yearning to get out and try something new. The road is going to be narrow but that is ok that only helps us keep our focus straight ahead, on the prize.

There are going to be some potholes, some wrong turns, maybe even a few crashes but if we will learn the Way we will arrive at our destination. If we continue forward we will receive the reward. The further down the road we get the easier it becomes. Everything we need will be provided. We will pick up tools that will help us as we go forward, tools that fit each situation as we encounter them.

Are whole journey has been planned we need to make the decision to go on a trip of a life time. It is quite possible we may even come across someone who is lost or stranded alongside the road. Imagine we have what this person needs to continue on his journey.

The Apostle Paul whose name was Saul hated Christians. Saul took great joy in persecuting Christians. Saul had such great hate for Christians that Jesus finally had to come down and have a talk with him.

Saul was on the road to Damascus when a great light flashed all around him and he heard a voice calling out his name. Jesus said, "Saul why do you persecute me?" Paul took Jesus' offer and exchanged his old ways for a new way of life.

After Paul's encounter he began a new journey. Paul went from persecuting Christians to trying to help them see the light, the same light that transformed him. Paul's life changed so much he ended up being the author of thirteen of the twenty-seven books in the New Testament (NT).

We are all sinners and I am certainly no exception. I abused alcohol, experimented with some drugs, committed adultery, dabbled with idolatry, and I enjoyed fighting.

The Lord has given me the ability to remember where I came from and yet through His grace I have been able to bury those old haunting memories. My past no longer defines who I am because I am a new creature.

I try to never look back on the negative things I have done. For me to continually look back would be reliving all those memories. It would be a constant reminder of the things I did that no longer define who I am. Those memories have been washed away by the blood of Jesus Christ never to haunt me again.

Regardless of where you are in your walk with Christ the Ultimate Ultimatum was written so you may find hope and comfort in Jesus Christ. I believe the Ultimate Ultimatum will help you answer a lot of questions you have or will encounter on your journey.

I believe the Ultimate Ultimatum will be a good reminder to mature Christians because often we forget what it was like when we first started our walk with the Lord. This will be a good refresher and hopefully remind many of us of the mindset of someone who is spiritually dead or the mindset of a new believer.

As God lays out the lessons I have learned in the Ultimate Ultimatum I trust the Holy Spirit will guide you and speak directly to you. You are reading this book because the Holy Spirit knows there are lessons that will help you on your journey. Amen (Amen simply means we agree)!

You will learn how I escaped from the very pit of hell. I escaped from hell and now I am on a road that leads to eternal life. We are all on the same road. Some people are in front of us, others are beside us, many people are behind us, and a lot of people remain at the very beginning of the road still in park. There are others who haven't even stuck their key in the ignition. It doesn't matter where we are or where we have been. Where are you? It doesn't matter how you start. But it does matter how you finish. We have the opportunity of a life time to embark on an awesome journey so buckle up and let Jesus do the driving!

CHAPTER 1

Bereshith-In the Beginning

Bereshith means "In {the} Beginning" in Hebrew. My journey began the year I was born, 1967. God had a plan and a purpose for me from the very moment I was born. Unfortunately, like the majority of us I had my own plan. I knew what was best for me.

I look back at my life and ask myself how did I get from there to where I am today? Of course I know God deserves the glory because I was incapable of rescuing myself. In the course of sharing with you it will never be my intention to dishonor my mother or father in anyway. But with that said to really relate to what I am saying you need to understand a little bit about my upbringing.

The Bible was not a book readily available in our home and God was never a conversation piece at the dinner table or anywhere else around the house for that matter. The Bible was thought to be too thick and it had too many Thou's and Thou Shall Not's and beside that the text was too small.

Growing up we never went to church as a family. I went to a few church functions when I was in junior high but it wasn't to hear the word. I went for the food. I am not proud to admit this but I could be persuaded to attend a nightly event when the word "potluck" was tossed out there.

I had heard about church potlucks and if they didn't care I was only there on those occasions when they were offering free food well why should I deprive these people of my company? Everything would be fine as long as they don't ask me any questions, or expect me back for a regular Sunday service.

I lived by two unwritten rules growing up. I only read Sports Illustrated and the sports pages of the local paper. It is a miracle I can read.

My second rule was Sunday's were made for recovering from the last six days and how better to do that then laying around watching sports all day long. I believed church, Bible, and all that religious *stuff* was not for me, I thought I would leave that stuff for those other people.

The potlucks came to end the first time there was a short service prior (I was tricked) to eating and I saw a person flopping on the floor like a fish out of water. Hey, I like food but that was too much. I still don't know what that was all about. Nobody seemed to be concerned or willing to help the person so I determined it wasn't anything medical. But that pretty much put an end to the potlucks for me and ended my church attending days if that is what I can call it.

For the next sixteen or so years the only time I entered a church was if there were a wedding or a funeral. Neither of which occurred very often. Oddly, there were times when I felt I wanted to be somewhere where I could spend time with this God I had heard mentioned a few times.

My college football coach always offered prayer time before each game on Saturday mornings. For some strange reason I often felt this internal tugging to attend those meetings. I never knew why I wanted to be at those meetings. Why, was I drawn to these gatherings? After all I am not one of these people.

God is always working in our lives we just don't always see what He is doing. Two significant events happen in my life in February of 1991 that started me on the journey I am on today. February 10th, 1991 was the date when my dad passed away and it was also the year and month when I had my very first date with Kelli.

I met Kelli that winter while going to college. Kelli became a rock for me to lean on during this time of grieving, sadness, and anger. Kelli and I will be celebrating eighteen years of marriage on our next anniversary.

I graduated from college in June of 1992 and moved back home. I had been hired by the Forest Service as a wildland firefighter the two previous summers and I was going back for another summer. Twenty plus years later I am still a wildland firefighter and still employed by the United States Forest Service (USFS).

Kelli had one more year of college before she would graduate. We tried the long distance relationship for awhile but eventually called it quits. It was not working out because of the distance. I don't recall there being a big ugly break up it just happen due to the distance and lack of seeing each other. I believe we were both enjoying our freedom anyway.

After Kelli graduated she moved to Portland and found a job. After a few miscellaneous jobs Kelli landed a job with a home mortgage company. Prior to Thanksgiving in 1993 Kelli and I started dating again and even making plans to have Kelli move up to North Idaho in the fall.

Shortly after the new year Kelli saw a job opening in Coeur d' Alene, ID which is fifty miles west of Mullan, ID where I was raised and living at this time. It was a long shot and if she did get the job it would change our whole time table for her moving up to North Idaho. I wasn't too concerned believing the odds were insurmountable with her being new to the profession. I wanted her to move up but I wanted to stick with the time frame we had discussed and wait until the fall.

Kelli applied for the job and to our amazement she ended up getting the job. We moved her up from Portland in the spring of 1994 (Yes, living together is a sin but let's take baby steps for now). Shortly after the move I realized I had made the mistake of my life. What was I thinking? I was only twenty-seven years old and tied down. I did not like the situation I was in. I believed the problem was she was smothering me. Can you imagine she wanted to spend time with me whenever I wasn't working!

The fire season of 1994 was one of the worst fire seasons we had ever experienced as a country. From the middle of June until early October I was pretty much gone on fire assignments. The trend was to go on a fire assignment for ten to sixteen days come home for a day or two and then go on another assignment.

One or two days off did not give me a whole lot of time to see what the buddies were doing, go fishing, and attempt to get in a game of golf. Kelli had these crazy expectations that we were to spend time together when I was home. How was I going to work in some time for her? Talk about selfish . . . what was she thinking?

Let me recap the situation. Kelli has moved up to be with me which was a big adjustment for her and I am gone all the time. She left her friends and a good job, a sacrifice for sure. Add in the fact she didn't know anybody and you have the ingredients for a lot of quarrelling to take place on those valuable days off I had desperately earned.

Kelli didn't seem to understand I had priorities I needed to get accomplished. My thinking was that I didn't have time to waste squabbling with her since I had things to do that didn't necessarily include her.

We purchased our first home in the fall of 1994 making it Kelli's third move in about seven months which can cause a person to be a little stressed. We paid $19,600 for our first one bath two bedroom home. It was a fixer upper but it was an ok little home. Nothing permanent but it would work for awhile.

It became excruciating obvious this new lifestyle (single to living together a definite lifestyle change) was not working. We needed a new plan. We were both miserable. We talked about it and after a few hours of discussion we came to the conclusion the best thing to do would be to . . . get married!

We had our two dogs and now we were waiting for the day we would be happily married. Here we are two adults with college degrees and the best solution we could come up with was to buy a home and get married. Oh! Boy!

Marriage was going to be the cure for all this bickering and fighting that was taking place between us. Being married would create this new affection and love for each other. We just needed more of a commitment. A piece of paper saying we are Mr. & Mrs. Terry Zufelt. Yes, a piece of paper would be the answer to all our problems. After all, life couldn't get any worse, could it?

Listen! If you are currently not getting along do you think adding the stress of making wedding plans is the answer? From experience let me tell you, no! We could not agree on anything. Who would be my best man, how many bridesmaid and groomsmen would we have? I probably didn't really care I just didn't want her to have it her way. Solution! There has to be a solution. Think! Got it! The next brain storm we came up with was to fly to Reno and get married. The situation was still intolerable but we would soon be married.

So on March 25th, 1995 we were married in Reno, NV. Real small wedding only our immediate family members were there, it was over in ten minutes. Is anybody up for a little Black Jack? We occasionally look back and laugh at the situation. Kelli and I admit prior to our wedding we did not really love each other and to tell you the truth I am not sure we even liked each other.

Come on, she was trying to convince me life was not all about me and what I wanted. We even had a fight on the way to the airport when we were going to get married. Kelli went as far as to try and kick me out of the car. First, why go if you kick me out of the car? Secondly, who was Kelli going to marry? She definitely didn't think things through. Ha!

I can still remember what the fight was about. We purchased our flight tickets early and they were sitting on the counter for about a week. Somehow the tickets got thrown away. I blamed her and she blamed me so on our way to get married we both said some very hurtful things to each other. For the record I am positive Kelli made the mistake and threw the tickets away (Not really we'll never know for sure). Ha!

The craziest thing happened after we were married. We still fought like the Hatfield and the McCoy's. You didn't really think things were going to get better just because we got married did you? We had our reception about a month later in Mullan. Lots of family and friends showed up and we all had a good time. Until Kelli suggested it was time to go home. Why call it an early night, I was having fun. It was only one or two o'clock in the morning. Yes, the night of our wedding reception ended in a fight.

The weeks were just kind of going by and our lives pretty much stayed on this course for the next few months. There were a few good times but they were nothing compared to the bad times. We had good jobs, although we seemed to be broke a lot, we fought a lot, and just sort of tolerated each other.

The 1995 fire season went down in history as one of the worst (no fires) seasons ever. It was extremely slow. Things remained status quo between Kelli and me but we had to talk about something so we decided it was time to upgrade our living quarters.

God blessed us and we actually made a small profit on our house (we did not give God the glory at the time). We moved across town into a nice two bedroom home in January of 1996. But can you believe our marriage remained on rocky soil even after buying a new home and moving? I am being facetious of course. We were both still miserable. Why? We were buying our second house; we had dogs, cats, good jobs, but something was still missing. What was wrong with us?

Another fire season had come and went and it was now the fall of 1996. The 1996 fire season was ok. It was one of those fire seasons where I was gone for awhile and then home for awhile. Life merely existed. I was trying to survive and make the best of a bad situation. I was stumbling forward with some peaks but mainly valleys. Our marriage was on life support. I didn't feel like I was living life the way it was meant to be lived. I had this awful void that wasn't being filled. It was like a big pit that nothing could fill. A wife couldn't fill it; dogs, cats, new homes, and cars couldn't fill it. What was it going to take to fill this emptiness in my life?

Something was beginning to blow in the wind and the times were about to change. My journey was about to shift into high gear, of course unannounced to me. I came home from work one day in the fall and Kelli was on the porch. She said, "We need to talk." In reality she ended up giving me an ultimatum. She said she wanted to start going to church or she wanted a divorce (again not very scriptural) because she could not live like this any longer.

An ultimatum, I had to make a decision. It wasn't a life or death choice but significant for sure. Do I take the bailout right now and walk away or do I make a sacrifice and agree to attend a church?

Kelli and I had already endured one marriage counseling session and we both agreed one session was enough. After all we could sit at home and talk to each other at a designated time and have more of a conversation than we did with the counselor and that would be a lot less expensive.

Seriously, counseling sessions can be very beneficial. Kelli and I were not ready or committed to being counseled.

When I think back to the day Kelli gave me the ultimatum and knowing how I felt I am really surprised I didn't jump on the opportunity to get divorced. I am thankful I agreed to go to church. I had no expectations of church it was just another avenue to try.

I am being honest when I share with you it was my full intent to go along with this absurd idea and when it failed I would be free. In my mind the catch was I could feel good about telling everybody we tried everything to make this marriage work but we are too different, we are just not compatible.

My view on marriage was that it was simply a process in which you received a piece of paper stating we were lawfully married. It wasn't sacred to me. I had no idea of marriage's biblical significance.

I was thinking two maybe three trips tops to church then when nothing changed she would bring up the subject of divorce again and I would be free. What a plan! Her ultimatum was my way out! I would be able to say with a clear conscience I tried everything to make my marriage work. I even tried going to church with all those perfect Holly Rollers. You know them folks, those who were born with a silver spoon in their mouth. I honestly believed I was making the ultimate sacrifice.

Imagine! I am going to give up my time on a Sunday to make my marriage work. Remember it is fall which means football! Could there be a greater sacrifice then giving up a morning of football? I think not. The town folk will have pity on me. Some might even think of me as a hero. Surely they will know I gave this marriage every opportunity to work but it wasn't meant to be.

I figured Kelli would quit her job and move back to Oregon. She would be out of my sight, mind, and life. I want to make it clear I didn't hate Kelli; I just didn't like being married and tied down. You know the old ball and chain (I really never have used that) as our single friends like to remind us.

I was unaware of some things that had been happening at Kelli's work. Doors kept opening for Kelli and she was only working six miles from home. She had her own office and was a loan consultant. Kelli was pretty busy and needed help at work so by the grace of God He delivered a couple of Christian women into her life. There were many people to choose from but through work God brings two Christian ladies into Kelli's life.

God placed two women who began to speak to Kelli about His kingdom whenever the opportunity arose. There is no doubt in our minds Evon and Carolyn entered our lives through God's divine wisdom. We still refer to them as Saint Evon and Miss Carolyn. They are both very important in our lives and we love them.

Evon began to subtly share what the Bible would say about situations in our lives. She was never pushy with Kelli and we now realize she was being directed by the Holy Spirit on what to share and when to share it. I have never asked Evon but I bet she prayed for our salvation many times.

Carolyn is a "Prayer Warrior!" Carolyn and her husband Gordon attend the same church we attend. The cry of Carolyn's heart is to faithfully seek and hear what God is saying. We thank God so much for placing a strong Christian couple like Gordon and Carolyn in our lives.

Like Evon, Carolyn began to seize opportunities to talk to Kelli about God and how with God in her life she could have a better life. They assured her a positive change was possible if she would begin to lean on God and trust His way. They captured Kelli's attention and she began to imagine she could have a better life. Their subtle teachings were what finally led Kelli to give me the ultimatum. Kelli, began to wonder why live in this hell if there was an opportunity or a way that would make life better, more livable?

The bait was on the hook. Kelli was nibbling but she wasn't quite convinced to take a bite. It was going to take a little more bait before she was going to throw away her life for something she had no understanding. Something she believed would require her to make a drastic change in her life, a life she wasn't even enjoying. Isn't it odd we can be miserable, think life stinks, not have any answers, and still be hesitant to make a change? We won't step out there in faith and take a chance there is something that will work. I know it is not easy.

Kelli had an appointment scheduled with a gentleman who was looking to purchase a house. He was friendly, bubbly, and appeared to be an all around nice guy. He turned out to be a pastor, Pastor Kent Roberts. We didn't know it at the time but he would be the final piece of bait God would use to lure Kelli into finally biting the hook.

One fishing line was cast but two fish would eventually be hooked. All that needed to be done now was for the hook to be set, and then we needed to be gently reeled in so we would not flip off the hook.

The amazing thing about the whole process was it wasn't an easy loan. Kelli and Pastor Kent had to meet and speak several times. These were opportunities the Lord provided so Pastor Kent could offer a little more bait and finally it worked.

Pastor Kent was there for a home loan but God had sent him on a fishing trip. Pasture Kent had recently began to pastor at Christian Life Center (CLC) in Kellogg which was approximately sixteen miles from our home in Mullan. At some point in the loan process he invited Kelli to church.

For months people in Kelli's life had been planting little subtle seeds and those seeds were on the brink of germinating into something life changing in both of our lives. The seeds were planted and being watered.

I agreed to give church a *chance*. Since then things have moved so fast I don't ever recall discussing with Kelli if she thought I would agree or disagree to go to church. Maybe she was thinking the same thing I was.

It was now the first part of October and the ultimatum was on the table. I agreed to go to church and it made sense to attend Pastor Kent's church. After all what a coincidence this pastor is getting a loan the same time we decide to attend a church. We weren't about to go to a church in Mullan somebody we knew could see us. They would really think I went off the deep end. I am sure most of them would have come to the conclusion I was dying or preparing for Kelli's death. Remember no Bible, no understanding of the Bible, and no expectations.

You might be wondering if this whole *finding Jesus thing* has to take place in a church and the answer is no. You can stop right now and ask Jesus Christ into your life. In fact, if you have not done so stop right now and do it. How? What do you do? These are common questions. God made it so easy and the process does not have to be perfect. Try saying this, "Father I know I am a sinner. I believe Jesus Christ is the Son of God. I confess with my mouth that I receive Jesus Christ into my heart and I make you (Jesus) my Lord and Savior." Amen! Congratulations!

Wasn't that easy? Yes, but we will see in later chapters that the word believe has a much greater meaning than we realize. Now begin to trust Jesus Christ and learn to lean not on your own understanding but on his understanding. Your next step should be to start looking for a church so you can grow spiritually and receive the equipping you will need on your new journey.

Kelli and I were taking the big step, our first day of church, which was also my first step back to reclaiming the life I had left behind. I'll be back to hanging out with the buddies, drinking, and flirting with the women all those things I did before *she* ruined my life.

I entered the front door with the expectation there would be a strong earthquake and the walls would tumble down on me but as I slowly walked forward nothing happened. Strange, the walls seem to be holding up, I better walk lightly.

It was a cold fall day but the sweat was rolling down my forehead like a creek in the flooding season. I quickly observe some people are dressed really nice, shirts with ties. Some ladies are wearing dresses others are in casual attire. Okay, there are some people in tie dyes and sandals, and lots of people wearing jeans. Hum! I am thinking I am dressed like the rest. I am dressed appropriate. I am not standing out. This is good. Wait a minute! What is that? That guy over there has long hair and immediately I spot another guy who has an earring. All right this is okay. I didn't have an earring and I had short hair. I was stereotyping but I figured if long haired people with earrings were not getting struck by lightning I just might survive!

I kept saying to myself it is okay I can do this. I didn't anticipate seeing these kinds of *people*. Let's find a seat and slide into obscurity. This whole thing will be over in a couple of hours (most of the services I have attended have been over in an hour and a half max.). We have nearly made it through the foyer and all I have had to do is nod my head a few times. This is good. Almost sitting down, no I made eye contact with somebody. Great here they come. Sorry but even to this day I lean a little to the introvert side. But God is working on me. Torture, can you imagine someone wants to say hi and know my name. Woe! After a good wipe of the sweat off my forehead it looks like I survived that encounter but one more might be more then I can handle.

We found a seat in the back of the room and sat down quietly. I was trying not to bring any attention my way. I began to wonder when I was going to hear that loud voice; you know the voice that is going to say, "Get out!"

I knew any second I was going to hear that voice that came from behind the curtain on the Wizard of Oz. The voice was so frightening it made the Cowardly Lion take off running. "I am the great and wonderful God, leave! You are not welcome here."

I never did hear that voice but I think I would have felt better if I could have stood up and ran out the door. Most of us do not enjoy being uncomfortable. Remember lifestyle change brings us out of our comfort zone which is why we are so resistant to a lifestyle change and attending church definitely requires most of us to change our way of living.

Ok! Looks like they are about to get this show on the road, I see some people going on the stage and they are picking up musical instruments. There are some guitars, a drummer, piano, and various other instruments. What is this about? There were no instruments when Charles Engels took his family to church on Little House on the Prairie.

Some of you may be too young to remember or you chose not to watch the television series but either way talk about tough times. When my girls think they have it tough or if they think life is real bad I tell them to go watch a few episodes of Little House on the Prairie. Those kids had it rough. But they were always thankful. When they received a sock for Christmas they were elated and already looking forward to next Christmas when they knew they were going to get the mate to that one sock.

Honestly, the instruments, music, or any of that stuff did not matter to me. Music is not my calling. Remember Steve Martin in the Jerk? Well, I am like the character he played, Nathan. I cannot clap and sing at the same time. To this day

I sing the lyrics to about three different songs during a single song and cannot keep a beat for the life of me.

The piano player who was the lead singer and the other musicians began to play. It wasn't Motley Crue, Garth Brooks, or "The Boss" but it was ok! It wasn't anything like I had imagined. I imagined you would pick up a book from under the seats and the pastor would tell you to turn to a song on page so and so. I was waiting for all those *professional church goers* to look over at me when the singing began so they could roll their eyes at me when I didn't know the words to the songs.

I think back now and wonder why they would need the books if they knew the words? Nobody even paid attention to me. There wasn't an Edna in the whole church. Have you heard the stories of Fred and Edna? Fred's and Edna's can be found in every church. The following is an example of a Fred and Edna conversation that took place after a church service.

Fred and Edna were driving home after a church service. "Fred, Edna asked, "did you notice that the pastor's sermon was kind of weak today?"

"No, not really," answered Fred. "Well, did you hear how flat the choir was?"

"No, I didn't" he responded. "Well, you certainly must have noticed that young couple and their children right in front of us; with all the noise and commotion they made the whole service! I am sorry, dear, but no, I didn't." Finally in disgust Edna said,

"Honestly, Fred, I don't know why you even bother going to church."

There didn't appear to be a bunch of Edna's in church, nobody seemed to be concerned with what I was doing. I know because I wasn't about to sing so I spent my time checking people out. The majority of them were focused on singing and not really paying any attention to anything else around them. At this point my blood pressure was beginning to get back under two hundred.

They sang four or five songs and then we all sat down as the pastor took center stage. Again, my blood pressure began to increase and perspiration began to accumulate on my forehead. I was thinking this is it. This must be the time when all these goody two shoes come after me. Is this pastor going to point me out and bring some kind of attention to me? I imagined him pointing at me and saying, "Son of the devil change your evil ways."

I continued to remain motionless so I wouldn't draw attention to myself. I was thinking if I am really still maybe they won't notice me. It was kind of like when we (for some of us anyway) were in high school and the teacher would start calling on students to answer questions. We would get that lump in our throat because we knew there was a very good chance we were not going to know any of the answers.

Do you remember how we thought if we looked straight ahead and didn't move the teacher couldn't see us? Somehow our lack of motion made us invisible and since the teacher couldn't see us she couldn't call on us? Well relax because pastors are there to teach. They don't stop and ask questions during their sermons. It was such a relief when I realized I would never be called on during a Sunday service to answer a question which was good because there was no way I would have an answer to any question. I was absolutely blind to the word of God.

The first several times we stepped in church I was as nervous as a long tail cat in a room full of rocking chairs. I was out of my comfort zone. It was hard for me to relax. But there was my master plan and I was determined to make it look like I tried everything to save my marriage. Things were shaping up real nice it was just a matter of time. I was executing my game plan to perfection. At least that was my understanding. But God was preparing to shape and mold me.

God was prepping me for some reconstructive surgery. People pay millions for surgery that will change their looks but I was about to get it for free. I was going to be operated on the inside by a cardiologist.

We continued to test the waters and it seemed like each one of the sermons applied directly to me. I really began to believe someone was sharing the story of my life with the pastor. I was thinking somebody had to be revealing things to him about me and if I ever find out whom that person is they are going to be seeking God for some healing if you know what I mean. How else could he be teaching on these areas so applicable to my circumstances?

God was getting my attention via the pastors Sunday sermons. I cannot recall what Pastor Kent preached on that first Sunday or any of the proceeding Sundays but I do recall sharing with Kelli, "He was talking to me. How did he know all that and how could it be so specific to my life? How can he know this is where I am in my life and this is how I feel? This is not possible. Nobody in this church knows anything about me." At least that was my understanding. But God did know me and He was doing some work on me.

We were going to church but it was easy to talk ourselves out of attending on more than a few Sunday mornings. Hey, winters are extremely bad in Mullan which can cause the roads to be very dangerous or was it that tricky Satan who was still influencing us? After all he wanted us to remain in his kingdom, misery.

We remained what I have coined as dippers. Dippers are people who aren't quite sure they want to commit to the whole idea of church so they attend once in awhile. They dip in now and then. There are CE's who basically only attend church on Christmas & Easter and a step up from CE's are CEO's. These are not Corporate Executive Officers they are those who attend church Christmas, Easter, and Occasionally.

I had my master plan, I was exhausting all avenues including getting *right with God* and then as Mel Gibson would say "Freedom" back to the "Born to be Wild" days. It was a great plan. There was only one problem. God fully aware of my devilish scheme had another plan and His plans are perfect. His plan was to get me into church and kick my journey into overdrive.

Although it made absolutely no sense to me I actually discovered I liked the way I felt when I attended church.

There was no pressure to attend church. Nobody called us on those Sundays we didn't make it to church. The pastor did not call us up and ask us where we were. It is not easy when you have been living a certain way for so many years to all of a sudden begin a new way of life.

Our conscience and moral compass began to show us we were off course and Kelli and I stopped doing a lot of the things we were accustomed to doing. A lot of these activities didn't seem to quench our appetite any longer.

For example, the whole bar seen and getting drunk didn't seem as fun as it did in the past. Kelli and I both began to think there was more to life than watching television all week then heading off to the bar on Friday and Saturday. For us it came down to a life style change. Was our current life really that great we didn't want to leave it behind? No!

My plan went to the wayside. Kelli and I's marriage began to turn around we actually wanted to be around each other. Our marriage was taken off life support and we were actually breathing on our own. Jesus was the oxygen we needed. Unfortunately, taking that breath was still our choice and we weren't replenishing that O_2 consistently.

We were starting to believe there really was something to this *religion* thing. We had not killed the old self completely which meant we were still operating in the flesh a lot of the time. We began to feel better about ourselves and each other. We simply began to respect each other. I was learning life was not all about me. In other words I was being a lot less selfish.

I had a football coach in college who would always go around yelling "every day is a holiday and every meal is a banquet when you are an Eastern Oregon Mountaineer." I have to tell you it didn't seem like it when I was a part of a twenty-seven or it might have been twenty-eight game losing streak.

I don't recall thinking life was a holiday during three a days (three practices a day) in the fall in Eastern Oregon. Triple digit heat on some days and lots of sprinting. How that was considered a holiday I couldn't tell you. This was especially true the time when this horrible smell kept blowing into the field. This smell made us all gag.

I knew where the smell was coming from but there was no way I was going to fess up to being responsible for that foul odor. A few days before practices were to start my roommate and I killed a salmon. We thought we would get a few free meals.

We told a few of the natives we were going to eat this big fish we had killed which prompted them to inform us it was too late to eat the fish. They said the taste would be appalling. We didn't know what to do with this huge fish so we dropped it off on a little road that went right behind our practice field. After a few days in the heat that smell was bad! We were reaping what we sowed. Unfortunately, so were the other one hundred and fifty players and coaches.

Honestly, in spite of the heat and smell I loved it. Playing college football was a great experience. I would go through those hot days again if I were younger. My point is with Jesus as my Lord and Savior life does seem like every day is a holiday and the meals He prepares for me daily makes me feel as if I am at a banquet.

Psalm 23 says, "The Lord is my shepherd, I shall not be in want. He makes me lie down in green pastures, he leads me beside quiet waters, he restores my soul. He guides me in the paths of righteousness for his name sake. Even though I walk through the valley of the shadow of death, I will fear no evil, for you are with me; your rod and your staff, they comfort me. You prepare a table before me in the presence of my enemies. You anoint my head with oil; my cup overflows. Surely goodness and love will follow me all the days of my life, and I will dwell in the house of the Lord forever" (NIV). God is a good Father He wants the best for His children.

You may be thinking at this time I was saved and everything was great from that day forward. No! Walking with the Lord is a journey and each person's journey is different. Our journey will read like a book.

We get to write are own book. It is up to us to decide the beginning, how each chapter will read and the ending. Nobody else can write our story for us. Every chapter is important but no matter how your book reads as long as you get the ending right His grace is sufficient because we serve an awesome God.

It would be awesome if we all entered church, immediately believed, and accepted Jesus Christ. I have no statistical facts but I believe I can say not too many people change overnight. Yes, there are the testimonies where individuals have shown up to a gathering and instantly began a journey never to look back. We can read about the miracles in Acts where three thousand and five thousand were added to the church daily. God can do what He wants when He wants. God is not the obstacle, we are. We're our own worst enemies.

Before we are even a thought in our parents minds God has an awesome plan for each and every one of us. Jesus said, "I have come so that you may have a full and meaningful life." By our very nature we are sinful and if we try to live without Jesus we will die. Jesus is the only provision God provided to restore our fellowship with Him. He is the beginning and the end. He is the Alpha and the Omega!

CHAPTER 2

Lining up with God's Will

For Kelli and me our old ways were disappearing. Life had meaning to us now that we had Jesus Christ directing and guiding our lives. New ways were being birthed inside of us. These new ways were more fulfilling. Alcohol and worldly ways did not get the job done but being drunk on Jesus did. We were learning to trust and lean on God. We were also learning what it meant to line our will up with the will of God. In order for us to receive God's fruit it is essential that we line up with His will.

Kelli and I talked about how far we had come spiritually, fully acknowledging God had performed a miracle in our lives. We believed we were on the right track and our next move should be to start a family that is what married couples do, right!

God performs miracles all the time. There are two great but very different miracles He performs. There is the birth we are all familiar with which is the birth of a baby in the flesh. The other miracle when referring to birth is called being born again in the Spirit.

In my humble opinion being born again is the greatest miracle and the greatest gift God can bestow upon any of us today. Leonard Ravenhill said, "The greatest miracle God can do today is take an unholy person out of this unholy world, and make that person holy, put that person back into this unholy world and keep that person holy." (We will talk about what it means to be born again in the next chapter).

So life was pretty good and it was time to have children. No problem! You get married and have children, it is automatic. Well having a baby was not automatic for us. Boy did we take birth for granted. I believe a lot of people do. People often want to see a miracle from God but we don't recognize all the miracles He performs on a daily basis. Having children is something we expect to happen. I guess that is why ladies who are pregnant always hear the comment, "I see you're expecting."

God performed over four million miracles in the United States in 2007 which was fifteen thousand more births than 1957 during the baby boom. That is a lot of miracles. Figure 1 shows the four million births in 2007 broken all the way down to miracles per hour.

FIGURE 1

Unit	Births
Year	4,000,000
Month	333,333
Day	913
Hour	38

We did not know at the time but Kelli and I were about to enter a journey that would forever change our thinking about having children. This journey awakened our minds and hearts to the truth, conception is a miracle. Our frame of mind was okay time to have a baby so let's have one. Well it wasn't that easy.

We tried desperately for two years to have a baby. "Just relax" and "You are trying too hard" were not great words of comfort or biblical wisdom but people meant well.

We were growing spiritually but by no means had we "arrived" at a place in our relationship with God where we trusted Him completely. Our relationship with God was good but not yet solid enough where we had completely weaned ourselves from the ways of the world.

We were so desperate to have children we started looking at alternative options like invetro-fertilization. I am not saying invetro-fertilization is wrong or bad I am reflecting on the point we were desperate to have a child. If you have ever looked into invetro-fertilization you know how expensive it is. It was going to cost ten thousand dollars (probably inexpensive by today's standards) and it was best if you could go back to back to back months. I am not a mathematician but I know that adds up to a lot of money. It was money we certainly did not have. Would adoption be an option? Adoption is also expensive.

I wasn't too fond of the adoption option due to my lack of maturity and wild imagination. I had some crazy ideas at the time about adoption. I remember thinking to myself could I really love this child if he/she turned out different from my expectations? What if the child didn't share my ideologies, or beliefs? What if we adopted a boy and he didn't like football or any sports? Would I be able to handle it if the baby we adopted had a serious health problem? I know these are horrible thoughts but they were running rampant through my mind. I was haunted by these thoughts and really didn't want to consider adopting.

God began to speak to us about our situation through others. It was amazing! One day at work Carolyn shared with Kelli she had a dream. We were going to have a baby girl and her name was going to be Rebekah Marie. I still get cold chills and want to cry every time I think about it. Really, God spoke to you in a dream? Does God really speak to us through dreams? Yes!

God speaks to us! He told us through the prophet Joel, "'And afterward, I will pour my Spirit on all people. Your sons and daughters will prophesy, your old men will dream dreams, your young men will see visions. Even on my servants, both men and women, I will pour out my Spirit in those days'" (Joel 2:28-29 NIV).

One Sunday at church Pastor Kent from the pulpit told us he believed God wanted us to have children. He said, "Kelli and Terry I believe God wants you to have children." He later shared he immediately thought to himself what am I saying. I could be crushing this young couple if they don't have children. But he was obedient and spoke what the Lord put on His heart.

During the latter months of 1997 Kelli began seeing Dr. Smentek, a fertility specialist in Spokane, Washington. What a blessing he has turned out to be. We did the usual tests on both of us and it was determined the problem was some scarring in Kelli's fallopian tubes. The scarring was preventing the process of the egg being fertilized.

On February 18th, 1998 Dr. Smentek performed a surgery that had a chance of being successful. He was trying to be optimistic but we could tell it was a long shot. But he said there was hope. We were still spiritually immature at this time but we did pray fervently that the surgery would be successful. Thank God He has plans for us and they cannot be thwarted. It is only by His grace. Amen!

Following the surgery Dr. Smentek performed another test where he shot some dye into the fallopian tubes to see if the dye could get through. To our dismay very little dye made it through the fallopian tubes. He suggested we give it a few months and see what happens. If we didn't have any success we could look at other options.

We were using ovulation kits so we would know when Kelli was ovulating. We were very faithful when it came to praying this would work, Kelli more so than I. Notice I said praying. In our time of crisis we began to lean on Jesus more and more. Every crisis is an opportunity to seek Christ.

We were desperate and had nowhere to turn. I reflect back and think man we were using Jesus. Do I feel bad for turning to God when I wanted something? I don't believe He thinks that way. He wants good things for us. I try to remember to thank Him every day for being a God who answers prayers.

We had been on fertility drugs for two months. I think the plan was to try them for six months if necessary. May rolled around and with it came an early fire season for our friends north of the border. Canada was experiencing a bad fire season and put out a call for help. Like good neighbors we responded. I agreed to go as the assistant crew boss on a crew assigned to a large fire North of Edmonton.

I was slated to take a few summer courses at the end of May-beginning of June to continue my education. Prior to accepting the assignment I informed my supervisors I would have to be back before the end of May to attend these courses. No problem was the answer I received.

The assignment was winding down but it was beginning to look like the crew was going to need to stay up in Canada for a few more days. I made some phone calls reminding people I took the assignment after explicitly telling them I would need to be back by a certain date which was quickly approaching. I informed them I needed to have arrangements made to fly home.

My pleas were falling on deaf ears. I kept getting the same answer, "There is nothing we can do you will have to come home with the crew." I was discouraged and began to accept the idea I was not going to make it home on time.

Then out of nowhere these travel plans were handed to me. I was to head to Edmonton, stay the night, and fly home the next day. I recall thinking how did this happen? I didn't think anything about it at the time but now I know God stepped in because He can. His word says, "Then you will be able to test and approve what God's will is—His good, pleasing, and perfect will" (Romans 12:2 NIV). It was God's will I make it home and He made it happen.

I made it home in time to begin school but that was not the miraculous thing. I didn't share this with anyone else at the time but there was another reason I desperately needed to be home. According to the chemistry kit, I mean the ovulation kit Kelli was going to begin ovulating soon and we didn't want to miss a month while on fertility drugs.

Let me recap this whole situation for you because there was clearly some higher intervention taking place here. I am calling my home unit reminding them I needed to have arrangements made to fly home but my pleas are falling on deaf ears. Then out of nowhere I get an itinerary handed to me having me home the next day. I arrived at home and was able to fulfill my commitments. The miracle in all this is Rebekah Marie Zufelt was born February 18th, 1999.

Rebekah was born exactly one year after the surgery but she was conceived when God made it possible for me to return home from Canada when I did. See nobody can thwart God's plans for us. Thank you Father. We worship an awesome God. Amen!

The amazing thing is we were still not making a full commitment to God. We had taken big steps but it would still be a couple years before we would surrender all our old ways and commit fully to God. We were receiving good things from God; I don't want to say His best because I know we haven't even begun to tap into what He has for us.

We were still lukewarm at this time but getting warmer. I am so thankful we didn't stay at lukewarm. The Bible tells us in Revelation 3:16, "So because you are lukewarm—neither hot nor cold—I am about to spit you out of my mouth" (NIV).

Rebekah is thirteen years old now and not only is she a miracle but she is a tremendous blessing to her mother and me. All I remember for the next little while is being overwhelmed with joy that we had a little baby girl. I wish I could say the birth of Rebekah brought about a stronger commitment to God but it didn't. Not the way it should have. Our only defense was a lack of wisdom. Forgive us Father for we know not what we do or say.

Our lives were definitely different and we were heading in the right direction but we had a ways to go. Remember it is a journey. I realize the miracles God has performed for my benefit, a person who did not even understand His ways. I was only a degree or two past lukewarm, yet God was gracious enough to give me a healthy baby girl.

At the time we were still dismissing these things as coincidences and good luck. We were so blind not to see God's blessings that were being bestowed upon us. Come on God went as far as to give Carolyn a detailed dream that included the name of the baby girl we were going to bring into this world. God even had Pastor Kent stop his sermon and tell us, "Terry and Kelli I believe God wants you to have children." Why didn't He just move on? Because He loved us and He still loves us. We are no more special than anyone else.

There are millions of people who can relate to our story. God will show you the same kindness, regardless of what you have done. He wants the best for His children. We are children of the Most High God!

People who go to church are not perfect. In fact, they likely have a lot of faults but who doesn't. It has been my experience that they do not lack generosity or love. The first week we brought Rebekah home from the hospital proved to us that God's people do not lack these two qualities.

I don't know who organized it but somebody from church delivered a meal to our house at dinner time that whole week. That was awesome. It wasn't the food that made it special although the meals were great. It was the idea that people were taking time out of their own schedules, using their own means to bring meals to us. That was an act of love and compassion that I could not recall ever being bestowed upon me before. No, Christians are not perfect but I have no doubt they do genuinely have good hearts.

We really began to see fruit when we made a commitment to the local church. We were becoming a part of God's family. We were going to church on a regular basis and we were even tithing, although not biblically correct according to God's word. Kelli came home from work one day in the fall of 1999 and shared with me Carolyn asked her if Rebekah was ready to have a little sister or brother. She told Kelli God had given her another dream. Yes, we were going to have another child soon but this time God did not reveal if it was a boy or a girl.

The gender of the baby didn't matter anyway. At this point we were praying for a healthy baby. When I was operating strictly in the flesh it mattered. I wanted a boy who would be the greatest athlete ever to walk this earth or at least good enough to play college sports. Fortunately, that whole way of thinking went away as the flesh went away.

Thankfully, God did bless my daughters with tremendous gifts and athleticism.

Kelli and I had decided without consulting God, we would wait awhile before deciding if we wanted to try to have another child. All the emotion we went through trying to conceive Rebekah had basically drained us.

Dr. Smentek had informed us the scarring in Kelli's tubes would probably scar back and we may only have one child. If it was God's will that we would only have one child we were still going to be very thankful for the one child God provided. Thankfully, God wanted to keep on blessing us and we received the "official word" that we were going to be blessed with another child.

I shared in the introduction that I am a wildland firefighter. I am currently an Assistant Fire Management Officer (AFMO) on the Coeur d' Alene River Ranger District. I am responsible for helping manage the fire and fuels program on 750,000 acres of public forested land.

Ten years prior (99-2008) to becoming an AFMO I was on an Interagency Hotshot Crew (IHC). I worked my way up from Squad Boss, to Assistant Superintendent, and then in 2004 I became the Superintendent. I led nineteen young men and women into battle that were highly skilled, in excellent physical condition, and extremely motivated. Our job was to travel throughout the United States, mostly in the Western United States and assist in suppressing the largest, highest priority fires that were burning out of control. Interagency Hotshot Crew's are the special forces of firefighting. They are the best of the best. It is a demanding and physical job to say the least.

The summer of 2000 was my second year on the Hotshot Crew. Kelli had several false alarms while I was on fire. I would receive a call informing me Kelli was having the baby. I would race back home praying the whole time to be there for the birth. Every time I would arrive home and hear the words 'false alarm'.

Dr. Smentek would do his evaluation and assure us everything looked like it was on schedule for the due date.

Finally, it was late September and we were camped out in the Frank Church Wilderness where there was no cell service. After a few days we were heading to a fire camp when Kelli was able to get me on the cell phone and tell me she thought the baby was going to be born early. I recall thinking oh man what am I going to do?

The Superintendent at the time drove me to the Incident Command Post (ICP) located in Salmon, ID. Early that next morning I was on a little plane heading for home. I kept asking God to let me make it home for my child's birth. Obviously, it is the only chance I would ever get to see Olivia come into this world. Watching the birth of a child is amazing!

I made it home only to hear 'false alarm'. I decided it was time to stay closer to home so no more fire assignments for the year. After all those false alarms Olivia Grace Zufelt was born right on her predicted date of October 21st, 2000. God is good and Carolyn's dream was right on. Olivia was conceived a few months after the Lord revealed to Carolyn in a dream we were going to have another baby.

It was shortly after Olivia's birth when I applied for the vacant Assistant Superintendent position on the crew and was offered the job. This gave us an opportunity to sell our house in Mullan and move closer to my new station that was located in Coeur d' Alene. We split the difference so neither Kelli or I had to drive too far. We bought a three bedroom house in Pinehurst which was a move of about twenty-five miles so it worked out well.

We started attending a Bible study at Mark and Carey Schrams. Mark was an elder at CLC. Mark and Carey had been going to church there since they were saved twenty plus years ago. The two of them ended up discipling Kelli and me. They put a lot of time and energy into teaching us what the Bible said and how to live a Godly life. I believe we were part of their home group for three years.

Kelli and I were growing spiritually and beginning to obtain a little biblical knowledge. I recall showing up at home group with several sheets of paper full of questions. I was reading the Bible from Genesis to Revelation which was generating a whole lot of questions.

I was thirsty for biblical knowledge and wisdom. To this very day I still ask God to give me biblical knowledge and wisdom. I believe if I can begin to apply His wisdom that comes from searching and understanding His word everything in my life will fall in order. We should all ask God for wisdom. God's word says those who lack wisdom need to ask Him for it and He will freely give wisdom.

King Solomon was one of the greatest kings God ever put on a throne. Solomon became king after his father David passed away. God told King Solomon he could ask for anything and He would grant it to him. Whatever he wanted God was willing to give him. King Solomon asked for wisdom and understanding to rule God's people wisely and justly. God loved King Solomon's answer and said he would receive all of that and all the wealth imaginable. God liked this answer so much because wisdom is connected to the heart.

King Solomon became so famous people traveled from far and wide to hear his wisdom. When the Queen of Sheba went to visit Solomon she was amazed at his wisdom and wealth. She told Solomon the reports she had been told about his wisdom and wealth were inaccurate because his wisdom and wealth was far greater than she had been told. Solomon was blessed by the hand of God.

Unfortunately, King Solomon began to intermarry with other nations whom God said not to marry. God had warned the people they would forget Him and begin to worship other gods. Solomon took seven hundred wives and began to worship in idolatry. Even with all of his wisdom Solomon failed to listen to God. He failed to follow His commands but he didn't lack wisdom just judgment.

The amazing part of King Solomon's story is he was born out of a relationship that started with a desire. King David decided not to go off to war with his army which was the tradition every spring time.

One evening when he could not sleep David took a walk out on the palace roof and soon noticed a beautiful woman, Bathsheba taking a bath in the moonlight. She was very attractive and he desired to have her so he sent for her. King David slept with her and shortly after he received notice she was pregnant. This was not good news because she was married to one of David's mighty men, Uriah the Hittite.

King David sent for Uriah and on two different occasions he tried to get Uriah to go sleep with his wife Bathsheba. Uriah being a man of honor and character refused to lie with his wife because the other men were at war and sleeping on the hard ground.

Now David really had a problem so he sends a note back with Uriah to Joab the commander of his army. The note tells Joab to send Uriah to the front lines and have him get close enough so the arrows can reach him. David sentenced Uriah to death because of his own desires.

The Bible says, "Then, after desire has conceived, it gives birth to sin; and sin, when it is full-grown, gives birth to death" (James 1:15 NIV). This is exactly what David did. He desired to sleep with Bathsheba birthing sin. Then he lies and tries to manipulate Uriah which was his sin fully grown, and eventually he has Uriah killed. Because of David's actions the son that was born to David and Bathsheba out of desire and sin died shortly after his birth.

David repented and was forgiven by God's grace. Repentance is a foundational teaching of the Bible. To repent means we quit sinning. We make a commitment to quit doing the act that causes us to sin against God and leads us to death. Repentance is a change of one's will and mind arising from heartfelt sorrow for sin.

David moved Bathsheba into the palace and took her for his wife. They conceived Solomon who would inherit the kingdom from his father. God took a bad situation and made something good out of it but there were still consequences.

We were settled in at CLC. If the church doors were open we were there. Our lives, our marriage were so much better. Unfortunately, we began to feel like we were no longer getting fed at church and we were hungry. What was going on? We could sense something was happening but we didn't have a clue to what that was. We were reading the Bible and began to believe maybe everything we were being taught was not lining up with the scriptures we were reading.

We were showing up on Sunday's excited and expectant to hear and see what God was doing but we were leaving wondering how that sermon was even applicable to anything that was in the Bible. I recall Kelli and me looking at each other when we got in the car and saying, "I don't understand how that sermon relates to anything that is in the Bible or has to deal with God's kingdom."

I was definitely sensing and feeling something was not right. What do we do? Do you go to another church? Can you leave the church once you have been going regularly? I didn't know. I was never churched this was all new to me. What I did know was my life had changed so much I wasn't sure I wanted to risk leaving CLC to find another church.

My fear was I would quit going to church. I was nervous because I didn't want to risk going back to the old life. Kelli on the other hand wanted to start visiting other churches. She even began to visit another church when I was traveling on fires.

Word spread quickly we were thinking of leaving and we soon received a visit from the pastor. The pastor and his wife were such great people but this high we were riding was dissipating because of whatever was going on behind closed doors.

Something was not right and people were aware of it. People were bailing out right and left sensing the church was going down like the Titanic. Attendance on Sunday was down significantly. There were about twelve people attending on a regular basis. Reflecting back twelve is a pretty cool number considering Jesus chose twelve men who he would disciple. But the Bible says to be fruitful and multiply which was not happening.

We don't always understand why God does some of the things He does. We are not capable of understanding because He is all knowing and we are not. His ways are not our ways. There are times when we just can't explain it. God had His reasons for taking CLC in a new direction and that new direction came in the way of the Associate Pastor Ralph Lowe and his wife Susie becoming the senior Pastors in the fall of 2002.

This move would end up being significant in my life. When Pastor Ralph took the helm at CLC it was the initial step by God to start me down the road to becoming an elder at CLC.

An elder is like a board member of a company. Churches have different names and their duties and responsibilities may be different depending on the church you attend.

God began to bring some pretty powerful guest ministries into the church. I began to receive prophecies about how I was going to be a new man. In fact, one prophecy said Kelli would not even recognize me in two years. Another prophecy said I would become the man she had always dreamed of marrying, what did that mean?

"In a year or two years, your wife will look at you and say, "This is the man that I dreamed I would be married to." "This is the guy." (May 23, 2004).

What? How is that even possible? How can a person change so much when he has been set in his ways for twenty-eight years? That is what the prophecy said and that is exactly what happened.

Pastor Ralph began to seek God's vision and direction for CLC. He began to re-teach on some subjects where we had strayed away from what the Bible teaches. It wasn't kooky far out stuff it was some doctrinal issues that needed a little tweaking. Pastor Ralph was lining our will up with God's will.

The twelve of us who were left became committed to seeking and asking the Lord for guidance on how to rebuild the foundation at CLC. The reason God took us down to twelve before building us up only He knows. Regardless this was a major step in developing my journey.

I believe we all matured a great deal by going through the rebuilding process. We were committed as a group to continue God's work, to carry out His will. When we line ourselves up with God's will then we will begin to see the fruit of our labor and that is what we were beginning to see at CLC. CLC was about to embark on quite a journey and this was going to greatly influence my personal journey.

In 2003, I began a year of training into eldership at CLC. At the end of one year I was confirmed as an elder. Being an elder was not a position I sought after or coveted. I didn't even know this type of thing happened in churches. I didn't even know what an elder was when I first started attending church. Seven years ago I wasn't even going to church. I was in a dark prison where no light was allowed in because light was bad. Light didn't represent the way of the devil. Reflecting back I do believe I was called to be an elder but I certainly never saw it coming.

I had gone from never attending church to actually participating and helping where I was asked to serve. Since entering church for the first time I have preached sermons and taught Sunday school for various age groups. My resume also includes being in charge of water baptisms, coordinating membership classes, and organizing our local outreach activities.

Kelli became the Worship Leader and rotated in as the nursery babysitter. She has also taught Sunday school. Together we were the organizers for Kids Club for a year, taught parenting classes, lead home group, and we served on the finance committee together which I chaired (Kelli was really doing the work I just ran a few meetings). All these opportunities exposed us to a lot of situations and learning experiences in a short period of time.

I now realize God had His hand on me way before I recognized He did. He chose me long before I made a decision to choose Him. My prayer is light will flood into the hearts of people and they will understand the hope that is given to all of us when God chooses us. Then you will discover the glorious blessings that will be yours together with all of God's people (Ephesians 1:18).

For the next several years I stayed engaged in God's word. The Bible was the only book I read. I did not feel released to read any other books. I read the Bible front to back three times from 2001-2004 which is not great compared to a lot of people but I felt pretty good about it.

The first time I read the Bible I was looking to simply conquer it. Then I read back through it again writing down the immediate questions I had. They were very elementary questions but that was ok. I was beginning to form some basic beliefs. The third time I read through the Bible I began to study things out to solidify my beliefs and memorize scriptures. God had me focused on His word and only His word. I really did begin to look like a different person.

My whole philosophy about life changed. I did a complete metamorphous. Actually through the filling of the Holy Spirit I gained a conscience. I could no longer do the immoral things that once blinded me and kept me in the dark.

Prior to attending church I was very judgmental towards other people. I had a long haired hippie people with earrings need not apply sort of attitude. They were automatically weird or bad people. Punk rockers didn't seem to irritate me anymore. I began to find myself having compassion for people whom at one time I could care less about. Sad stories on television began to break my heart.

Cussing seems foreign to me. There are rare occasions when a cuss word comes out of my mouth and I will feel horrible. I am not putting myself on a pedestal and I am not saying everybody is this way but for me it just is.

Kelli and I's marriage was doing wonderful. We had Jesus and our two girls, life was good. It was amazing how our priorities had changed and how our lives were so different. When I look back at where I once was I cannot believe how well things are going. I owe all the glory to God. Things have turned one hundred and eighty degrees for us.

Our lives were going so great we decided to beat all the odds and we started talking about having another child. After praying for quite awhile we both felt God wanted us to have a third child. May of 2004 we found out we were pregnant. We were excited and felt really good about having another child.

I received an order to take the crew down to Arizona on June 16th. We got an early start that day hoping to get past Salt Lake City. Kelli had a routine checkup scheduled for that day but we had made a decision I would take off because everything would be fine.

I was just outside Dillion, MT when I got a call from Kelli. I instantly knew something was wrong. She managed to tell me the baby did not have a heartbeat. I knew in my heart things would be ok but I felt horrible because I wasn't there with Kelli. It tore me up she had to hear that news alone. I immediately got turned around and headed for home.

Having the miscarriage knocked us for a loop but we leaned on God. Everything would work out. It definitely hurt and we began to have second thoughts about having a third child. We had two healthy children and life was good maybe that was enough. We went back and forth for months trying to decide if we wanted to have another child. We decided to take a wait and see approach.

Kelli really struggled because she felt like God wanted us to have another child. The problem was our flesh was pretty content with having two healthy, beautiful girls. It was hard not to think if God wanted us to have another child why did we have a miscarriage? Were we not hearing His voice correctly?

We were up at Mark and Carey's around Christmas of 2004 sitting around a table sharing what God had been doing in our lives. Kelli shared she was getting really frustrated trying to figure out God's will. She finally said, "I wish God would just show me a burning bush or something if He wants us to have another child."

Instantly this decorative paper that was around the bottom portion of a candle hanging on the wall caught on fire. It was amazingly hilarious. Kelli asked for a burning bush or something like it and there it was.

There were no more questions about whether to have another child or not. Amazing! Our hearts were now lined up with God's will and we knew we were to have another baby. September of 2005 we learned we were pregnant. Sophia Marie Grace Zufelt was born May 12th, 2006 blessing us with three wonderful daughters. God is true and faithful to His word.

Remember I mentioned I was reading the Bible and praying for wisdom. Recently I learned that Sophia means wisdom in Greek. How cool is that! I was praying for wisdom and asking God if we should have another child and we get Sophia—wisdom.

We no longer expected God to line up with our will. We submitted ourselves to His will. We were trusting God to guide us, comfort us, and to provide for us. We were giving God the glory He deserved and we were thankful He showed His love for us.

I have been so blessed and I want to give the glory to God. This is why I want to be obedient and do whatever God tells me to do. I trust Him. He is my Rock and my Refuge. It has been an awesome journey. My heart's desire is to see others get on their own path. It is not an exclusive club. Begin to trust in God. His ways are perfect!

CHAPTER 3

The Devil is a Worthy Foe

Sporting events are played every day in our society. Professional and collegiate sports have become such a big business that owners of franchises, presidents of universities, athletic directors, and coaches look for whatever advantage they can to increase their chances of winning.

Scouting opponents is one area where coaches spend time and energy trying to gain an advantage over their opponent. The more they can learn about their opponent the better the game plan they can prepare to defeat them.

When I was playing college football every Monday the offense would spend the first hour looking at game film from the previous week. We would review the plays we executed correctly and discuss the plays we could have executed better. Once that hour was over all of our focus went towards our upcoming opponent.

I enjoyed watching film so I would find time to watch three or four hours of film throughout the week. I would look for anything that could give me an advantage over my opponent. The better I knew my opponent the greater the chances I had to be successful and help my team.

The Bible gives us this same advantage. The Bible clearly describes the devil's game plan. The Bible among other things gives us a scouting report on our opponent, the devil. We need to know how the devil operates and what schemes he likes to run. What are his tendencies? What are his strengths and weaknesses? We have to read and study the

Bible if we are to get a clear understanding how we defeat the works of the devil.

Our goal is to prevent Satan from scoring. We can bend but not break. Satan knows how to play so he is going to be able to call some plays that will work and be successful. We need to be offensive minded and keep Satan on the defensive.

Satan is a tough opponent we need all the advantage we can to defeat him. We need time in the classroom before we take on our opponent. We need to read our text book or scouting report, the Bible. We need to talk and formulate a game plan which means we are prayed up. If we tried to blindly take on Satan there is a good chance he would crush us.

If we look at our team we will see our best player is God. He can do anything and cannot be stopped. He is very gifted and understands the game. God's knowledge of the game is so amazing. He is always out in front, way ahead of everyone else. He knows when things are going to happen before they happen. His intelligence and understanding of the game is like that of a person who has played the game forever. The more you play with Him the more you realize He could win this game by Himself. But He likes to see the commitment of His teammates and their hard work payoff.

God is the ultimate team player. He is a coach on the playing field. God knows the rules better than anyone and He never breaks them. He will make sacrifices in order to give the team a better chance at winning. God knows His teammates cost Him some victories but He won't give up on them. He will never forsake His players He loves them too much.

Our next player is Jesus. This guy is tough! He can take a beating and still get back on his feet. Jesus' strength is he loves the people who are on his side and are engaged in the game. If somebody makes a mistake he reaches his hand out and picks them up. He would do anything for his teammates. He would even die for his teammates if asked. Jesus has all the talent but his strength is that he loves playing with his teammates. When Jesus is in the game he can do all things. He has no limit.

Jesus can be spit on, called names, bruised, and bleeding but he will not quit. He is dedicated to the plan and he is going to carry it out. He has a desire to do the will of his Coach that is nothing like you have ever seen.

Next we have the Holy Spirit. This guy is a star but never seems to get the recognition or the glory he deserves. He is the forgotten player. He does everything Coach asks him to do and he doesn't need the glory. For him it is all about doing what he can to make his Coach happy. He is a team player who is always there to motivate and encourage his teammates. Win or lose if we are on his team he is going to root for us and comfort us. Oddly, he is really popular with some teammates but other teammates seem to avoid hanging out with him. Many of his teammates fail to get to know him. They acknowledge he is part of the team but they fail to comprehend his role and what he brings to the team. The Holy Spirit is underutilized.

All the other players are ordinary. Each one brings something to the field. They are valuable assets to the team. Without each and every one of them the team would be weaker. Some of these players are playing out of position to fill a void. There are individuals who have the talent and gifting to play the position but they have not joined the team. Unfortunately, the team roster is incomplete. Incomplete or not the members of the team are ready to take on their opponent.

Our opponent's game plan is to win. Not only win but he truly desires to hurt, maim, and kill anybody who stands against him. He does not have a set of rules because he does not play by any rules. He will do whatever it takes to hurt his opponents and win the game.

He never lacks players who are of the same mind set as him. He takes good players and convinces them it is his way and no other way. Morale is low and self esteem cannot be found among his players. He doesn't inspire he despises and criticizes.

Fortunately life is not a game. Life is war. Jesus said, "The thief comes only to steal and kill and destroy; I have come that they may have life, and have it to the full" (John 10:10 NIV). Satan has one purpose: To take down as many of God's creation as he can. Satan desires to frustrate God's creation. He wants nothing more than to drive a wedge between God and humans. It is his cold heart's desire to populate his prison with as many prisoners as he can. Jesus wants to give good things and Satan wants to take those good things away.

Our enemy wants to steal anything that is good. Any good seed that is sown in us he wants to take it away. It is Satan's desire to kill us. Jesus said he wanted to do the will of his Father which was that none of us shall perish. Satan desires the opposite. His desire is that we would all perish. Lastly, he wants to destroy our lives. He wants us to live in hell on this earth. Satan does not have the authority or power to destroy our lives but if he can keep us from hearing the word and if he can keep us from turning to God he knows he can win some battles and capture many prisoners.

The outcome of the war is Satan and his band of followers will be thrown into the lake of fire. But until that time he is looking for some prisoners to sentence to hard times. Alcatraz will seem like a picnic. He does not want us to have eternal life in heaven that would mean we belong to God. He wants everything that belongs to God.

The deceiver wants to destroy our marriages because marriage is sacred to God. He wants to destroy our families. A weak and broken family does not make time for God. He wants us to lose our jobs so we will lose everything. Satan wants us operating at the highest possible stress level.

He wants us stressing about our jobs, relationships, retirement, homework, bills, and every single thing in our lives. Anything to keep our attention from Jesus.

If he can break and destroy our lives he knows from years of studying our habits a large majority of us will turn to other things like alcohol and drugs. These potentially addictive drugs can destroy many lives for many generations. If we turn to drugs Satan knows he has turned the tide in his favor.

In football blockers are taught to knock their opponent to the ground and once they get them down they are taught to keep them down. Satan and his militia have the same philosophy. If they sense they have dealt us a blow they become relentless. Satan and his militia do not have a mercy rule. We have a tendency to give up when we keep getting knocked down. This is the attitude Satan wants us to have. Woe me nothing works out for me. I have never done anything and never will. Life stinks. You know all those clichés.

"When Jesus spoke again to the people, he said, 'I am the light of the world. Whoever follows me will never walk in the darkness, but will have the light of life'" (John 8:12 NIV). Knowing this Satan wants us to live in darkness. What makes us live in darkness? Sinning!

This worldly system we live in has so many things that can tempt us and cause us to sin. These temptations can be so strong that we can end up living a life of sin. This world is Satan's playground! This world offers lots of 'activities' that can distract us and keep us from the light.

Have you asked yourself lately, "where did the day go" or "where did the time go" or how about "time just seemed to pass me by today?" If Satan can keep us occupied with things that are not of God he knows he is winning.

We have a tendency to lose track of time and get caught up in so many activities and so many things we don't make time to visit our Father. Typically most of us won't make time to pray or read our Bible. We live such busy lives we don't take time to talk to someone God have put in our path. In fact, we have become so busy Monday through Friday we need to take evenings and weekends off and make them about us.

Going to church and spending time with our heavenly Father should not take the back seat in any situation or for any reason. Time management or lack of is a strategy of the devil. The devil is so successful at this we all have to have day planners. If it were possible he would have stock in companies who make day planners.

The devil (slanderer or accuser), Diablo's, Serpent, Satan, or Enemy which ever name we chose to characterize him understand he is not stupid. He's cunning, shrewd, crafty, deceitful, and heartless. Yes, he certainly is stupid for picking a fight with God and believing he can match wisdom with Him. But when it comes to this world he is pretty crafty and dialed in. Don't be fooled! This isn't one of those cases where you keep your friends close and your enemies closer. No, we want to distance ourselves from Satan. We need to know how he works, what his resources are, and what he is capable of doing. We need to recognize and understand the devil has two strong advocates we know as "world" and "flesh."

Before we look at how he uses "world" and "flesh" let's first gain some insight into who this enemy of ours is. Satan in Hebrew is translated into 'adversary.' Therefore, Satan is the one who opposes God. God stands for good which means Satan opposes anything that is good.

Satan, also known as Lucifer, was an angel before he tried to over throw God. The Prophet Isaiah gives great insight into Satan's life. "How you have fallen from heaven, O morning star, son of the dawn! You have been cast down to the earth, you who once laid low the nations! You said in your heart, 'I will ascend to heaven; I will raise my throne above the stars of God; I will sit enthroned on the mount of assembly, on the utmost heights of the sacred mountain. I will ascend above the tops of the clouds; I will make myself like the Most High.' But you are brought down to the grave, to the depths of the pit" (Isaiah 14:12-15 NIV). Satan desired to become greater and more powerful then God. He wanted to rule!

Satan is responsible for the first act of sin. The very existence of sin was birthed in heaven. Can you imagine that? Satan became prideful and was not happy or satisfied to be a follower of God and to do the work that God asked of him. He wanted to be the leader no matter the cost.

The Bible tells us Satan was the Worship Leader in heaven. We read in Revelation 12:3 that Satan was powerful and wise and while still in heaven he led a rebellion against God. Satan is a fallen angel who lost his place in heaven when God cast him to earth.

Satan saw God's mightiness and power and desired it above all other things and when he didn't get it he rebelled until he had to be kicked out of heaven. This is very insightful because it gives us a hint as to how he operates. He likes pride, rebellion, and he has a thirst for power that is not rightfully his.

Satan and his band of followers now inhabit the earth. They roam from here to there to spew out evil. He is not omnipresent which means he cannot be in more than one place at a time. Satan is not omnipotent, all-powerful. The only power he has is what God gives him and he is certainly not omniscient, all knowing.

We need to know Satan is on a leash and we have inherited the authority to rebuke him. The authority belongs to Jesus. Satan cannot keep us behind his bars. He does not have the authority to hold us. Jesus proclaimed he has the keys to the gates of hell and that hell will not prevail. "Then Jesus came to them and said, 'All authority in heaven and on earth has been given to me'" (Matthew 28:18 NIV).

Jesus says *all* authority has been given to him. All means all. If Jesus has all authority that means there is none left over for Satan, none. Jesus departed and gave the righteous this same authority. "When the righteous thrive, the people rejoice; when the wicked rule, the people groan" (Proverbs 29:2 NIV). When we apply the authority given to us we rejoice because we are in God's will.

Although he is not all-powerful, all knowing, and he cannot be in more than one place at a time the devil is a master psychiatrist's. He knows our behavior. He has studied us for many generations. Satan's ways at times seem to go past what our human minds can phantom. There is a very good chance he received some insight into our human nature when he was still in God's good graces. After all these years of studying he has developed his game plan. He has evolved, changed tactics, added new tactics, and adjusted to the times.

Satan wants us to act independently of God. We can gleam a lot from the following four scriptures that give us some insight into the personality of Satan.

- "You belong to your father, the devil, and you want to carry out your father's desire. He was a murder from the beginning, not holding to the truth, for there is no truth in him. When he lies, he speaks in his native language, for he is a liar, and the father of lies" (John 8:44 NIV). Remember Satan is a master psychiatrist.
- "'Simon, Simon Satan asks to sift you all as wheat'" (Luke 22:31 NIV).
  There is not a single person who has ever lived that Satan did not try to separate from God.
- "For the accuser of our brothers, who accuses them before our God day and night, has been hurled down" (Revelation 12:10 NIV). Divide and conquer is his game. If he can keep us pitted against each other than he will have success.
- "'In your anger do not sin': Do not let the sun go down while you are still angry, and do not give the devil a foothold'" (Ephesians 4:26-27 NIV). He is always around hiding, crouching like a lion ready to attack do not give him the opportunity.

Those verses are admonishing us to join and stay with God. Don't even give the wily devil an opportunity. You might be saying to yourself this all sounds good but how do we avoid him? How do we avoid letting him in?

We need to understand Satan is a fisherman of people just like those who follow Christ are asked to be. He cast a little doubt hoping to spur a little rebellion. If he gets a nibble he will use everything in his tackle box to hook that person and reel them into his kingdom. He is a king over a kingdom of darkness and destruction. Satan's followers are living in a world of darkness. There are a lot of us who were in the same place. We each chose to stay behind the bars and live in his kingdom. It was our free will that put us there and our free will that keeps us there. The gate is unlocked we have to push it open and run towards the horizon. We need to make a decision to belong to God's kingdom and stay far away from Satan's kingdom.

The following are some of the other names Satan is referred to in the Bible.

Liar	Beelzebub-Lord of Flies	Enemy of all that is
Thief	Great dragon	good
Murderer	Prince of darkness	Father of lies
Tempter	Prince of this world	That ancient serpent
Evil one	Sower of discord	Angel of light
Prince of demons	Belial-wicked one	Imitator
Destroyer	Roaring lion	Oppressor of Saints

If we look at the synonyms for adversary we will get a good picture of the description of our foe. Synonyms for adversary include opponent, challenger, rival, enemy, and antagonists. Satan is all of these things to us and God. He is one hundred percent evil. He is not capable of doing anything good. Destruction is the business he is in and havoc is what he sows and in the end destruction is what he will reap.

First and foremost understand everything Satan stands for and represents makes him our enemy. Why? He has one purpose in life and that it to convince us that we do not need anything God has to offer. He wants us to believe there is no God. If he can deceive people into believing there is no God then he doesn't need to spend any time or resources on these people.

Atheists are defeated and need no attention from Satan. The Bible calls them antichrists. 1 John Chapter 2 verse 22 says, "Who is the liar? It is the man who denies that Jesus is the Christ. Such a man is the antichrist—he denies the Father and the Son" (NIV).

Our society is being kind or politically correct to refer to those who don't believe in God as atheist. In fact, by their very nature they are advocates for Satan. The disciple John whom the bible tells us Jesus loved said that those who don't believe in the Father and His son are antichrists. That may seem harsh but Jesus said if you are not for me then you are against me. There is no such thing as being on the fence in God's kingdom. Jesus said, "I know your deeds, that you are neither cold nor hot. I wish you were either one or the other! So, because you are lukewarm—neither hot nor cold—I am about to spit you out of my mouth" (Revelation 3:15-16 NIV).

Mark Twain said it well many years ago when he said, [1]"We may not pay Satan reverence, for that would be indiscreet, but we can at least respect his talents. A person, who has for untold centuries maintained the imposing position of spiritual head of four-fifths of the human race, and political head of the whole of it, must be granted the possession of executive abilities of the loftiest order." Satan is good at what he does.

I teach our young firefighters that they shouldn't fear fire but they better not underestimate the power it has and the damage it can cause. Likewise we should not fear Satan but at the same time we should not underestimate him.

God is who we should fear. "Therefore, since we are receiving a kingdom that cannot be shaken, let us be thankful, and so worship God acceptably with reverence and awe, for our 'God is a consuming fire'" (Hebrews 12:28 NIV). The key word in this scripture is "reverence," which means respect for, admiration of, and awe at His mighty presence.

We read in the beginning of Genesis that God created the heavens and the earth. Genesis reveals that there were living creatures on earth at this time and one of those creatures was the crafty Serpent, Satan. Satan was craftier than any of the wild animals the Lord God had made.

The next thing God did was create man, Adam. Then God created man a suitable helper, Eve. God had created a beautiful garden on the east end of the Garden of Eden.

In the middle of the garden God had planted two trees. One tree was the tree of life and the other was the tree of the knowledge of good and evil. "And the LORD God commanded the man, 'You are free to eat from any tree in the garden; but you must not eat from the tree of the knowledge of good and evil, for when you eat of it you will surely die'" (Genesis 2:16-17 NIV). God said when you eat of it. He knew what was going to happen.

God gave Adam and Eve a commandment not to eat from the tree of knowledge of good and evil. They were given a test in the garden and they failed. The first exam ever given and Adam and Eve failed it miserably.

It was through the conversation with the Serpent that Eve started allowing herself to be tempted. She began to see the fruit was good for food, her body would like it. She also saw that the fruit was pleasing to her eye, and it was desirable for gaining wisdom. When lust has been conceived, it births sin and when sin has ran its course, it brings forth death (James 1:15). Remember God's warning to them? When you eat of the tree you will surely die. Do you see the connection between sin and death? "For the wages of our sins is death, but the gift of God is eternal life in Christ Jesus our Lord" (Romans 6:23 NIV).

Eve was deceived and we need to realize deception is a strategy of Satan's. The Serpent's words to Eve were, "Did God really say you could not eat from that tree?" He deceived Eve by using one of his greatest strategies. He made her question God's word. This is the exact strategy he still uses today when he says, "Does the Bible really say we should do this or we shouldn't do that?"

Another strategy of our nemesis is to convince us that the Bible is old and written by man. Satan tells us God couldn't have known we would be this smart and so the *old* Bible doesn't apply to our situation in the twenty-first century.

The Serpent deceived Eve in the Garden of Eden and both Adam and Eve ate the forbidden fruit. What we need to realize is that eating the fruit was not the initial sin. Eating from the tree of knowledge of good and evil brought the fall of humanity and the death penalty. The original sin was disobeying a command God gave them to not eat from that particular tree.

So why did Adam and Eve disobey the direct word of God? Did God not speak clearly? Was it merely a case of Adam and Eve misunderstanding which tree God was talking about? I don't think so because they hid from God after they ate from the tree. They knew that was the tree they were to not partake of. They knew they were busted because God commanded them not to eat from the tree of knowledge of good and evil. Were they deceived? Yes, but why did they disobey a direct command from God? Was it a learned behavior? No, they were the only people on earth and life on earth began with them. They had nobody to teach it to them. They were God's first creation.

Before we start blaming Adam and Eve for the big "fall" that affected all of mankind we need to know they were the first but by no means the last to be deceived by Satan. Only twenty-seven percent of adults are convinced Satan is a real force and only forty-percent of born again believers believe Satan is a real force. Those are extremely low numbers and they give us a good perspective why Satan is a worthy foe.

Isn't it interesting Lucifer was the first sinner in heaven and the root of his sin was he desired to be like God? Eve was the first person on earth to be deceived by Satan leading her to sin and the root of her sin came from the desire to have wisdom like God. Did she believe she could become like God?

The question that keeps coming to mind is why would God create angelic hosts and man that would sin? If Adam and Eve would have passed the test would that have been the end of Satan or would he have been allowed to keep slithering around until he got someone to sin? Adam and Eve's son Cain killed his brother Abel making him the first murder on earth. We all agree Adam and Eve sinned but if earth was going to be perfect why cast Satan down here?

Eating from the tree that God said was forbidden was the result of their flesh having a built in law to disobey God's word, to sin. I believe the flesh has a built in law of failure, making it impossible for the natural man to please or serve God. What did I just say? You read it correctly. It is true! We fail to understand that our human nature is to oppose God and our nature is prone to sin.

There was the original order that was designed by God that had the Spirit, the Soul, and the Flesh. Our flesh or body was to be subservient to our Spirit and Soul. This order got flipped upside down and our flesh is now in control and our soul and spirit are suppressed making it necessary for us to kill our old selves and become new creatures in God. When we become new creatures the order is restored back to God's original intent. The Bible talks a lot about needing to be born again!

The words "born again" literally mean "born from above." It is a change of heart. It is a spiritual transformation. Basically, to be born again is very similar to repent. The term in the original Greek of the NT was translated "be converted" which means to "turn around."

To be converted is used thirty-nine times in the NT. Eighteen of those instances it is used in the sense of turning from sin to God. Conversion in the NT means we turn away from those "worldly" things that are not of God and we start filling our lives with the ways of God, making Him first in our lives.

Nicodemus who was a Pharisee (Pharisees kept the Law of Moses) spoke to Jesus and said, "'Rabbi, we know you are a teacher from God. For no one could perform the miraculous signs you are doing if God were not with Him.'"

"In reply Jesus declared, 'I tell you the truth, no one can see the kingdom of God unless he is born again'" (John 3:2-3 NIV).

Nicodemus had no understanding of what it meant to be born again. The doctrine of being born again was introduced by Jesus. Nicodemus was dumbfounded and asked Jesus how a man can enter back into a mother's womb and be born again. "Jesus answered, 'I tell you the truth, no one can enter the kingdom of God unless he is born of water and the

Spirit'" (John 3:5 NIV). When we accept Christ into our heart we are starting the process of being born again.

How did this order get out of whack? What happened? We don't know for sure. It is one of those things we may have to wait and ask God when we get to heaven. We have established that by exercising free will in the Garden man came under the death penalty. Some would argue that our inner desire to sin was inherited from man's fall. But why did Lucifer, the bright and morning star fall? Why did Eve disobey God's commandment? Both of these incidents were prior to the fall of man. All the guilty parties made a decision to rebel against God. Is there a common denominator? Is it that God gave us free will?

Let us look at the concept of free will. We don't know for sure but it looks like free will played a huge role in the original sin. God gives us the choice to decide whether to believe and follow His ways or to live our lives as we see fit with no intervention from Him. Free will means we have the power or discretion to choose. We have the ability to choose freely. Free will is the belief that man's choices ultimately are or can be voluntary, and not determined by external forces.

God created us but He didn't hardwire us to automatically believe and follow His way. Isn't that interesting? Why would God give us the choice? This wasn't something He overlooked. God could take anyone of us and turn us in the direction He wants us to go. Unlike Satan God is omnipotent, omniscient, and omnipresent.

God's desire is that we will make a conscious decision to make a commitment to follow Him. He wants the decision we make to believe in Him and follow Him to be from our own hearts not because He makes us.

Our Abba Father loves us and because of His great love for us Jesus, God's only son stretched out his arms and died on the cross for all of mankind. God loves us so much He had His one and only son willingly stretch out his arms and take all of the world's sins with one act of compassion.

God does not want to create robots designed or hard wired to serve Him. He created us in His image and God can do whatever He wants. He has a free will so we have free will. If I possessed God's ability and created you I would have made it mandatory you believe in me. I would have hard wired it right into your brain. But my ways are not His ways.

God in His infinite wisdom gave us free will to choose right from wrong. He gave us the choice to believe, to follow, and fulfill our purpose or to simply shrug our shoulders and turn the other direction. Unfortunately, we often turn in the direction of the enemy who rebelled against God. Satan is aware of this and takes full advantage of it. God made the decision ours whether to follow Him or go the journey alone.

As previously mentioned Satan is the great deceiver. He knows our weakness. He definitely knows God allowed us free will. Satan counts on the fact that our flesh will desire the things of his kingdom. Satan is the head of an army of dissidents just like himself who carry out his will and they make his influence felt over all the earth. He has blinded the minds and hearts of unbelievers.

We are told unbelievers belong to him. "He who does what is sinful is of the devil, because the devil has been sinning from the beginning. The reason the Son of God appeared was to destroy the devil's work. No one who is born of God will continue to sin, because God's seed remains in him; he cannot go on sinning, because he has been born of God. This is how we know who the children of God are and who the children of the devil are: Anyone who does not do what is right is not a child of God; nor is anyone who does not love his brother" (1 John 3: 8-10 NIV).

Children of the devil are the only ones Satan is allowed to carry out his works unless God allows him. We read in the Book of Job where God did allow the Serpent to try to prove Job was not a righteous man.

Job was blameless and upright; he feared God and shunned evil. In fact, the Bible tells us he was the greatest man among all the people of the East. He was the ultimate family man having seven sons and three daughters. He also owned thousands of various livestock.

We learn in the very first chapter of the Book of Job that some angels came to present themselves before the Lord, and Satan happen to come along with them. "The Lord said to Satan, 'Where have you come from?'"

"Satan answered the Lord, 'From roaming through the earth and going back and forth in it'" (Job 1:7 NIV). God knew what Satan was up to because the next thing He asks Satan is if he has considered His servant Job. There was no conversation God knew Satan's thoughts.

When I read that I am thinking have you considered Job for what? God repeats that Job is blameless and upright; he feared God and shunned evil. We have to completely capture the next couple paragraphs between God and Satan because I cannot give the story justice by paraphrasing.

"'Does Job fear God for nothing?'"

"Satan replied. 'Have you not put a hedge around him and his household and everything he has? You have blessed the work of his hands, so that his flocks and herds are spread throughout the land. But stretch out your hand and strike everything he has, and he will surely curse you to your face.'"

"The Lord said to Satan, 'Very well, then, everything he has is in your hands, but on the man himself do not lay a finger.'

Then Satan went out from the presence of the Lord" (Job 1:9-12 NIV).

What? God has put everything of Job's in Satan's hand except for Job himself. Why? So we could have this story handed down from generation to generation to demonstrate to us Satan cannot do anything against us if we are under God's authority. We have authority to refuse Satan and his tactics.

God still maintained control of the leash He had on Satan by not allowing him to lay a hand on Job. This demonstrates Satan has to operate within the boundaries set forth by God. This whole seen is setup to show that even though Satan took everything from Job and tried to ruin his life Job never even considered turning from God. Job's story is an excellent testimony that shows us we can be committed to God especially when times are tough.

This did not stop Satan from attempting to prove his point and attempt to show God that He was wrong. Satan begins his attack. First, Job's oxen and donkeys were carried off and his servants were put to the sword. Immediately after hearing that news Job is told that a fire of God fell from the sky and burned the sheep and the servants. It's not over yet because right when that guy is done speaking another servant is there to tell Job his camels have been taken and all his servants were put to the sword. Yes, waiting in line with more news is another servant who is about to give Job the most devastating news yet, his sons and daughters were in their house having a feast when a mighty wind came and blew the house down on them and they are all dead.

Job did not blame God or disown Him, he praised Him. How many of us would react in that way? What was Job's response? He said, "'Naked I came from my mother's womb, and naked I will depart. The Lord gave and the Lord has taken away; may the name of the Lord be praised'" (Job 1:21 NIV). The story is not over.

Satan goes to the Lord again and they basically have the same conversation as they previously had but this time he tells the Lord, "'A man will give all he has for his own life. But stretch out your hand and strike his flesh and bones, and he will surely curse you to your face'" (Job 2:4-5 NIV). This time God tells Satan he may do what he wants to Job but he must spare his life.

Satan leaves the presence of the Lord and afflicted Job with painful sores from his head to his toes. Job's wife had had enough and encourages him to curse the Lord. Job makes a profound statement at this time when he says, "Shall we accept the good from God, and not trouble?" Job would have none of that foolish talk so he took a piece of broken pottery and scraped his sores. After everything he went through Job did not sin. That is integrity! Job had so much love and faith for the Lord he would not consider cursing the Lord even after losing everything and being stricken with sores.

Job's faith should witness to all of us. He proved to Satan there was a person on earth who would not curse God no matter what was thrown at him. Job was given two tests and he passed them both with honors. Could we do the same?

If we fast forward to the end of Job's story we learn the Lord blessed the latter part of Job's life more than the first. He had more sheep and camels and he was blessed with seven more sons and three daughters. Job lived to see the fourth generation of his family because God blessed him for his faithfulness. What a beautiful lesson we learn from Job. Amen!

If we are going to truly understand the big picture we need to know there is a universal war that has been waged since the beginning of time. Man is at war with both God's spirit and Satan's spirits. God is at war with the evil of man's flesh and the evil spirits of Satan. Satan and his spirits are a war with man's spirit and the spirit of God. This is, in fact, the real battleground of good and evil; right against wrong. Good against evil. God is always looking for people who are willing to serve Him. In fact, He is looking for an army of good people. God is a recruiter who asks us to join His army. He does not have a draft it is an all volunteer army. If we look at the definition of recruit we will see it is a fascinating word. It means:

- To engage persons for military service
- To strengthen or enlist an armed force by enlistment
- To supply with new members or employees
- To enroll in support of an idea
- To renew or restore
- A new member of a body

Can you see why God is looking for recruits? Those are all great definitions but let's look at the last two. First, to renew or restore: These are perfect words to apply when referring to God and His kingdom. We hit the nail on the head. When you peal everything away this is what is at the core of God's message. God is saying I can make you new. Remember John 3:5, "'I tell you the truth, no one can enter the kingdom of God unless he is born of water and the Spirit'" (NIV). God wants us in His army so we can become a new creature. Nothing but the blood of Jesus can make us whole again. He will heal our wounds and forgive our transgressions.

Our transgressions are our violations of God's law and commandments. Transgression can also be the violation of not performing our duty. Are you beginning to see God's wisdom? Prior to surrendering our will to Him and letting God be in charge of our lives we are AWOL in His army. We are not performing the duties we are designed to perform. We are not deserters but we are sinners. We are all sinners who need to be part of a body.

Recruit means to become a new member of a body. God uses the body metaphorically in the Bible many times. "The body is a unit, though it is made up of many parts; and though all its parts are many, they form one body. So it is with Christ" (1 Corinthians 12:12 NIV).

Being a recruit means we are becoming a member of an army that Jesus is the leader. "Just as each of us has one body with many members, and these members do not all have the same function, so in Christ we who are many form one body, and each member belongs to all the others" (Romans 12:4-5 NIV). This tells us there is a role for each member of the body of Christ.

God has a place and a role for each one of us in the body. The scriptures also tell us God sets the members of the body, as it pleases Him. Jesus is the supreme leader because he only speaks what God will have him say. Christ is the head of the church.

Our human body was created to act and respond in a certain way. If we take something away from our body it does not function as it was meant to function. For example, I wouldn't function the same way if I were missing one of my arms. That missing arm is no longer a part of my body. It had a purpose to fulfill and the arm is no longer there to fulfill its role.

God designed every one of us with a purpose in mind which was to supply or fulfill a role in His body, the church. Like a good General He adapts and improvises when we fail to follow His will but none the less we were designed to fill a need. Let me use the example of a church that desperately needs a worship leader and God gave you a voice that makes the angels dance. He gave you that voice to fill a need in His body. The idea is to make the body strong so it can do the glorious work of the Lord. There is strength in numbers. A strong body will be a healthy body if it is following and applying the word of God.

We are stronger together than when we are apart from each other. To illustrate this point at a county fair one year in a horse pulling competition the champion horse pulled 4,500 pounds and the runner up 4,400 pounds. For entertainment and because they were curious the organizers decided to hook the two horses to the same sled and see how much they could pull. Together they pulled 12,000 pounds-an increase of more than thirty-three percent over their combined individual efforts. That is quite an effort. The Lord's body would accomplish a lot more for His kingdom if we would hook up together. Our enemy knows this and he spends all of his energy trying to keep the body from forming. Satan thrives on creating division wherever and whenever he can.

Remember the devils' two advocates or partners in sin: world and flesh. Through the years Satan has became very sophisticated and adapted very well at using his two pawns world and flesh. We will get incredible insight if we look into how the devil uses these two venues to create havoc and keep sin alive and well in this world.

As we talk about world and flesh visualize an exercise ball that we see in the gym and imagine it as the world. Imagine our body, our flesh mending and bending to that ball. We are able to lean forward, backwards, and sideways on the ball. Our flesh can conform to it. If we are exercising this is great but in this context conforming to the ways of this world is sinful. It can lead us to destruction, hell. God tells us we are in this world but we are not of this world. We have a purpose while on this earth and that purpose cannot be fulfilled if we conform to the things of this world.

The Bible speaks of the "world" in a few different contexts. It speaks about the world as being a place that is sinful, rebellious, and of a worldly system. "Do not love the world or anything in the world. If anyone loves the world, the love of the Father is not in him."

"For everything in the world—the cravings of sinful man, the lust of his eyes and the boasting of what he has and does-comes not from the Father but from the world" (1 John 2:15-16 NIV).

John is talking about the rebellious sinful worldly system. We need to keep that in our mind when we are talking about the world in this context. The point is Jesus tells us not take part in this worldly system. Why? Jesus wants us to understand the world offers ways to keep us from fulfilling our purpose. John 3:19 says, "This is the verdict: Light (Jesus) has come into the world, but men loved darkness instead of light because their deeds were evil" (NIV). In this example world is being referred to in general terms as when we say the world is a big place. This verse is referring to the physical world and what occurs in it.

We can look at John 3:16, "For God so loved the world that he gave his only begotten Son, that whosoever believes in him shall not perish but have everlasting life." Clearly, Jesus was referring to the people who live in this worldly system.

Another example is the "Great Commission." "Therefore go and make disciples of all nations, baptizing them in the name of the Father, and of the Son, and of the Holy Spirit" (Matthew 28:19 NIV). It wouldn't do us any good to go to a deserted island somewhere in the world and have nobody to preach the good news to! So this is obviously a scripture using world as the people who inhabit the world.

Take a minute and think of the world we live in today. We have ventured so far away from our roots one has to wonder why God doesn't put an end to it. After all He only made a covenant that He would not destroy the world by water ever again. I guess it is because God sees the big picture.

The world is our flesh's playground. The world is the devil's recruiting ground. We fail to understand that this world (system) we live in is under Satan's control (1 John 5:19).

Jesus told Pilate his kingdom what not of this world. Jesus came to save the people in this world. We are merely visitors of this place God created. This is a big playground where school is always in session. We don't receive A's, B's, C's, or D's. There are only two grades. It is simple if we "receive" Jesus as our Lord and Savior we get a "P" pass to heaven. If we get an "F" that means we failed to receive Jesus and we receive a one way ticket to hell.

There is the way of the world and there is the way of the Word! We are to live according to the Word! "If you belonged to the world, it would love you as its own. As it is, you do not belong to the world, but I have chosen you out of the world. That is why the world hates you" (John 15:19 NIV). Jesus is talking about the world hating his disciples, those who follow him. Jesus came into the world but the world rejected him.

"Everyone who does evil hates the light, and will not come into the light for fear that his deeds will be exposed" (John 3:20 NIV). Jesus is saying we can't have it both ways. We cannot be a part of both worlds. In other words we must choose which world we want to be a part of. The two worlds were not created to work together.

The second pawn the devil uses is our flesh or the desires of our flesh. Our flesh is that part of our body that is distinguished from our mind or soul. Following God is contrary to our flesh.

Flesh is our physical or carnal nature. Carnal is that part of our nature that deals with our appetite for desires and wants. Get this! Carnal means earthly or worldly it is not spiritual. It is neither holy nor sanctified. Therefore our flesh or carnal nature desires things that are not from God.

There are many things in this world that feeds the flesh. When people are feeding the flesh it makes it so difficult to rescue them but it makes Satan's work easier. We either feed the flesh or we feed the Spirit. Those who feed the flesh are not living according to God's word. I was in the same situation. It is not easy to give up these desires that feed the flesh. It should be of encouragement to everyone to know millions of people have escaped from behind Satan's bars. These people resisted the devil, they refused to stay conformed to this world, and they asked their heavenly Father to rescue them.

We need to understand our flesh cannot be reformed. The flesh is intimately intertwined with our mind, our will, and our emotions. We are instructed to become new creatures. Our only hope is to destroy our flesh. Remember our definition of flesh.

The only way to escape the death sentence that is associated with the law of the flesh is the total execution of our flesh. We have to destroy our flesh and allow God's Spirit to take control. Our hope comes when we allow the Holy Spirit to take up residence in us.

Satan would like us to feed our desires with the things of this world but if we are going to line up with God's desire we must feed ourselves with His food. Jesus said, "Do not work for food that spoils, but for food that endures to eternal life, which the Son of Man will give you. On him God the Father has placed his seal of approval" (John 6:27 NIV). Anything that prevents us from walking with God and deters us from His will is not from God's kingdom. This is food that is perishable. If we would remember that it is all about God's will we would be a lot better off. There is a furious battle being waged in regards to whose will, will be in charge.

The Lord's Prayer does not say our kingdom come our will be done. It says Your kingdom come Your will be done referring to God's kingdom and His will. In its entirety it says:

Our Father who in heaven,
hallowed be your name,
your kingdom come,
your will be done
on earth as it is in heaven.
Give us today our daily bread.
Forgive us of our debts,
as we also have forgiven our
debtors.
And lead us not into temptation,
but deliver us from the evil one.

We briefly looked at sin and who it originated with but let's take a closer look at what sin is. Sin is a component of darkness that negates the power of the blood of Jesus. Sin expresses itself both as general and specific rebellion against God and His righteousness.

We read in Genesis that God knowing Cain was going to kill his brother Abel warns him about sin. He tells Cain sin is crouching at his door, and it desires to have him. God encourages Cain to learn to master sin (Genesis 4:7). We all need to heed this instruction and realize God could stick every one of our names in place of Cain's name because sin is always lurking and it does desire to control every one of us. "Terry, sin is crouching at your door, and it desires to have you, and you must learn to master it." Replace my name with yours and heed God's warning to us. God informs us sin is always going to be around. It wants us to mess up so it can own us but we can learn to defeat the temptation of sin.

In the fall of 2005 I took the crew down to preposition for the arrival of Hurricane Rita. If you recall Rita were a few months behind Hurricane Katrina. Our government received a black eye because many people claimed there was no help and the government was not prepared to help with the recovery process. You can determine your own thoughts on that issue. But it was those accusations that led to us being ordered down to San Augustine, TX.

We were cruising into the city about twenty four hours before Rita was predicted to make land fall and everybody else was getting out. Honestly, I have to tell you I am not sure riding out a hurricane while hunkered down in a motel room is something I want to go through again. We were able to do some really valuable work but I would certainly put a lot of thought into it before doing it again.

We had enough supplies for three days and probably even more but a few stores were still open when we arrived so I thought I would get a few extra snacks to get me through the hurricane. My eyes were opened when I noticed the items that were cleaned out (advertisement signs were still up). I began to pay attention to the items that were sold out and those that were left behind. I started consciously observing the shelves in order to perform an educated observation of the wants, needs, and priorities of people in stressful, crisis situations.

I don't know if you will think it was as odd as I did but I quickly noticed the items that were gone were the items I would say are craved by our flesh. There was no alcohol left, cigarettes were all gone. I am not sure what kinds of magazines were sold, but I can imagine, it didn't matter gone, all of them. The desires of our flesh scream for the things that are of this world. It would have been awesome if all the Bibles would have been sold out and any other reading material that was applicable to God's word. Our flesh because of its nature turns to those things that are of the world.

Here is the problem: Sin is controlled by Satan and organized against God. Does God expect us to live a life that is perfect? No! There is no difference, "for all have sinned and fall short of the glory of God" (Romans 3:23 NIV). Remember sin equals death and as sinners we deserve death but God sent Jesus to redeem those of us who accept Jesus as our Lord and Savior.

The first thing we need to do is submit ourselves to God. James the brother of Jesus had a little insight when he wrote resist the devil and he will flee from you. "Submit yourselves, then, to God. Resist the devil, and he will flee from you" (James 4:7 NIV).

Satan has no choice but to flee when we turn to God. Satan has to put his tail between his legs and leave or maybe he just slithers away. Why? Because greater is He that is in believers than he that is in the world.

A great example of this is in Matthew chapter four when Jesus was tempted by the tempter (Satan). After Jesus fasted for forty days he was hungry and weak. He was weak in the flesh but his spirit was strong. The devil thought he would be able to tempt Jesus during this time. He thought Jesus would be weak and succumb to the things of this world but Jesus rejected the devil's temptations with scripture. Jesus refused the devil and he fled. What did Jesus say to him? "It is written: 'Man does not live on bread alone, but on every word that comes from the mouth of God'" (Matthew 4:4 NIV).

Jesus defeated Satan two more times by quoting scripture. "It is also written: 'Do not put the Lord your God to the test'" (Matthew 4:7 NIV).

Jesus had enough and the third time Satan tried to tempt him "Jesus said to him, 'Away from me, Satan! For it is written: Worship the Lord your God, and serve him only'" (Matthew 4:10 NIV). Jesus instructs us to do the same.

One of the greatest weaknesses we have as a human race and one of the main areas that prevents us from signing on as recruits and joining God's army is our fascination with recreational activities. Our obsession with recreation is one of the greatest weapons the devil has. The devil is very aware of our fleshly pitfalls in this area. We live in a world that idolizes recreation. We spend billions of dollars on recreation in the United States every year. Let me explain what I mean before you throw the book down and never pick it up again.

The devil wants us emphasizing the RE in recreation. He knows we will lose our focus which should be on creation (he has a scouting report that is from the beginning of time through present). If Satan can keep us more focused on ourselves and less focused on God how can we grow spiritually? If Satan can keep us focused on recreation rather than creation and our Creator then he has accomplished his goal.

Recreation is fine in moderation but not at the cost of not fulfilling our purpose. We put fleshly things above spiritual well-being forgetting God created us for a higher purpose. We are living in a time when the majority of people in this country and probably this world truly believe their purpose is to have fun and that life is all about them. We will discuss recreation and our purpose in depth in chapter six.

We have become a world that has a "what have you done for me lately" mentality. This is contrary to the idea of "how am I serving my purpose?" For years our rally call as a nation was, "Ask Not What Your Country Can Do For You, But What Can You Do For Your Country." President John F. Kennedy spoke that now famous phrase at his inaugural address on January 20th, 1961.

"For man holds in his mortal hands the power to abolish all forms of human poverty and all forms of human life. And yet the same revolutionary beliefs for which our forebears fought are still at issue around the globe—the belief that the rights of man come not from the generosity of the state, but from the hand of God. And so, my fellow Americans, ask not what your country can do for you; ask what you can do for your country.

My fellow citizens of the world ask not what America will do for you, but what together we can do for the freedom of man. Finally, whether you are citizens of America or citizens of the world ask of us here the same high standards of strength and sacrifice which we ask of you. With a good conscience our only sure reward, with history the final judge of our deeds, let us go forth to lead the land we love, asking His blessing and His help, but knowing that here on earth God's work must truly be our own." Do we no longer heed those words?"

Our rally call should be "Ask not what God can do for us, but ask what we can do to increase His kingdom." Now that is a rally call. God wants us to enjoy life. He is our

Father, our Creator who wants good things for His children. He wants us to have a good time just as our earthly parents want us to enjoy life. The scripture tells us that our Father in heaven wants to give us good gifts even more than our earthly father.

Another tool of the enemy is deceitfulness (remember Eve). He has convinced a large majority of our population that being a Christian is for the geek and the weak. Our enemy wants the world view of a Christian to be that we are uncool and stuffy people who do not know how to have fun. Unfortunately, he is having a lot of success.

We need to make the decision not to believe the great deception that life is all about us. This deception is a lie founded by the devil so his prison will remain full in this life and the next.

We have an adversary who doesn't want us to spend our eternal life with God and Jesus. Satan and his dissidents are very real and they are very strong. These forces of evil will quit a nothing to keep us from enjoying the life God has planned for us. Satan is going to use everything in his arsenal to keep us from receiving Jesus Christ as our Lord and Savior. We have to be prepared to fight our opponent on a daily basis and we do that through the power of Jesus Christ. He is our strength; our armor, our comforter, and our encourager that we need to overcome all things. All things should glorify His name!

CHAPTER 4

Heaven or Hell: It is a Choice

You might be wondering why we need to know how our adversary operates. The answer is when the sun sets on our lives here on earth we go to one of two destinations. One destination hell, is run by Satan our adversary. The other destination heaven is a place of perfection owned and operated by the very Spirit that created us.

These two destinations are operated very differently. Heaven and hell only have two things in common: They are for eternity and they always have vacancy. Once we enter our final destination our journey is over. Hell is a life of misery and torment. Heaven is a life of peace and serenity.

Satan wants the worst for his prisoners, hard times for certain. God wants to share His kingdom and make eternity euphoric. In hell you can never check out. In heaven you will never want to check out. Satan will never let you go and even if he would God could not let you in His kingdom, it is too late. We don't even like to talk about hell and many of us do not imagine life in heaven often enough. Reality is they both exist.

Kelli had given me an ultimatum that led me to face the ultimate ultimatum. It is the ultimate ultimatum that every person ever born is faced with. There is no escaping this ultimatum that is presented to us by God. Accept Jesus as our Lord and Savior or chose to go through life as our own boss. One choice has a reward, eternal life. The other choice has a consequence, eternal hell.

Our denial, unwillingness to think about hell or just not accepting it does not matter in the end. Jesus is going to hand down our sentence and it will not be up for appeal. There is no appeal process. Jesus will render a decision quickly and fairly and that will be the end of it.

We are under God's judicial system. It doesn't matter if we are an atheist, devil worshipper, Muslim, Pagan, Mormon, white, brown, yellow, gray all people past, present, and future we all have a predetermined court date with Jesus as our judge. We will not be able to blame the sentence we receive on anyone else but ourselves. We are responsible for the sentence we receive, we script our own destiny.

What many of us fail to understand is we are on probation while we are on this earth. Some of us have been on probation before and we know how it works. We got in trouble with the law and depending on the crime a judge gave us a sentence of probation, actual jail time, or the judge may have sentenced us to probation after we served out our jail sentence.

I don't believe anybody knows the age at which time we begin our "probation" here on earth but it *might* be safe to say it is around the age of twelve. Studies have suggested most people's minds are made up, and they believe they know what they need to know spiritually by the age of thirteen. Studies also indicate a person's moral perspectives and foundations are largely in place by the age of nine. After the first nine years most people simply refine their views as they age.

This *theory* and that is all it is seems to be supported by biblical scripture that may verify our probation would begin around the age of twelve. The gospel of Luke gives us the story of when Jesus tells his parents he is doing the work of his Father.

Jesus had gone with his mother and father to Jerusalem where they went every year during the feast of the Passover. "When he was twelve years old, they went up to the Feast, according to the custom. After the Feast was over, while his parents were returning home, the boy Jesus stayed behind in

Jerusalem, but they were unaware of it. Thinking he was in their company, they traveled on for a day. Then they began looking for him among their relatives and friends. When they did not find him, they went back to Jerusalem to look for him" (Luke 2:43-45 NIV).

"After three days they found him in the temple courts, sitting among the teachers, listening to them and asking them questions. Everyone who heard him was amazed at his understanding and his answers. When his parents saw him, they were astonished."

"His mother said to him, 'Son, why have you treated us like this? Your father and I have been anxiously searching for you.'"

"Why were you searching for me?" "he asked."

"Didn't you know I had to be in my Father's house?"

"But they did not understand what he was saying to them" (Luke 2:46-50 NIV).

We generally start thinking about heaven and hell when someone who we are close to dies. I know it was that way for me. I really started thinking about the two alternatives, heaven, or hell when my mother passed away in 2006.

I had already experienced the death of my father in 1991 but I really didn't give heaven or hell much thought because I didn't know Jesus, God, or anything about the Bible. My focus was on me and how I felt about losing my father.

I was walking with the Lord at the time of my mom's death and so heaven and hell were on my mind. Specifically, I wondered where my parents ended up following their deaths.

I believe my parents thought there was a God but they did not have a relationship with God. I remember asking Dad questions about what religion we believed and he would answer back, "We are Jack Mormons." I would think to myself what does that mean? But that was about the end of the conversation. I have since realized that meant we did not belong to any religion but my parents once lived in an area where Mormonism was the dominant religion so by default we were Jack Mormons or people who did not live according to the Mormon religion. I was clueless and if the conversation came up where somebody asked me my religion I would answer "I am a Jack Mormon."

Growing up I can recall numerous occasions when some of *those door to door religious people would show up*. We had this big window in our living room and we could look right down on the road where people had to park if they were going to come visit. It was common practice if we heard car doors closing somebody would get up and look to see whom it was. If it were those *two men in suits* the alarm would sound and we would all scatter to our favorite hiding places throughout the house and wait for the all clear sound to ring out. I am sure they wondered why we left the lights and television on when we were not home.

I believe my dad may have had some teaching about the Bible while growing up. There were a few times when we got surprised by those gentlemen caring the Bible. I believe Bible thumper is what we commonly called them. There were a few times when we were forced to open the door (only because we were not quick enough in sounding the alarm) and we would have to indulge these *intruders* and listen to what they were preaching. The nerve of some people, why would anybody want to share a message of gentleness, goodness, joy, love, meekness, patience, hope, peace, and temperance? I remember Dad was able to answer some of the questions they would ask. He seemed to be familiar with some of the stories they mentioned, although he never discussed them with us kids. Not that I can recall anyway.

On the other hand I do not believe Mom knew too much about religion. (Incidentally doesn't religion sound like something cold or far away? We will address this in chapter six). I don't remember Mother being present during those times we were snoozing and got caught red handed by those Bible thumpers.

I cannot recall having any conversations about religion with my mother until we had the conversation that saved her life. Through God's grace I was able to lead my mother in the sinners' prayer shortly before her death in March of 2006.

My mother's health had been deteriorating for a few years and she had a prolonged stay in the hospital in November of 2005. I was at the church meeting with my pastor, his wife, and the wife of another elder when Kelli called and told me my mom had been admitted to the hospital. The pastor prayed for me and then I proceeded to the hospital to be with my mom.

I went to the hospital to see how she was but I knew I had a greater mission. It was up to me to share with my mother the ultimatum she was facing. Did she want to spend life in hell or have eternal life with Jesus in heaven? Remember this whole topic had been off limits to me for thirty-eight years.

If you are wondering if I was nervous the answer is a resounding yes. When I reflect back I think how odd to have that mind set. She was my mother, whom I loved, and yet I was nervous to speak to her about Jesus. It wasn't like she could beat me up, why was I so nervous?

There was no beating around the bush I just came out and asked her if she believed there was a God? She looked at me and firmly said, "Yes, I do. I don't want to go to hell." At that point I knew it was going to be a lot easier than I thought. I told her I wanted to lead her through a prayer that would make sure she didn't go to hell. I started leading her through the prayer and she was silent. I stopped and said Mom you have to repeat after me which she did.

The doctor tried to be optimistic but it was obvious Mom was pretty sick. The doctor told us she was suffering from congenital heart failure. When she passed away four months later I was at peace. When I went to the funeral home to say goodbye the Lord spoke to me. God said, "Be still, and know that I am God." I could not recall ever hearing that before so I looked to see if it was scripture and sure enough it was Psalm 46:10. What a comforter!

I shared with those in attendance at my mother's funeral service that my mom and dad's deaths were like night and day to me. It was a story of two totally different funerals. When my dad passed away I was not walking with the Lord. Dad's death left me angry, lost, and hurting.

My notes from the service read, "As I visited with Mom I was reminded of Dad's funeral and how much I did not understand death. I was angry God had taken my dad away from me at such a young age. I had so many negative emotions and somebody was to blame so I blamed God. I feel so many different emotions now that I have a relationship with Jesus Christ. The anger I felt when my dad died has been replaced by new emotions. I feel peace, hurt, pain, sorrow, happiness, and joy to mention a few."

I went on to say, "On March 8th my mother went to be with our Lord. We can be sure of this because the week before last Thanksgiving when I was visiting with her in the hospital Mom accepted Jesus Christ as her Lord and Savior. Her obedience is our assurance that her name is written in the Book of Life. She is now a resident of heaven!"

I felt different during Mom's death because I understood what Jesus did for her. I understand the significance of Jesus going to the cross for all of us who have received him as our Lord and Savior. I know he has made eternal life possible. I know my mother is in the heavenly kingdom.

Heaven is a place where there is no more suffering, no more loneliness, no more sorrow, and no pain. It is a place of joy and comfort. It is a promotion when we enter into heaven. Think about this! The roads are paved with gold!

The pain of my mother's death still hurt. Death of our loved one's will always hurt. God created us to have compassion and to love people. Hurting over the loss of a loved one is fine and expected. Having God in my life was the difference between the two deaths and why my emotions were so different.

Nobody gets a free pass or a get out of hell card they can use in the future. If we had a free pass why was there such a high price to pay? Jesus was sacrificed so his blood would redeem those of us who receive him. We can't have a free pass. A free pass would mean Jesus died for no reason which is unacceptable.

Satan's greatest deception of all time is he has deceived about ninety-percent of the world's population into believing the majority of us go to heaven. Simply not true. If we read a series of scripture from Matthew we will be enlightened and learn many go to hell and few go to heaven. "Enter through the narrow gate. For wide is the gate and broad is the road that leads to destruction, and many enter through it. But small is the gate and narrow the road that leads to life, and only a few find it" (Matthew 7:13-14 NIV).

This is how that same passage reads in the Message Bible. "Knowing the correct password—saying 'Master, Master,' for instance—isn't going to get you anywhere with me. What is required is serious obedience—doing what my Father wills. I can see it now—at the Final Judgment thousands strutting up to me and saying, 'Master, we preached the Message, we bashed the demons, our God-sponsored projects had everyone talking. And do you know what I am going to say? You missed the boat. All you did was use me to make yourselves important. You don't impress me one bit. You're out of here. These words I speak to you are not incidental additions to your life, homeowner.'"

When Pharaoh finally let the Israelites leave Egypt about two million people headed out to follow Moses including the rabble. Rabble was the name given to the non-Israelites who followed the Israelites out of Egypt. The rabble were not blind they witnessed the power and awesomeness of God. They wanted to follow the God of the Israelites.

Because of the Israelites rebellion and lack of faith God had them wonder through the desert one year for every day the spies spent checking out the land God had promised them. After wondering the desert for forty years how many Israelites from that generation were allowed to enter the Promised Land? Two, Joshua and Caleb were allowed to enter out of two million. I would say that is few not many. Not even Moses the leader entered the land God had given them. The Israelites did not trust God and were disobedient to His word. God is a God of His word. Many do not enter into heaven! Do not be deceived.

Jesus gave us the parable of the wedding banquet to illustrate that all do not make it into heaven. The Master of the house (God) invited a large number of guests (all of us) to a wedding banquet (heaven). Most of the invited guests made excuses and did not want to go to the banquet.

Everyone ever born is invited to the wedding banquet but most of us make excuses and fail to do our part. We fail to take the time and put forth the effort that is required of us, we miss out.

How many times have we dreaded going somewhere or to an event but we end up going and in the end we were glad we went? If we trust His word we will be glad we did. If we make the commitment to attend the banquet He has invited us to be a part of we will be thankful.

Let me see if I can illustrate this with two scenarios. There is this big room and in the middle of this room is a big throne where Jesus will sit when every person ever born will come to bow down before him and be judged. "It is written: 'As surely as I live,' says the Lord, 'every knee will bow before me; every tongue will confess to God'" (Romans 14:11 NIV). Jesus is the Judge! The Day of Judgment is the great reckoning day when God will bring all men before His throne to give an account of their lives while on earth. We find this in the following scriptures:

- "For he has set a day when he will judge the world with justice by the man he has appointed. He has given proof of this to all men by raising him from the dead" (Acts 17:31 NIV).
- "This will take place on the day when God will judge men's secrets through Jesus Christ, as my gospel declares" (Romans 2:16 NIV).
- "By the same word the present heavens and earth are reserved for fire, being kept for the day of judgment and destruction of ungodly men" (2 Peter 3:7 NIV).
- "He will judge the world in righteousness and the peoples in his truth" (Psalm 96:13 NIV).

When our judgment takes place we will be separated into three classes the: "Sheep" and the "goats" "the just" and "the wicked" "the Saints" and 'those who do not obey the Gospel'. We decide which class we are in by our obedience to His word. Obviously, we don't want to be the "goat" "wicked" or those who "disobey" the gospel.

In our scenario we have two individuals who are about to begin a new journey but first they have to go face their judge, Jesus Christ. The first guy who chose to go through the wide gate and travel the broad road struts up to the throne feeling pretty confident; he believed the foolish lies of this world: Do your best. There is a quota. Do good. Have fun there is no heaven, we just die. What happens in Vegas stays in Vegas. But since he has no understanding of God's word he feels pretty confident walking up to Jesus' throne. He gets to the throne and reality sets in. Is this really happening or am I dreaming? No dream!

Jesus already knows his name is not written in the Book of Life because if it were he would recall the memories of the time the two of them spent together. But Jesus goes through the motion and looks at the guy with tears in his eyes and says, "I don't know you." The guy quickly straightens up and realizes this is serious stuff. He tries to utter a few words but Jesus repeats, "I don't know you." The guy tries to defend his actions while on earth but it does not matter, it is simply too late.

Jesus' heart is broken but it is too late for this guy. Faced with the ultimate ultimatum he made the wrong choice. Jesus shows him all the times he reached out to him practically begging him to receive his mercy, to accept his grace, to grab eternal life before it was too late but he turned a blind eye every time.

Instead of receiving and accepting Jesus' offer this guy held on closer to the ways of the world. Jesus said, "Ask and it will be given to you; seek and you will find; knock and the door will be opened to you" (Matthew 7:7 NIV).

Jesus even went to this guy's door and knocked but he would not let him in. "Here I am! I stand at the door and knock. If anyone hears my voice and opens the door, I will come in and eat with him, and he with me" (Revelation 3:20

NIV). Jesus shows him the scars on his hands, feet, and side and says, "I bore these inflictions for you but you went down a different path. My passion was to die for you but you failed to accept me."

Reality has set in for this guy or so he thinks wait until he actually gets to hell. He begs Jesus for another chance. He pleads emphatically with Jesus to let him go to heaven but God's word is His word. We reap what we sow. If we sow evil we reap evil. Jesus points to the path he must now walk. From the throne there are two paths. One leads to the right and the other to the left. Dejected, scared, and sobbing uncontrollably the man heads down the path Jesus pointed to. His path is to the left and he immediately comes to a gate and above it reads, "WELCOME TO HELL—YOUR NEW ETERNAL HOME."

Jesus did not send this man to hell. His actions and defiance to accept Jesus Christ as his Lord and Savior sent him to hell. Jesus had to be obedient to the word of God.

The next person is already coming up the path towards Jesus. This is the guy who took the narrow path. He kept his eyes focused on Jesus. Jesus immediately begins to smile. He recognizes this person. This person knows whose thrown he is about to bow down to. He is humbled as he approaches the throne of Jesus. He reverently begins to express to Jesus how he knows he could have done more to help others and he is sorry he didn't do better but Jesus stretches out his arms and says, "Son you are forgiven, your name is written in the Book of Life. Welcome! Take the path to the right we have eternity to talk." Wow! That is it! You are even more awesome than I ever imagined. This guy sprints down the path to the right. He has more joy and peace then he has ever experienced in his entire life. He gets to the gate and above the gate it reads, "WELCOME TO HEAVEN—YOUR NEW ETERNAL HOME!"

In this story one guy receives salvation and the other guy a life of literal hell. Both faced the ultimate ultimatum and one chose correctly. Look at how hell and heaven are described in the Bible. Let's first look at hell.

The Hebrew word for hell is Hades or the world of the dead, including its inmates. Inmates, isn't that interesting. Remember the story of Alcatraz from the introduction? It is a grave or pit. Hell is the place of departed souls. It is the physical place where those who do not accept Christ as their savior go. Hell is an everlasting punishment. "Death and Destruction are never satisfied, and neither are the eyes of man" (Proverbs 27:20 NIV). Satan's home always has the vacancy sign posted right above the gate but he doesn't leave the light on for his patrons. There is no light.

There is some confusion or some who believe hell is the valley of Hinnom; gehenna, which means hell. This was a valley on the outskirts of Jerusalem where the pagans (worship earth, wind, and fire) sacrificed their children. There was a big gorge and the pagans did sacrifice their children in the valley of Hinnom but it is a different place then the hell where we can be sentenced for eternity if we fail to accept Jesus Christ as our Lord and as our Savior.

The Bible gives us a testimony of a poor beggar whose name was Lazarus. Lazarus's testimony is an eye witness account of hell so we won't be deceived that hell is not a real place where we go if our name is not written in the Book of Life. I am going to take the story in its entirety. It is Jesus himself who is sharing this testimony in Luke.

"There was a rich man who was dressed in purple and fine linen and lived in luxury every day. At his gate was laid a beggar named Lazarus, covered with sores and longing to eat what fell from the rich man's table. Even the dogs came and licked his sores.

"The time came when the beggar died and the angels came and carried him to Abraham's side. The rich man also died and was buried. In hell, where he was in torment, he looked up and saw Abraham far away, with Lazarus by his side. So he called to him, 'Father Abraham, have pity on me and send Lazarus to dip the tip of his finger in water and cool my tongue, because I am in agony in this fire.'

"But Abraham replied. 'Son, remember that in your life time you received your good things, while Lazarus received bad things, but now he is comforted here and you are in agony. And besides all this, between us and you a great chasm has been fixed, so those who want to go from here to you cannot, nor can anyone cross over from there to us.'

"He answered, 'Then I beg you, father, send Lazarus to my father's house, for I have five brothers. Let him warn them, so that they will not also come to this place of torment.'

"Abraham replied, 'They have Moses and the Prophets; let them listen to them.'

'No, father Abraham,' he said, 'but if someone from the dead goes to them, they will repent.'

"He said to him, 'If they do not listen to Moses and the Prophets, they will not be convinced even if someone rises from the dead'" (Luke 16:19-31 NIV).

It should be clear that this is not a gorge where children were sacrificed because the rich man is still alive. He is in hell, eternal torment. He failed to listen to the words that were spoken by Moses and the Prophets. We have the Bible that has gathered all of Moses teachings and the words of the Prophets in one book. We have no excuses for not knowing God's word.

I have always found it interesting that the rich man first asked for water. I think I would have asked for a second chance. I would have been begging, "Please let me out, I am sorry." I believe the rich man knew hell was forever so why bother asking. Can you imagine the torment? You know how you do something stupid and at first you hope it was just a dream or you wish you could have a redo? This guy knew there was no hope. He knew hell was for eternity!

Unfortunately, we have relegated the word hell to just another word in our vocabulary. In fact, it might be a top ten word that is used on a daily basis. What sense does it make to say, 'What the hell'? Is it a statement or a question? I don't know. If we stick the synonyms for hell into that same sentence look at what we would be saying.

- What the torture
- What the misery
- What the torment
- What the agony
- What the nightmare
- What the anguish

Hell is nothing to laugh at but if you replace hell with those synonyms it is kind of funny how "What the hell" became such a popular saying in our society. We should be afraid of hell, afraid enough we fear God.

Jesus tells us to fear God because He alone determines our final destiny. Jesus told us to fear Him who is able to destroy both body and soul in hell. Hell is real! It is a physical place where we go if God decides we are not fit for His kingdom.

Peter admonishes us by writing even angels, listen even angels go to hell if they sin. "For if God did not spare angels when they sinned, but sent them to hell, putting them into gloomy dungeons to be held for judgment;" (2 Peter 2:4 NIV). We need to believe if God will send angels to hell then He will surely send the unrepentant and unbelievers to hell. If we believe His word we will know hell is real.

This is how hell is described in the Bible:

Valley of groans,
weeping, & wailing
Fire & brimstone
Horrible torment
Continual ascending
smoke
No light

Fire is never quenched
No peace or joy
"The worm" of the
conscience never dies
Last for eternity
Eternal jail for the wicked

No righteousness, nor
salvation
Everlasting shame and
contempt
Furnace of fire-HOT
No life

Who goes to hell? Hypocrites, serpents, vipers, the wicked, and unrepentant are "salted" as sacrifice to eternal destruction. Those whose names are not found in the Book of Life go directly to hell along with those who failed to choose correctly when faced with God's ultimatum.

The Bible does not give us a lot of information about heaven. I do not believe we are capable of comprehending the true awesomeness that awaits believers in heaven. We have nothing to compare it to because of its beauty, tranquility, and splendor. We know the city needs no sun or moon because the illumination from God's glory will shine so bright. We also know Jesus will be there and he will be our shepherd. "For the Lamb at the center of the throne will be their shepherd; he will lead them to springs of living water. And God will wipe away every tear from their eyes" (Revelation 7:17 NIV).

"He will wipe every tear from their eyes. There will be no more death or mourning, or crying, or pain, for the old order of things has passed away" (Revelations 21:4 NIV).

There will be no hunger or thirst because on the side of the river is the tree of life that provides everything. We know the city streets are paved with gold. The gates are made of pearl and precious stones. But we receive the greatest news from Revelation 21:3, "And I heard a loud voice from the throne saying, 'Now the dwelling of God is with men, and he will live with them. They will be his people, and God himself will be with them and be their God'" (NIV) Woe! That sounds pretty amazing to me.

This is how heaven is described in the Bible:

Place of happiness	Eternal light	Love
New heaven and earth	No unrightcousness	Holiness
New Jerusalem	Eternal life	Righteousness
Tabernacle of God	The redeemed will see	Joy
No more death	His face	Peace
God's glory	You will serve God and	No sin
Worship centered around	the lamb eternally	No hate
God	It is glorious	No sorrow

Our destination is decided by what we do or fail to do on this earth. We have to learn to persevere. We are going to face roadblocks and obstacles. Too often these roadblocks and trials cause us to quit or lose hope in Jesus. If we lose hope we may be sealing our fate and earning a one way ticket to hell.

Does the Bible, God's living word promise us a perfect wonderful life with no obstacles? No! In fact, James Chapter 1 verses 2-3 says, "Consider it pure joy, my brothers, whenever you face trials of many kinds, because you know the testing of your faith develops perseverance" (NIV).

Obstacles, road blocks, difficulties, and tough times can come from God or they can come from the devil: But they are very different. Have you faced some obstacles? God wants us to persevere through some things so we will lean more on Him. "Not only so, but we also rejoice in our sufferings, because we know that suffering produces perseverance; perseverance, character; and character, hope. And hope does not disappoint us, because God has poured out his love into our hearts by the Holy Spirit, whom he has given us" (Romans 5: 3-5 NIV). He desires for us to grow-up spiritually.

God often creates obstacles for us so we will have opportunities to overcome and grow. God wants us to become mature. God's obstacles are for growth and He provides tools that will help us overcome. Satan's obstacles serve only one purpose, to beat us down and keep us down.

God's Obstacles:	Devil's Obstacles:
Wants us to succeed	Wants us to fail and give up
Knows we can persevere	Causes us to stray from the Way
Leads to maturity	Wants us to remain spiritually dead
Has a reward-heaven	Has a reward-hell on earth
Gives us tools to succeed	Attempts to keep us alone in the dark or
Brings a light to come beside us	bring someone who is operating in the dark beside us

We can deal with obstacles. Waves will subside and we will no longer be tossed around by them. When we learn to trust Jesus, "Then we will no longer be infants, tossed back and forth by the waves, and blown here and there by every wind of teaching and by the cunning and craftiness of men in their deceitful scheming. Instead, speaking the truth in love, we will in all things grow up into him who is the Head, that is, Christ" (Ephesians 4:14-15 NIV).

God declares to us in His living word how we can avoid hell. It starts by us seeking something very precious to Him. This is a riddle from Proverbs see if you can guess what it is that is being described in Proverbs 8 verses 1-36.

Listen! I am calling you out.
Does not understanding raise her voice?
On the heights along the way,
where the paths meet, she takes her stand;
behind the gates leading into the city,
at the entrances, she cries aloud:
"To you, O men, I call out;
I raise my voice to all mankind.
You who are simple, gain prudence;
You who are foolish, gain understanding.
Listen, for I have worthy things to say;
I open my lips to speak what is right.
My mouth speaks what is true,
for my lips detest wickedness.
All the words of my mouth are just;
none of them is crooked or perverse.
To the discerning all of them are right;
they are faultless to those who have knowledge.
Choose my instruction instead of silver,
knowledge rather than choice gold,
for I am more precious than rubies,
and nothing you desire can compare with her.
I, dwell together with prudence;
I possess knowledge and discretion.
To fear the LORD is to hate evil;
I hate pride and arrogance,
evil behavior and perverse speech.
Counsel and sound judgment are mine;
I have understanding and power.
By me kings reign

and rulers make laws that are just;
by me princes govern,
and all nobles who rule on earth.
I love those who love me,
and those who seek me find me.
With me are riches and honor,
enduring wealth and prosperity.
My fruit is better than fine gold;
What I yield surpasses choice silver.
I walk in the way of righteousness,
along the paths of justice,
bestowing wealth on those who love me
and making their treasuries full.
"The Lord brought me forth as the first of his works,
before his deeds of old;
I was appointed from eternity,
from the beginning, before the world began.
When there were no oceans, I was given birth,
when there were no springs
abounding with water;
before the mountains were settled in place,
before the hills, I was given birth,
before he made the earth or its fields
or any of the dust of the world.
I was there when he set the heavens in place,
when he marked out the horizon
on the face of the deep,
when he established the clouds above
and fixed securely the fountains of the deep,
when he gave the sea its boundary
so the waters would not overstep his command,
and when he marked out the
foundations of the earth.
Then I was the craftsman at his side.
I was filled with delight day after day,
rejoicing always in his presence, rejoicing
in his whole world
and delighting in mankind.

"Now then, my sons, listen to me;
blessed are those who keep my ways.
Listen to my instruction and be wise;
do not ignore it.
Blessed is the man who listens to me,
watching daily at my doors,
waiting at my doorway.
For whoever finds me finds life
and receives favor from the Lord.
But whoever fails to find me harms himself;
all who hate me love death."

Are you serious? Look at this list.

Truth
Better than silver, gold and jewels
Insight
It honors God
Hates evil
Fewer waves
It detests wickedness
Council
Brings prosperity
Sound judgment
It is not crooked, perverse, prideful, or arrogant

Lord gives it
Knowledge and understanding
Right & just
Discretion
Saves you from wicked people
Prolongs your life
Saves you from adultery
Lord's discipline
Riches
Honor
Peace
Prudence

Blessed
Confidence
Protection
Health
Insight
Precious
It is everywhere and all we do
Fear of the Lord
Nothing you desire compares
Power
Love

What is this list missing? Nothing! Do you want success and a fruitful life? Do you want eternal life in heaven? Do you want to know what it is? All those things we just read describe wisdom. Wisdom! We will become mature when we seek the wisdom of Christ. His living word says seek wisdom first before anything else. God created us in His own image-God is wisdom; don't fall short.

Wisdom is an awesome word. The root word of course is wise which means to have discernment for what is true, right, and lasting. Wisdom is to know what God's word says so you can have ever-lasting life. The Apostle Paul told us to try to learn what pleases the Lord. Spending our time searching for wisdom pleases the Lord. Wisdom is not the best kept secret anybody can have it. "If any of you lacks wisdom, he should ask God, who gives generously to all without finding fault, and it will be given to him" (James 1:5 NIV).

There are two types of wisdom. There is wisdom from heaven that we should seek and wisdom from this world that is not pure and not worth obtaining. "But if you harbor bitter envy and selfish ambition in your hearts, do not boast about it or deny the truth.

"Such "wisdom" does not come down from heaven but is earthly, unspiritual, of the devil. For where you have envy and selfish ambition, there you find disorder and every evil practice. But the wisdom that comes from heaven is first of all pure; then peace-loving, considerate, submissive, full of mercy and good fruit, impartial and sincere" (James 3:14-17 NIV). We need to gain some heavenly wisdom.

There are things we can do to gain this wisdom. We need the full armor of God. The Apostle Paul instructed us to put on the helmet of salvation and the sword of the Spirit, which is the word of God and pray about everything. God's word says to pray in the spirit on all occasions. Pray! If we do not consult, we insult God. When we pray we must believe and not have any doubt.

Heaven and hell are real physical places and Jesus really is a judge. If we accept him he becomes our redeemer. We have to make a choice during this life time, a choice that has grave consequences if we make the wrong choice, but very rewarding if we make the right choice. Do you understand why it is the ultimate ultimatum? It is not good enough we are wise in our own eyes; we have to be wise in the eyes of God. We need to stop being deceived and send a message to the great deceiver that our eyes have been opened to his deception.

We are always looking for that miracle pill. A pill we can take to lose all of our unwanted weight so we can look skinny or the miracle cream that will reverse our aging. God has a pill that is more precious than any of those things, Jesus. Guess what! Jesus is wisdom! If we seek Jesus we will receive wisdom and eternal life that comes with knowing him.

We must make a decision before it is too late to join the wedding banquet. We must knock on the door that opens automatically when we receive Jesus. Residence in heaven comes from the choice we make. If we fail to make Jesus the way there is only one option left-hell. Depending on our choice we either secure our room in God's mansion or we spend eternity getting tortured and mocked. We really don't want to imagine how bad hell is. We need to make a decision today to allow Jesus to be Lord of our lives. Chose the ultimatum correctly and secure your inheritance as a child of God. Secure your room in heaven by knowing Jesus Christ!

CHAPTER 5

Salvation

I had always believed in God although I had no idea what that meant. I didn't know anything about Him or our Savior Jesus Christ. I only knew what un-churched men told me the Bible said. I know it is crazy but in my late teens, early twenties and in an impaired vision and slurred speech my buddies and I conversations would turn to religion.

I had two very good friends whose grandfather planted some biblical seed in the both of them. They shared a lot of what their grandfather taught them with me. After a few drinks the conversation would usually turn to God and what the Bible says.

The only church we knew was located in the mountains. My pastors were two guys who didn't go to church whom I never saw read the Bible. Yes, I am chuckling! Our pews were usually the seats of four-wheelers, jeeps, or trucks.

Our communion consisted of Doritos or some other chip and an inexpensive alcohol beverage. If they spoke it I believed it. Obviously, they messed a few stories up and had a few inaccuracies but they did ok (God bless them).

I am still amazed how man has made God's word to fit his thoughts, beliefs, and ideas. This is completely backwards but accepted by our culture as the truth. I am often left shaking my head when I see how readily we are to believe what we hear.

I am convinced that man's biggest down fall is we think we know or understand something about everything. Have you noticed that everybody is an expert in the field of weight loss? If you bring the subject of weight loss up in a group you will be hard pressed to find someone who will not have to add their expertise whether it is true or not. They mean well. They have heard it many times from other people and now they take it as the gospel. They begin to preach what they were told themselves. Yet, we are a country where over fifty-percent of our population is considered obese. Maybe we don't practice what we preach. We have a tendency if we hear something enough times we begin to believe it is true. We do the same thing with God's word.

For example, I can recall reading a story where an individual was sharing that he was beginning to wonder what he had to do to have eternal life. Like so many of us he turned to his secular (people without a biblical view) friends for the answer.

He goes to the first friend and asks him what he knows about receiving eternal life. The friend gives him the answer that God has a giant scale and as long as his good deeds outweigh his bad deeds he is good to go. Salvation was guaranteed. He likes the answer and he is feeling secure about his salvation.

He looks for a little reassurance and asks another friend the same question. This friend informs him that all he has to do is go get dipped in some water. The friend tells him that the water has an amazing way of forgiving him of all his sins. He will be washed clean of all his sins if he does this and that will get him to heaven. Again he likes the answer.

He decides to seek one more opinion and asks a third friend. This friend tells him he has to be better than fifty-percent of the people who die before him because God works on a quota. As long as he is better than fifty-percent he will get to go to heaven. The friend points out that there are a lot of murders, thieves, adulterers, and generally bad people in this world.

The man is feeling pretty good about all three answers. After receiving the answers from his friends he doesn't give it another thought because he is very confident he has at least one of those three answers covered and his life continues as normal.

There is no biblical truth to any of these three answers. The sad reality is this is a life and death question. I would be more accurate if I said it is a heaven or hell question. There are so many people living today who have never read or studied the word of God but they take man's word when it comes to their own salvation. When asked how a person could have eternal life "Jesus answered, 'I am the way, and the truth and the life. No one comes to the Father except through me'" (John 14:6 NIV). Jesus is the only way!

The Bible gives us the opportunity to understand exactly what Jesus says about eternal life. If we will read the Bible for ourselves and trust the Lord with all our heart we can each gain an understanding of eternal life.

We have hit all around the topic of salvation but now we are going to dive into this "complex" matter and look at what a person has to do to inherit eternal life. By now, you should have it in your head that you need to accept Jesus Christ as your Lord and Savior. However, what does that really look like? We need to get this in our head then get it transferred to our heart.

The Apostle Paul tells us in Romans that we need to have the word near us and we need to make an outward confession with our mouth. He instructs us to confess, "Jesus is Lord" and believe it in our heart that Jesus was resurrected. "That if you confess with your mouth, "Jesus is Lord," and believe in your heart that God raised him from the dead, you will be saved" (Romans 10:9 NIV).

"For it is with your heart that you believe and are justified, and it is with your mouth that you confess and are saved" (Romans 10:10 NIV).

"Everyone who calls on the name of the Lord will be saved" (Romans 10:13 NIV). We must call upon the Lord.

Metamorphous needs to take place in our heart. Salvation is a heart issue and God knows the heart of all men, He cannot be fooled. If someone is playing a game and going through the motions, God knows. If we are saying all the right things but we have not truly changed God knows. We are only fooling ourselves and in the end, hell awaits those who played the game.

Since becoming a Christian, I have struggled with the subject of how one receives eternal life. I have studied this subject searching intently on what I have to do to have eternal life in God's kingdom.

We have already established there is no quota and that few not many make it to heaven. We also have looked at where people go who do not make it to heaven and that hell is a real physical place. Hell is not the place we want to end up when our probation is over.

If it is written in the Bible it is important. If something is repeated by four authors in the Bible it is significant. Let me read each gospels account of receiving eternal life. "Whoever finds his life will lose it, and whoever loses his life for my sake will find it" (Matthew 10:39 NIV).

"For whoever wants to save his life will lose it, but whoever loses his life for me and for the gospel will save it. For whoever wants to save his life will lose it, but whoever loses his life for me and for the gospel will save it" (Mark 8:35 NIV).

"For whoever wants to save his life will lose it, but whoever loses his life for me will save it" (Luke 9:24 NIV).

"The man who loves his life will lose it, while the man who hates his life in this world will keep it for eternal life" (John 12:25 NIV).

Translation: If you want things your way, the world's way, if you put other things first then you will not have eternal life. But put Jesus first and you will have eternal life. You want salvation put Jesus and the gospel first and you will have it. Your life will be saved if Jesus is your first priority. Love your life more than Jesus and you will lose it, but the man who would go as far as to hate his life and not put himself first, will have eternal life.

The point: Do the things that God tells us to do, He scripted the game plan we just need to execute it. If we execute His game plan we will have eternal life. Don't wait until it is too late!

Teachers are required to spend four or more years learning how to teach in order to become an expert in the field they get certified. If a person is going to share God's word he needs to know what it says. This means we need to read and seek the wisdom of the Bible. We cannot afford not to learn what is taught in the Bible. Understand everyone can proclaim the gospel but not everyone can explain the gospel and that is ok. But everyone must read the Bible and trust that God will give us revelation about what it says.

Let's think about this. We read directions weekly on how to cook, or how to put something together, or how to fill out an important document but we don't take the time to read the instructions on how we receive salvation. This is absurd if we think about it. There is a detailed manual that tells us how to live a better life in all areas and how we can live forever. The Bible tells us how we can receive eternal life but many don't ever read it.

Eschatology is the study of end times. It is the study of heaven, hell, judgment, eternal life, and other subjects like that. I guess you can call me an eschatologist. I am goal orientated and my goal is to make it to heaven and on my journey try my hardest to help rescue others for Jesus.

This is what we have to understand about our salvation: It is not about us. What did I say? Our salvation is all about what Jesus Christ did for us. Again, Jesus said it clearly, I am the way, the truth, and life. You can only get to my Father if you accept me. It is all about Jesus!

We had an outstanding bill that needed to be paid. We did not have the correct currency to pay the bill. Jesus was the only accepted method of payment. The question is, "Did Jesus pour out his blood for no reason when it comes to you having eternal life?"

I recently heard a story that occurred back in the early 1930's about a father and the love he had for his son. The father's job was to lower and raise a bridge depending on the time of day. The barge's would stack up and wait for the bridge to rise so they could travel through to their destination. When the bridge was down it was the way the commuter train would travel over the river.

The father brought his young son to work one day and at lunchtime, they went down from the control room to enjoy lunch together. The father being so excited to share everything about his job with his son lost track of time. A commuter train scheduled to pass over the river at one o'clock was only a few minutes out. The father told his young son to stay there and he took off running up the stairs.

It was standard operating procedure before raising or lowering the bridge to look down into the giant gears that were below and on both sides of the operator. The operator was responsible for making sure the gears were free from any obstruction.

The father looked down into the giant gears and to his horror noticed that his young son had tried to follow him up the stairs but he must have fallen off the spiral staircase and landed on top of one of the sets of gears. The father immediately turned around and started running down the stairs. He quickly realized he could not rescue his son and get the bridge closed in time to prevent the train from wrecking and likely leading to the death of its' four hundred passengers. With time running out he hurled around, ran back up the stairs, and pushed the control to lower the bridge sealing the fate of his son.

The father watched the commuters as they were going by. He witnessed some commuters reading newspapers, others snacking on food, and yet others just gazing out the window oblivious to the sacrifice he had just made for their sake. The father sacrificed his own son so the others would live. It was the ultimate sacrifice for others. That is a true story. Does that sound like another story we know?

Many of us are often oblivious to the sacrifice that has occurred so we can have eternal life. We fail to grasp the significance that God sacrificed His son so we could live.

If we look at the beginning we can understand the ending. In the beginning God, Adam, and Eve are fellowshipping together in the Garden of Eden. No sin has taken place on earth at this time. Jesus has not carried out his program of action; he has not been born in the flesh on earth.

Now let's say the "fall" the sin that separates us from God has just occurred. This can be illustrated if we imagine the Grand Canyon forming. This big split has occurred and God ends up on one side and Adam and Eve end up on the other. They are separated forever.

Regardless how many years we go in the future or what kind of technology we develop this separation between God and humanity can never be crossed. We cannot go from one side to the other because we are sinful and since God is pure and sinless he will not come over to our side.

Enter Jesus and God's redemptive plan. Jesus is in heaven with God. "In the beginning was the Word, and the Word was with God, and the Word was God. He was with God in the beginning" (John 1:1-2 NIV).

Life is good for Jesus remember heaven is awesome. God comes up to His only son and says, "Son I have some good news and some bad news. The good news is I am going to send you to earth so you can hang out with those guys for awhile."

God tells His son he is going to be born to a virgin, walk the earth teaching, preaching, making disciples, and doing all kinds of miracles and wonders. That is great Dad! What is the bad news? Well son after thirty-three and a half years the people you are trying to save are going to brutally beat you, mock you, spit on you, deny you, drive some nails through your hands and feet, pierce your side with a spear and crucify you on a cross.

God continues, "Son these people have a debt to pay and nothing but your blood can pay for the debt." God says, "Son all of creation will remain on that side of the Grand Canyon forever unless you do this. They will stay on that side until they die and when they die the only option for them is to spend eternity with that rotten rebellious ex-angel Lucifer that I cast down to earth."

Jesus replies, "Okay Dad not my will but your will be done." Understand if it was God's will then it was Jesus' will.

Everything happened like God said it would. Jesus brought the Good News for all of humanity to hear. After thirty-three and a half years Jesus was betrayed and murdered by the people he was sent to save. Jesus was willing to carry out the plan of action. This is why he is the Messiah. Because of Jesus' obedience there is a bridge for us to travel across and continue our fellowship with God.

We can't see the bridge that goes across the Grand Canyon. It takes faith to know that it is there. It takes faith to step out over the Grand Canyon (symbolically) but if we take that step we will find the bridge.

The Bible says, "Consequently, faith comes from hearing the message, and the message is heard through the word of Christ" (Romans 10:17 NIV). Hebrews chapter eleven is called the chapter of faith. Chapter eleven mentions works of faith twenty-one times. This chapter reviews many scenarios where somebody did something out of shear faith. What is faith?

Hebrew 11:1 says, "Now faith is being sure of what we hope for and certain of what we do not see" (NIV). We pray for rain but faith is carrying an umbrella when nothing but sunshine is in the forecast. Faith is building an ark when everybody thinks you're crazy. Abraham had faith and was willing to sacrifice his son as instructed by God.

Having this kind of faith demonstrates to God we are worthy of salvation. In fact, the Bible says we will be rewarded for our faithfulness. We are asked to have faith. Early Christians were also asked to have faith and some of them recorded what they saw. Today we have their testimonies recorded in the Bible.

God accepts those who have faith and credits righteousness or justice to those who believe. Genesis 15:6 says, "Abram believed the LORD, and he credited it to him as righteousness" (NIV). Here in the first two sentences we have faith and believe. We need to recognize that faith and believe our synonyms in Hebrew. The Old Testament (OT) is written in the Hebrew language. Faith and believe are interchangeable in most cases. The Hebrew word for both of them is *awman* (faithful, to believe).

Salvation is not possible if we do not have faith in Jesus Christ, the son of God, and we must have faith that he was resurrected, and he is our redeemer. He was the sacrifice for all sin. Anytime we sin, we need to realize that Jesus' blood was poured out so we could have forgiveness and have eternal life in heaven. His sacrifice made it possible but did not guarantee eternal life for every individual, only those who know in their heart that Jesus is their redeemer.

Faith comes from taking a chance and making a decision that we are going to trust God. We finally get to that place in our lives where we surrender and say, "God I have tried so long to do things my way but now I am giving my life to you. I cannot live my life any longer without your presence. Come Father! Come into my life. I give you complete control to do your will." It takes faith to know that bridge exists and to seek that bridge, Jesus Christ!

If we take a quick snap shot of Jesus our Savior, we will see how amazing he is. If we would trust the truth, we would enjoy a beautiful journey. As Christians we are suppose to strive to be like Christ. If we are to emulate Jesus, we should understand a little bit about him. Actually we should try to find out all we can about Jesus. Remember this is just a snap shot of Jesus Christ.

- He was foreshadowed in every book of the OT
- Birth prophesied seven hundred years before he was born
- Wonderful counselor
- Messiah-carries out a program of action
- He is mighty, enduring, compassionate, a provider, warrior, and he is grace and righteousness
- He has divine power
- Everlasting father and the prince of peace
- He can bring healing to individuals and whole societies

- He had the will power to defeat temptation after forty days of fasting
- Preached repentance and the "good news"
- He is a leader
- Knows peoples thoughts
- He has authority to forgive sin
- Teacher on: authority, being blessed, salt and light, murder, adultery, divorce, oaths, love, giving, prayer, fasting, heaven, hell, forgiveness, judgment, seeking, narrow gates, fruit, how to build wisely, and he is wisdom

Jesus had great faith to command storms, drive off spirits, and heal all sickness, to rebuke winds and waves, bring the dead back to life, hearing to the mute, and faith to walk on water. Again, this is a snap shot. Does this sound like someone we can trust? It should because our lives are in his nail pierced hands. If we would come to a point where we understand what Jesus really did for us and share the hope with others we would see a greater light shining in our world.

I could not seem to get an answer from anybody I could accept or an answer that was conclusive enough based on scripture on what it took to make it into God's kingdom. I did a two-year study on salvation and then followed that up with another two-year study on eternal life. I would struggle with two scenarios I will share with you.

The first scenario: An individual says he believes in God but he does nothing to show he has anything to do with God. No church, no Bible, never prays, and does not fellowship with anybody who does those things. He is a good person and does what is right according to man's law. Is this person going to receive eternal life according to scripture?

Scenario number two: There is a pastor who believes in Jesus and it seems like he has accepted Jesus as his Lord and Savior but he lives a sinful life. He is supposedly happily married but he is having an affair. One day after meeting with his mistress, he gets in a wreck and dies before he had the chance to repent or ask for forgiveness. He is a pastor and he believes there is a God and Jesus died on the cross for him. Does he get to go to heaven? We will look at these two scenarios again and you will need to answer them yourself.

How do we get salvation? Is it through God's grace? Do we have to believe in the one He sent? What does believe mean and what does it look like? Do we receive salvation from following the Ten Commandments, knowing Jesus, works and deeds? Is it hearing the word, repenting of our sinful nature, being born again, or overcoming?

Do those who sin receive eternal life? Do we need to love God, do His will, or are we all blessed and all saved? Do we want to put more weight on the things Jesus spoke? There are scriptures in the Bible that pertain to every one of those topics and we need to look at scripture to determine how one receives eternal life in God's kingdom.

There is a tendency to over emphasize certain scriptures, disregard others, and or take some out of context. It is necessary that we understand Romans 5:18, which says, "Consequently, just as the result of one trespass (Adam) was condemnation for all men, so also the result of one act of righteousness (Jesus) was justification that brings life for all men" (NIV).

I like the way the same passage reads in the Message Bible: Here it is in a nutshell: Just as one person did it wrong and got us in all this trouble with sin and death, another person did it right and got us out of it. However, more than just getting us out of trouble, he got us into life!

Prior to Jesus' death and resurrection the wages of our sins equaled death. Jesus laid down his life so we can be set free from sin. Because of Jesus' action we now have the opportunity for eternal life. This is why it is about Jesus and not us.

Eleven scriptures refer to grace in the NT that is applicable to salvation. Interesting, Jesus does not talk about God's grace and mercy when referring to our salvation. God is merciful. Not because He tells us He is but because of His actions. Would any of us sacrifice our children because we loved the world (people) so much? "But because of his great love for us, God, who is rich in mercy, made us alive with Christ even when we were dead in transgressions—it is by grace you have been saved" (Ephesians 2:4-5 NIV).

"For it is by grace you have been saved, through faith—and this not from yourselves, it is the gift of God—not by works, so that no one can boast" (Ephesians 2:8-9 NIV).

Salvation is a gift for believers. I can buy a gift for you but until you receive the gift, it is not yours. You need to physically have the gift for it to be yours. The gift of eternal life operates in the same manner. We need to receive the gift for it to be ours. If we do not accept Jesus we are rejecting him.

Some scholars make the argument that we all go to heaven, every person ever born because God's grace is sufficient. True, His grace is sufficient but it is not a blank check so to speak. His love and grace provided the manner for us to have eternal life. I would argue that there is no logic in believing God had Jesus go through that horrific death for no reason. We are not taking anything away from God when we say it is not all about His grace. God's grace requires a response from each one of us. We all have to do our part. We must possess the gift by accepting His grace.

We have to believe God gave His one and only son for a reason. His grace is sufficient comes from His power to cover our sins. We can use the analogy that God has a big umbrella and every person who receives Jesus Christ as their Lord and Savior fits under this umbrella. It is sufficient and big enough to cover all of our sins, transgressions, and iniquities. That is what we are talking about when referring to His grace. The song Amazing Grace has a verse that says, "How precious did that grace appear the hour I first believed." His grace is always there and the hour we believe, we enter under that umbrella.

Before we go any further let us first define what it means to believe according to the Holy Scriptures. The Greek word for believe is Pisteos which means faith, trust, and to be committed.

Let's break it down even further. Trust means to have hope, confidence, expectation, reliance, and dependence in someone or something. In this case we are talking about Jesus. Do we trust Jesus?

If we put our confidence in Jesus, we can be confident in our salvation. If we lean not on our own understanding but on his understanding, we can expect to enter heaven when our time on this earth has ended. We need to understand that He who resides in us is greater than anybody we could lean on.

Actions speak louder than words. Have we heard this before? Jesus is the Messiah. He carried out a program of action. Believe is a verb that means we must express an action. Do you see the connection? Jesus carried out an action for us. In fact, he carried out many actions and in return, we must carry out an action to receive the blessing from his action. Are you thinking of scenario number one? What we do or fail to do matters.

We cannot put off our "actions" because we think we have time. If we fail to take action and pass from our current life Jesus will say, "I never knew you, be gone from me." If we really believe Jesus is the way, our actions and thoughts will be verifiable. Again, God cannot be fooled. He knows if we are playing games.

If you are unequivocally committed to making sure you have salvation than you need to make an effort and commitment to know what the Bible tells you. If you begin a journey to really seek and understand God's heart, under no false pretense, you will be amazed at the hope you will receive. You are not alone everyone who makes a commitment to Jesus Christ has to do the same thing.

If you really want to trust and commit to knowing what God says then you need to begin to read the Bible every day and make what you read applicable in your life. "But as for you, continue in what you have learned and have become convinced of, because you know those from whom you learned it, and how from infancy you have known the holy

Scriptures, which are able to make you wise for salvation through faith in Christ Jesus" (2 Timothy 3:14-15 NIV).

One of the definitions for commit means to give or hand over. Are you tired of trying to do things your way? Jesus says if you believe in me you will give your life to me, you will hand your life over and trust me.

When we look at the word believe we see it means more than it appears. Words are just words if they are not backed up with actions. We can say we believe in Jesus but that is not good enough. Action is required! We need to get our salvation settled and then start reaching out to others.

You may have to give up an hour of Biggest Loser, Survivor, or you may not be able to see who has been added to your Face Book every thirty minutes. You have to make time to get in the word or your journey will be short lived. You cannot afford to take time off. If you show this kind of commitment you will reap the fruit and God will take care of the rest. If you are not willing to give up some reality television now you may not like reality when it comes time to face our judge, Jesus Christ.

Secondly, you need to communicate with your heavenly Father-pray and listen. There is no reason for you to worry about what to say, He created you, start talking to God about how things are going in your life and how you would like to get to know Him and better understand His word. There is no way you can go wrong.

Find a quiet place and reach out to Him. Take the time to clear your mind and humble yourselves because you are about to enter into the presence of the Most Holy God. Time with the Lord will become precious to you. It will become so rewarding you will want to make it a habit. You will need it and if you don't make time for the Lord your day will seem incomplete.

Thirdly, begin to fellowship with like believers. Yes, that means you will have to start attending a local church (I will cover this in chapter seven). This may be the toughest step on your journey. I know how you feel. I survived and you will survive. You need to trust that God will develop new relationships for you. He will not fail you or desert you if you make this commitment.

Love is the foundation churches are built on because Jesus is all about love. He willingly spread his arms and died for each and every one of us because he loves us.

Fourthly, begin to change some habits. This one may seem insignificant and generally doesn't get a lot of emphasis but it is "huge." I will tell you right now you aren't going to like it. This may be the one you are not willing to change but you need to make this change. Begin to listen to praise and worship music. Yes, you need to start dissecting some of that "worldly" stuff out of your lives. Why music? God created us where music feeds either our spirit or our flesh and the less worldly things feeding our flesh the greater the chance for success.

I have never paid attention to artists and their music. I don't even listen to secular music. I could not tell you who have the top hits in country, rap, pop, rock, or any other kind of music. Kelli always listens to the newest songs. Praise and worship music is her passion. She passes on the new music to me and puts it on my iPod.

I have come to realize during that rare occasion when I hear a song from my past when I was all flesh, my mind will race back to those memories that were created when I was listening to that song. I am flooded with memories that more times than not make me think of all the immoral acts I have committed. The emotions begin to come back as if I were reliving them. When I was making those memories they felt good and I believed I was enjoying myself.

When anyone one of us begins to relive old memories those same chemicals that were released back when we made the memories begin to be released again. Before we know it Satan can start telling us that those times were not so bad. Come on back you don't want to give this up. You have plenty of time to worry about your eternal destination. Don't be an old stick in the mud. Worry about the next life later that is if you want to believe in that stuff.

Music is a tool Satan will use. He knows God designed us to enjoy music. If he can get us to focus on other music instead of worship and praise music he feels pretty confident in his chances of keeping us behind his bars.

If you talk to ex-tobacco users you will generally find out that one of the hardest times to deal with when quitting was after a meal. For years a tobacco fix came right after eating.

Our bodies crave that tobacco fix after eating. Food triggers that craving. Music works the same way. Music can help trigger all those old habits and memories we are trying to bury. Music can also induce fantasies if we allow ourselves to get caught up in the song.

If you were to hear a song that you listened to in high school or college your mind would likely be flooded with memories from those days. I am not saying those are all bad memories and we shouldn't reflect back. What I am saying is your new journey has to begin to operate in this manner. You need to listen to music that will make you think and reflect on Jesus and his way!

To this very day I enjoy worship more when they sing the songs that I was listening to when I really began to trust and commit my life to the Lord. It takes me back to that freshness that I felt when I first began my journey. Maybe this is the reason so many churches still sing all those classic hymns. It reminds them of that first feeling they felt when they accepted Jesus. Nothing wrong with hymns-if you are there to knap! Ha! Just joking.

Worship is not my area of expertise but I have learned a valuable lesson over the years. I have seen more people walk out the door of the church and never come back because of music than I have anything else.

Those *creative* people take their music serious (maybe too serious) and their feelings can easily be offended. Being a worship leader has to be a tough job because you probably can never please more than one-third of the people at any given time. There are too many choices. Personally, I like celebratory contemporary music that gets the Holy Spirit moving. But it is not about me.

Fifthly, begin (definitely begin sooner if you want) to share the Good News with other people. Share your testimony with them. Share the love and compassion you are feeling. Invite others to church. Sharing accomplishes three things. It reinforces the things you are experiencing. It shows God you are obedient and it helps the message of Jesus Christ get preached and shared. Maybe if it is God's will someone will begin their journey at the same time you are beginning yours. The objective is to fill as much time as you can with the things of God and to cut out the things of the world.

If you begin to apply these five steps I believe you will see your trust and commitment level in the Lord begin to increase. A positive transformation will begin to take place in your life.

The five steps we just talked about will help you in the process of being born again. We all enter this world spiritually dead. If we begin the born again process and continue to grow we go through four spiritual stages.

When we first accept Jesus we leave the spiritually dead stage and enter a stage of spiritual infancy. We are really messy and dependent on other people. We are very immature spiritually which is ok but we cannot stay in this stage.

After infancy we become spiritually young children. When we are in this stage we think the world is all about us but we are having some breakthrough in the ways of God.

The third stage we can refer to as spiritual young adults. As young adults we have a good foundation of the things asked of us as prince and princesses in God's kingdom.

Finally, we get to graduate and become spiritual parents. This means we begin to invest time in others and disciple them. As spiritual parents we spend our efforts building relationships for the purpose of helping others begin their spiritual journey.

Spiritual parents have walked the path and have been equipped to rescue lost souls for Jesus. They have shown God they have had a change in their heart. They have successfully transferred what they learned in their brain down to their heart. They have become new creatures.

Okay where is all this written and who wrote it? Initially, we will look at the words of four men who spoke and wrote about what it takes to have eternal life in God's kingdom. After all isn't that our goal? We will find out what three authors, two of whom are writers of the Gospels named after them, and another who wrote nearly half of the NT, and finally we will look at what Jesus himself told us about salvation. Three ordinary men and one extraordinary man will give us a detailed answer to our question, "What must we do to inherit eternal life?"

The Apostle John, the Apostle Jesus loved an eye witness to the accounts of the gospel and one of the original twelve disciples of Jesus Christ writes in depth about how we can receive eternal life. John hung out with Jesus. He was a companion to the King of Kings and Lord of Lords. He has direct quotes from Jesus. This is exciting and we should be salivating at the mouth in anticipation of what he says.

John is also the author of 1st, 2nd, and 3rd John, and Revelation. These books are his account of this historical time and a look into the future. John's books capture his testimony, what he wrote he lived.

John's main purpose was clearly to get people from every generation to understand that by believing in Jesus Christ, the son of God, you may have life in the name of Jesus. "Whoever believes in the Son has eternal life, but whoever rejects the Son will not see life, for God's wrath remains on him" (John 3:36 NIV).

"We accept man's testimony (affirmation of fact or truth), but God's testimony is greater because it is the testimony of God, which he has given about his Son. Anyone who believes in the Son of God has this testimony in his heart. Anyone who does not believe God has made him out to be a liar, because he has not believed the testimony God has given about his Son. And this is the testimony: God has given us eternal life, and this life is in his Son. He who has the Son has life; he who does not have the Son of God does not have life."

"I write these things to you who believe in the name of the Son of God so that you may know that you have eternal life" (1 John 5:9-13 NIV).

Notice that he says to those who believe he writes these things. Unbelievers are not going to read His word unless they are attempting to discredit what is written. These people have no part of God's kingdom.

You want assurance that you have eternal life? Listen to John because this became his purpose in life! It takes faith, God designed it this way.

It is not likely, although it could happen, that Jesus is going to physically come down and say to each one of us, "Yes it is true, please believe." He said have faith in my word. What is written is true.

Jesus told his disciples to preach and teach about faith and that we all have to accept Him as our savior or we will fail to have eternal life. Jesus knew full well that some would accept this teaching and others would not. "Yet to all who received him, to those who believed in his name, he gave the right to become children of God" (John 1:12 NIV).

"But these (miraculous signs recorded in the Bible) are written that you may believe that Jesus is the Christ, the Son of God, and that by believing you may have life in his name" (John 20:31 NIV). John could not make it any clearer. This should get us fired up. Nothing man says should trump what we just read.

Next let's look at Luke the author of both the third gospel and the 'Acts of all the Apostles'. Luke was a companion of the Apostle Paul. Luke's main purpose was to show the way to salvation by presenting the works and teachings of Jesus. Today we would call Luke a private investigator. Luke's actual profession was a physician. In order to write his gospel he relied on eyewitness accounts and the testimony from servants of Jesus. Luke relied heavily on the preaching and oral accounts of the Apostles.

Luke wrote, "All the prophets testify about him that everyone who believes in him receives forgiveness of sins through his name" (Acts 10:43 NIV). After investigating the testimony of eyewitness accounts and being a witness to the preaching of the good news Luke came to the conclusion and wrote that to have salvation we must believe in Jesus.

Luke records the incident when Paul and Silas were in prison praying and singing hymns to God and the other prisoners, when suddenly a strong earthquake shook the very foundation of the prison. The prison doors were flung open and the chains fell off the prisoners. The guard was so scared he was going to run his own sword through himself but Paul stopped him.

Experiencing this made a believer out of the guard and he asked Paul and Silas what he had to do to have eternal life. "They replied, 'Believe in the Lord Jesus, and you will be saved—you and your household'" (Acts 16:31 NIV).

Luke explains to us that Jesus is the one who can forgive our sins. In fact, get this, he says we must comprehend the fact that it is all about Jesus. We become vindicated when we accept what he did for us. "Therefore, my brothers, I want you to know that through Jesus the forgiveness of sins is proclaimed to you. Through him everyone who believes is justified from everything you could not be justified from by the law of Moses" (Acts 13:38-39 NIV).

The Law of Moses required the blood of bulls and goats to forgive sins. Thankfully, since Jesus came we no longer need the blood of animals because his blood is sufficient for all of our sins. "Therefore, when Christ came into the world, he said: "Sacrifice and offerings you (God) did not desire, but a body you prepared for me; with burnt offerings and sin offerings you were not pleased.

Then I said, 'Here I am—it is written about me in the scroll—I have come to do your will, O God'" (Hebrews 10:5-7 NIV). Jesus' blood is so precious that it is able to cover our sins. Nothing but the blood of Jesus can cover our sins.

Now let's look at what the Apostle Paul, whose name was Saul before his conversion, says about eternal life. We talked about Saul's conversion to Paul earlier. Paul is credited with writing thirteen of the twenty-seven books of the NT. He hated and persecuted Christians.

One day he is feared by all believers and then just like a flick of a switch the light turns on. Jesus met Saul on the road to Damascus and asked him why he keeps persecuting his people. The encounter was so intense that it changed Saul instantly.

After his conversion Paul understood the patience and compassion that God has for His people. He knew in his heart the righteousness of God. He wrote, "This righteousness from God comes through faith in Jesus Christ to all who believe" (Romans 3:22 NIV).

"But for that very reason I was shown mercy so that in me, the worst of sinners, Christ Jesus might display his unlimited patience as an example for those who would believe on him and receive eternal life" (1 Timothy 1:16 NIV).

Paul emphasizes that it is never too late to inherit eternal life (unless you die before accepting Jesus Christ) but why wait. Every sin we have committed can be forgiven. Paul says, "I am a good example. I use to persecute those who belonged to the Way, Christians." Paul was forgiven and he became a great disciple of Christ.

Paul urges us to understand Jesus died for each and every one of us. "And he died for all, that those who live should no longer live for themselves but for him who died for them and was raised again" (2 Corinthians 5:15 NIV). We must kill the old self which means we no longer live for our selfish desires and wants but we start living for Jesus.

Paul in his writings warns us against unbelief. He compares unbelievers to the Israelites who rebelled against God. "And to whom did God swear that they would never enter his rest if not to those who disobeyed? So we see that they were not able to enter, because of their unbelief" (Hebrews 3:18-19 NIV).

He tells believers we will not face damnation, we will not lose our souls like those who do not believe. "But we are not of those who shrink back and are destroyed, but of those who believe and are saved" (Hebrews 10:39 NIV).

The Apostle Paul teaches us that we are not to be ashamed of the gospel. We should not deny our faith in Jesus Christ. The greatest insult someone could ever say to me is, "I never knew you were a Christian." If we proclaim to be a Christian and someone ever says that about us it should tear us up inside. I have heard that spoken more than once about people. If those seven words are ever said about us after we claim to receive Jesus Christ I believe it is fair to say we are not committed to the ways of the Master.

We should not be ashamed of the gospel or be fearful of telling people we are Christians. We should fear the one who has the power to find us guilty or acquit us. "I am not ashamed of the gospel, because it is the power of God for the salvation of everyone who believes: first for the Jew, then for the Gentile" (Romans 1:16 NIV).

Paul tells us that unbelievers are evil and he warns them that they will perish. God knows that there are going to be many people who will believe the lie from Satan that there is no God so He allows them to be fooled. But they will be punished for being deceived because they chose to do evil and not believe the truth.

Doing evil instead of good is a choice we make. We all know the difference between right and wrong. If we make a conscience decision to do wrong we are basically spitting in the face of God. We are snubbing our noses at Him and in return He allows us to be fooled. What we fail to realize is whenever we do things contrary to God's word there will be consequences.

The Apostle Paul tells believers if we work hard and persevere salvation is ours. Our hope is in God, who sent the Savior into the world to save all those who believe. Believers will enter into God's place of rest and unbelievers will enter a chasm of never ending torture.

The three authors we looked at wrote that to have eternal life we must give and hand over our lives to the son of God, Jesus Christ. They are specific that if we believe in Jesus we are credited with having faith and we will inherit eternal life. It is critical that we grasp what these three men said. Our eternal life hinges on us understanding the truth.

The scriptures tell us that we must believe in Jesus and believe in what he testified. In fact, God's living word says we must believe in Jesus and receive the kingdom with full dependency. Lukewarm, half-heartedly, or on the fence is not acceptable. Full means complete, we must have a complete dependency in Christ. We do not have big enough shoulders to try and go it alone without God. He is the one with the big shoulders. We need to let go and become fully dependent on Him.

It makes sense that if we are going to believe in Jesus, as our savior then we would want to listen to what he has to say about eternal life. Jesus tells us in his own words his purpose and how we can inherit eternal life. Jesus preached a righteousness that comes only through faith in him and his work. Jesus referenced the word believe fifteen times when referring to salvation.

The following are Holy Scriptures spoken by Jesus. "He said to them, 'Go into all the world and preach the good news to all creation. Whoever believes and is baptized will be saved, but whoever does not believe will be condemned'" (Mark 16:15-16 NIV).

Jesus said, "For I tell you that unless your righteousness surpasses that of the Pharisees and the teachers of the law, you will certainly not enter the kingdom of heaven" (Matthew 5:20 NIV).

The Pharisee's (Jewish leaders) believed righteousness came from good works. They followed Mosaic Law and believed in the resurrection, angels, and spirits but they didn't understand that it was about Jesus not the works they did. The Pharisees were about the "show" and their works. They liked to draw attention to themselves. In other words it was all about them.

The Sadducees who were also Jewish leaders denied the resurrection. They denied Jesus was the son of God. They failed to believe angels existed and denied that there were spirits. We cannot deny the resurrection of Jesus Christ and enter into the heavenly kingdom.

Jesus says believe in the son and you will have eternal life. Look at the following scriptures. "'For God so loved the world that he gave his one and only Son, that whoever believes in him shall not perish but have eternal life'" (John 3:16 NIV).

"Whoever believes in him is not condemned, but whoever does not believe stands condemned already because he has not believed in the name of God's one and only Son" (John 3:18 NIV).

Unbelievers are under the death penalty because of their failure to believe in the one-of-a-kind son of God when introduced to him. "'I tell you the truth, whoever hears my word and believes him who sent me has eternal life and will not be condemned; he has crossed over from death to life'" (John 5:24 NIV).

"Jesus answered, 'The work of God is this: to believe in the one he has sent'" (John 6:29 NIV). Hear His words, believe and you will live.

To do God's work is to believe in His son. "'For my Fathers will is that everyone who looks to the Son and believes in him shall have eternal life, and I will raise him up at the last day'" (John 6:40 NIV).

"'I tell you the truth, he who believes has everlasting life'" (John 6:47 NIV). Ignorance of the law is no excuse.

It is not a coincidence that Jesus used the words live and die together in many sentences. He was making a point. "Jesus said to her (Martha), 'I am the resurrection and the life. He who believes in me will live, even though he dies; and whoever lives and believes in me will never die. Do you believe this'" (John 11:25-26 NIV)? If we do not believe Jesus is who he said he is we will not be forgiven for our sins and we will not inherit eternal life.

Jesus wants us to understand that life is precious. We could say it is the father in him coming out. He is saying, "Listen children I am giving you some instruction are you listening to me? If you trust and put your hope in me and my word you are my true followers." Jesus is the light and his desire is that we chose to come out of the dark.

Jesus knows the works of our enemy is to keep us from accepting and believing the word of God. He cautions us that following him will not be easy. Hell is no picnic either. Jesus told a large crowd the parable of the sower. He said, "'A farmer went out to sow his seed. As he was scattering the seed, some fell along the path; it was trampled on, and the birds of the air ate it up. Some fell on rock, and when it came up, the plants withered because they had no moisture. Other seed fell among thorns, which grew up with it and choked the plants. Still other seed fell on good soil. It came up and yielded a crop, a hundred times more than was sewn'" (Luke 8:5-8 NIV).

The seed is the word of God. The seed that landed on the path was the word and it was taken from them so they would not believe. Remember our enemy's game plan is to steal. He steals the word from us by deception. Does God's word really say you can do this or you shouldn't do that? Do we really have to trust and commit to Jesus to have life? There are consequences if we don't. The biggest consequence is that whoever fails to put their trust in Jesus is a prisoner and their permanent home is behind the gates of hell.

Trees and plants grow roots for stability and survival. It is in the roots where they store their food. We also need roots to survive and remain stable. It takes time to grow strong and mature.

When we are young spiritually we have shallow root systems. It doesn't take much for us to fall away from the word. A few trials and tribulations, we are bailing and reverting back to doing things our own way. As our roots grow we become more stable. We are able to store more food, the word of God. Remember the Bible says, "Do not work for food that spoils, but for food that endures to eternal life which the Son of Man will give you. On him God the Father has placed his seal of approval" (John 6:27 NIV).

The seed that fell among the thorns symbolizes those who hear the word but they are too concerned with the 'world'.

James (brother of Jesus) calls this "useless" faith or "dead" faith and this kind of belief is superficial and does not lead to salvation. Life is still all about them. These people fail to ever mature.

Jesus said, "But the seed on good soil stands for those with a noble and good heart, who hear the word, retain it, and by persevering produce a crop" (Luke 8:15 NIV). These are the people who heard God's message in their brain and then got it transferred to their hearts.

It is very conclusive that John, Luke, Paul, and Jesus speak specifically to trusting, committing, and putting our hope in Jesus. It is not our interpretation of what it means to believe that matters. It is what the Bible says believe means that matters.

If we believe in Jesus we have handed our lives over to him and we have made him Lord of our lives. He has become our king and we understand it is his kingdom we are advancing. To say we believe is one thing but to carry out, or live a life that shows we are committed is another thing. We must be honest when we ask ourselves, "Do I have eternal life according to the way John, Luke, Paul, and Jesus define how we receive eternal life?"

The point needs to be driven home that God sent Jesus so our sins would be forgiven. Our goal should be to live a life that is free from sin. We should try earnestly to obey the commandments even though God knows we will come up short. Again, it goes back to the sin in the garden. We needed a redeemer and that redeemer is Jesus.

Jesus was very direct when responding to the question of how we inherit eternal life. Jesus said, "Whoever has my commandments and obeys them, he is the one who loves me. He who loves me will be loved by my Father, and I too will love him and show myself to him" (John 14:21 NIV). Are the commandments important? Do we need to obey all of them? Can we just obey seventy-percent of them? How about fifty-percent? No, Jesus said commandments. Plural, we must obey all the commandments.

James the pastor said that we must keep all the laws. "For whoever keeps the whole law and yet stumbles at just one point is guilty of breaking all of it" (James 2:10 NIV). If we break the law, we will be punished. If we choose to stay in the darkness about Jesus, it is no excuse. He is our Judge! Turning a deaf ear to the message of the gospel is signing our own death certificate.

Knowing his time was coming to an end on earth Jesus told his disciples he was giving them a new command. "'A new command I give you: Love one another. As I have loved you, so you must love one another. By this all men will know that you are my disciples, if you love one another'" (John 13:34 NIV). Jesus was emphasizing the importance of loving one another.

The Apostle Matthew who was one of the original twelve disciples of Jesus, wrote his gospel with the purpose of proving to the Jews that Jesus was the Messiah. He tied Jesus to the OT Scriptures. Matthew writes that when asked about the greatest commandment Jesus' answer dealt with love.

"One of them, an expert in the law, tested him (Jesus) with this question: "Teacher, which is the greatest commandment in the Law?" Jesus replied: " 'Love the Lord your God with all your heart and with all your soul and with all your mind.' This is the first and greatest commandment. And the second is like it: 'Love your neighbor as yourself.' All the Law and the Prophets hang on these two commandments" (Matthew 22:35-40 NIV).

John Mark the author of the Gospel Mark arranged his book from the teachings of Peter. Mark's account is very similar to Matthew's. Mark makes it clear we are to love the Lord with everything we have. We are to hold nothing back when it comes to loving the Lord and loving our neighbors.

Jesus' greatest quality is that he loves his sheep with all his heart, soul, mind, and strength. The two greatest acts of love that sets the standard for all of us was first God so loved the world that He gave His only son that whosoever believes in him will not die but have everlasting life. The second greatest act was Jesus said not my will Father but your will be done and he went to the cross for our sins, our iniquities, and our infirmities. These two acts display to all of us the true meaning of love.

Love our neighbors as we love ourselves. Does that seem complicated or hard to do? Some people feel horrible about themselves and they think their life stinks. How can they love their neighbor like they love themselves? Love Jesus first that is why it is mentioned first. If we love Jesus first and foremost we will be amazed how everything else starts to fall into place. Jesus needs to be first. Falling in love with him needs to be our priority. If we love Jesus we can't help but to love ourselves and our neighbors, trust him.

Neighbors are not just those we live near. We need to understand that the Greek word for "neighbor" is "plesion," which means "fellow man." Literally, we are to love all of human-kind. This is an OT Scripture given to Moses from God. "Do not seek revenge or bear a grudge against one of your people, but love your neighbor as yourself. I am the Lord" (Leviticus 19:18 NIV).

What is love and what does it look like? We have lost this in our culture. The Greek word for love is Agapao which is likely the same as the Hebrew word aw-gab' which means to breathe after. Love is a noun and a noun is a word used to denote or indicate an act. Earlier we identified believe meant we had to take action. If we are to show love we have to take action. Does this mean we can't just say the words I love you? Actions speak louder than words, haven't we heard that before? God is looking at our actions to "verify" that we love Him and our neighbors with all our heart, soul, mind, and strength.

The Apostle Paul says love is patient and kind but it is not envious, boastful, arrogant, rude, irritable, or resentful. Paul says love is about compromise. It doesn't rejoice in evil or wrongdoing but instead, it rejoices in the truth. "It always protects, always trusts, always hopes, and always perseveres" (1 Corinthians 13:7 NIV). Real love never fails and since God is love He never fails.

This hit close to home one day when we were at our home group. We were asked to put in order who we love the most. I wrote down Kelli, my girls, Jesus, and God in that order. We started going around the room and I quickly realized everyone had Jesus and God before their family. All eyes were going to be upon me soon. What was I going to do? I had to suck it up, be bold, and share what I had written down. No not really. I quietly pulled my paper back appearing like I was doodling but in reality I was changing my order to match everyone else's. The discussion that ensued made me change my whole way of thinking.

I realized by putting Jesus first and loving him more than anything else, it would allow everything else in my life to be even better. I would have even more love for my wife and children. I would want what is best for them even more which is for my family to know and love Jesus. This has turned out to be so true. I love Kelli and my girls more with each passing day.

Last Thanksgiving Sophia, my youngest daughter and I were hanging out and I said to her, "Let's say what we are thankful for." I went first and I said, "I am thankful for my wonderful family." It was Sophia's turn and she said, "I am thankful that Jesus died for our sins." Wow! I have to believe that put a smile on Jesus' face.

As I search and seek God's wisdom and grow in faith my love for my wife and children continues to grow. One of my favorite things I like to do is watch my girls as they sleep. I can get lost thanking God for them. I can become overwhelmed with how much God loves me and how much He has blessed me.

God is all love right! How can we be condemned? If God loves us so much why did He give us a potential death sentence? Yes, God is love but He did His part. God doesn't even ask us to go half way. He took all the steps necessary and we need to take one step toward him, one! Allowing your only son to be the sacrificial Lamb for all of humanity is quite an action! Would you agree?

Matthew, Mark, and Luke all respond with similar answers when they share the story about when Jesus was asked about receiving eternal life. Since they are all very similar we will only look at Matthew's account. Jesus tells us that obeying the Ten Commandments are essential to our salvation.

"Now a man came up to Jesus and asked, "Teacher, what good thing must I do to get eternal life?" "Why do you ask me about what is good?" Jesus replied, "There is only One who is good. If you want to enter life, obey the commandments." "Which ones?" the man inquired. Jesus replied, "'Do not murder, do not commit adultery, do not steal, do not give false testimony, honor your father and mother,' and 'love your neighbor as yourself'" (Matthew 19:16-19 NIV).

It is safe to say that Jesus wanted to convey that it is important to obey the Ten Commandments if we want to have eternal life. There is a correlation between us obeying the Ten Commandments and receiving eternal life. I want to reiterate that God knows we cannot live a sinless life but since He knows our heart He knows if we have received His son as our savior and He knows if we are trying to be obedient to His commands.

If Jesus said eternal life depended on obeying the Ten Commandments we had better know what they are and what they mean. If we look at the Ten Commandments and break each one of them down we can get a good understanding of what they mean.

The commandments were given to Moses from God on Mount Sinai while leading the Israelites through the desert. If we are obeying the Ten Commandments as instructed by Jesus we are performing an act, they require an action on our part.

1. Have no other Gods before me.
2. Have no idols except me.
3. Do not misuse the name of the Lord.
4. Remember the Sabbath.

5. Honor your father and mother.
6. Do not commit murder.
7. Do not commit adultery.
8. Do not steal.
9. Do not give false testimony against your brother.
10. Do not covet what others have.

If we look at the Ten Commandments it is easy see why we often hear people say, "There are too many Do's and Do not's for me to follow that religion stuff." We have all heard similar comments. Too many Do's and Do not's is a poor excuse and will not be accepted by Jesus come judgment day. My reply to these people is simple. Really, you're asked to obey ten commands and that is too many? What if Jesus would have said no to the beating he endured? What if Jesus would have said no to the spikes that were driven into his hands and feet? What if Jesus would have said no to being crucified on the cross?

I believe what Jesus went through was a lot harder than me being faithful to my wife or me not taking something that doesn't belong to me. Asking us to be obedient to ten laws so we can have eternal life seems pretty fair. Would you agree?

"'You shall have no other gods before me'" (Exodus 20:3 NIV). God is saying make Me number one. He created us and He is a jealous God. We are His creation and if we go around worshipping other god's we are disrespecting the One who made us.

I believe it comes down to a heart issue. If we love God we will not be able to worship anyone or anything but God. This is why God makes it personal. He knows if we are worshipping other god's then we have not truly made Him the Lord of our lives. We have not trusted, committed, or put our hope in Him. We have failed to believe and eternal life is not yet ours.

"'You shall not make for yourself an idol in the form of anything in heaven above or on the earth beneath or in the waters below'" (Exodus 20:4 NIV). Any object of ardent (warm or intense in feeling) or excessive devotion or admiration is defined as an idol.

An idol can be something we pin-up, perhaps on our walls or we may have pictures on our desks at work. I am not talking about family photos or anything like that. I am talking about that big poster of the guy jumping the ridge top on his snow machine and all he can think about is hitting the powder on Saturday and Sunday forgoing spending any time with Jesus or with his own family. That's absurd isn't it? Is it?

Take a minute and see if anything comes to your mind that may make you feel warm and fuzzy. Is there anything that gives you an intense feeling? Is there anything that you put before God?

It seems like we can always find time to sit around and read hours of material so we are informed on what movie stars and professional athletes are doing. We can read where they have been, who they were with, what they have been wearing, and what they eat and drink but many of us will not read the **B**asic **I**nstruction **B**efore **L**eaving **E**arth.

We will watch hours of television that feeds us with information on these "idols" and we soak it up and we cannot wait for more. Do you spend more time watching or 'worshipping' them then you spend praying to God?

Don't we love to idolize singers? We even have reality television shows called 'American Idol'.

We separate idolatry and enjoying something by the excessive devotion factor. Excessive is defined by extreme, unnecessary, and too much. We can define devotion with the words loyalty, dedication, and commitment. To sum it up and put it all together if we are spending too much time with the things of this world and not enough time focusing on God's word then our commitment is in the wrong area. It is quite possible the judge may find us guilty of idolatry.

I believe the key is in the definition, any excessive devotion, or admiration. If we are willing to stand in a line to get a look at Paris Hilton or some other star, we are either idolizing or getting real close and God says do not do that.

If something continually keeps us away from God and His word it is probably considered an idol in His view. That snowmobile that keeps you away all winter or the camp trailer that keeps you preoccupied all summer, probably an idol in God's mind.

If we go skiing all winter or take multiple Sunday's off from church to watch the big NASCAR race Jesus is probably going to have a problem with that. I am not saying we have to be in church fifty-two Sunday's or whichever day you may choose to go to church, out of the year. I am saying we need to be careful what we make a higher priority. If in God's eyes we are putting Him on the backburner He will see it as idolatry.

Let me share a situation we see all the time in the church. A man leaves his wife and she turns to the church for consoling and counsel which is great! After the divorce is final a new man usually enters the picture at some point and the lady is not heard from again. The love and comfort she was receiving from God is replaced by the new man in her life. Unfortunate, but it is what it is!

If we are not making God number one that means we are filling our time with something other than Him and He finds that offensive and it breaks His heart. We must be committed to Him and the things of His kingdom.

To me the following sounds like a pretty stern warning, what do you think? "You shall not bow down to them or worship them (idols); for I, the Lord your God, am a jealous God, punishing the children for the sin of the fathers to the third and fourth generation of those who hate me, but showing love to a thousand generations of those who love me and keep my commandments" (Exodus 20:5-6 NIV).

I believe there are some key words in those sentences: I am the Lord. Again, God is saying I need to be the priority. If you are asking yourself if He thinks our lives are suppose to revolve around Him the answer is yes! Does it say half or some of our love? No, it says, "I demand all your love."

If you decline or snub me there will be hell to pay, literally. Isn't that what God is saying? In fact, He is saying it is going to be bad for you and depending how far I want to go, three or four generations, it is going to be bad for your children. "And he passed in front of Moses, proclaiming, 'The Lord, the Lord, the compassionate and gracious God, slow to anger, abounding in love and faithfulness, maintaining love to thousands, and forgiving wickedness, rebellion and sin. Yet he does not leave the guilty unpunished; he punishes the children and their children for the sin of the fathers to the third and fourth generation'" (Exodus 34:6-7 NIV).

God says if you hate me I will punish you to the third and fourth generation. Hate, this is a strong word but we know unbelievers are those who hate Him. If my father and/or grandfather were sinning, rebelling, and were wicked people do I have to pay for their sins? I would be thinking where is the mercy? What about what Moses writes in Deuteronomy? He says we die for our own sins. "Fathers shall not be put to death for their children, nor children put to death for their fathers; each is to die for his own sin" (Deuteronomy 24:16 NIV).

The Prophet Ezekiel also says a father will die for his own sin and a son will die for his sin if they have kept the Lord's laws and decrees. "The soul who sins is the one who will die. The son will not share the guilt of his father, nor will the father share the sin of the son. The righteousness of the righteous man will be credited to him, and the wickedness of the wicked will be charged against him" (Ezekiel 18:20 NIV).

What is God saying? If we love God we will be credited for that love and He will not hold the wickedness of our parents and grandparents against us, they will be responsible for their own sin as will we.

God knows if parents fail to believe in God and if they fail to obey His commandments then the odds are very high the following generations will likely fail to obey the Lord as well because these attributes were not instilled in their children. These parents failed to disciple their children so until a generation is raised who obeys God's commandments they are under what we can call a curse.

This was demonstrated when God refused to allow the first generation of Israelites who came out of Egypt to enter into the Promised Land. God made them wander the desert until all of them except Joshua and Caleb had passed away and a new generation had been raised up. The first generation rebelled and disobeyed God's word and they paid for their rebellion but the second generation received the land and today that land is called Israel.

I recall a story of a mother who called into a radio station to ask a pastor about Exodus 20:5. The mother had an adulterous affair earlier in her marriage but she later accepted Jesus as her Lord and Savior and had a daughter with her husband. She was devastated and heartbroken to believe her sin had caused a curse to be on her daughter and her grandchildren. She was gripped with pain and remorse. The answer she received was God's grace is sufficient to cover your sin. God knew her heart and the hour she received Jesus His grace abound. Amen!

Commandment three states we are not to misuse the name of the Lord our God. We are not to swear falsely in the name of God. This is profaning His name. Jesus tells us to keep our word and to not swear by anything under heaven or on this earth. Jesus said, "And do not swear by your head, for you cannot make even one hair white or black. Simply, let your 'Yes' be 'Yes,' and your 'No,' 'No'; anything beyond this comes from the evil one" (Matthew 5:36-37 NIV).

Do you know that famous and often used saying that starts with God and ends with a big barrier that holds water? Yes, those two words! Not a good habit to get into saying. Every time you say that you are disobeying commandment three. It doesn't matter that it is just a part of your vocabulary and you mean nothing disrespectful to God. You are misusing His name. Incidentally, those two words often come out of the mouth when someone is frustrated or angry and God says we should be slow to anger.

The Lord said, "Six days you shall labor and do all your work, but the seventh day is a Sabbath to the LORD your God. On it you shall not do any work, neither you, nor your son or daughter, nor your manservant, or maidservant, nor your animals, nor the alien within your gates" (Exodus 20:9-10 NIV). Sabbath is also referred to as the Lord's Day.

God told the Israelites this day is so special if you do work on this day you must be put to death. They had to gather enough food on the day before the Sabbath so they would not have to perform any labor on the designated day of rest.

There are times during the summer when I am required to work on the Sabbath but I certainly don't want to disobey God's word and I really don't want to die when I work on the Sabbath. Wildfires do not quit burning and creating destruction because it is the Sabbath.

Good news! Jesus is Lord of the Sabbath and he told us we could do good on the Sabbath. "Then he said to them, 'The Sabbath was made for man, not man for the Sabbath. So the Son of Man is Lord even of the Sabbath'" (Mark 2:27-28 NIV).

"One Sabbath Jesus was going through the grain fields, and as his disciples walked along, they began to pick some heads of grain.

The Pharisees said to him, "Look, why are they doing what is unlawful on the Sabbath?"

Jesus answered, 'Have you never read what David did when he and his companions were hungry and in need? In the days of Abiathar the high priest, he entered the house of God and ate the consecrated bread, which is lawful for only priests to eat. And he also gave some to his companions'" (Mark 2:23-26 NIV).

Jesus even healed on the Sabbath. He asked the Pharisees if any of them had a sheep that fell in a hole on the Sabbath would they not do what is necessary to rescue it. Jesus said, "How much more valuable is a man than a sheep! Therefore it is lawful to do good on the Sabbath" (Matthew 12:12 NIV).

I am very thankful we can do good on the Sabbath. God is awesome and He thought of everything. If Jesus would not have been deemed Lord of the Sabbath doctors would not be able to help patients, police officers would have to allow crime to take place, and snow plows would have to let the snow stack up until the next day before they could plow. Pilots could not fly anybody to their destination until the following day and the list would go on and on.

The fifth commandment; "'Honor your father and your mother, so that you may live long in the land the LORD your God is giving you'" (Exodus 20:12 NIV). I often just ask my girls if their actions honored their mother and I when they have done something inappropriate.

Knowing they disappointed us and failed to obey God's word is usually all the punishment they need. I believe it is good to apply God's word in all situations possible.

God made us parents and in doing so He gave us the responsibility to disciple our children. We are to train our children in the way of Jesus so when they are older and making their own decisions they will not part from the way they were taught, which is to trust Jesus (Proverbs 22:6).

Train means we are to dedicate them to the Lord. Raise them so they understand the word and know who Jesus is. We can buy everything for them and send them to all the great sports camps but our number one responsibility as parents is to disciple our children. We are to teach them to be devoted to the way of the Master.

We will be judged on how we raise our children. We won't be responsible for their sins but God is watching to see if we raise them to be biblical or secular.

The Apostle Paul reminds the church at Ephesus that commandment five is the first commandment with a promise—"that it may go well with you and that you may enjoy a long life on the earth" (Ephesians 6:3 NIV). As a parent I like the fact life will go well for my children if they obey Kelli and me.

To honor means we respect. If children are taught to respect their parents this instills a strong foundation for children to respect authority. If parents fail to get this instilled in their children they often learn they are the leader in authority. Life becomes about them and there is a very good chance they will not make time for God in their lives.

Does this sound like something the enemy would like us to fail at as parents? Very much so!

I don't know of any studies but it stands to reason if you fail to respect those in authority and God is all about obeying and accepting His authority then you will not have any foundation to accept God's authority. That of course is a sentence in Satan's prison.

The next commandment, commandment six seems straightforward and it only consists of four short words. "'You shall not murder'" (Exodus 20:13 NIV).

Like so many other scriptures commandment six is not that straightforward. "Anyone who hates his brother is a murderer, and you know that no murder has eternal life in him" (1 John 3:15 NIV). John definitely throws a wrench in this commandment. Well, God did say love your neighbor as you love yourself and we learned neighbor is all fellow man.

Look! Some pretty terrible things can happen to us in this world. We will talk about this when we address the church's role in our culture but for now we need to understand we are not allowed to hate anyone. I do not even like to imagine this but if someone was to do something despicable to one of my girls I would have to forgive that person and learn not to hate him.

If you have read "The Shack" you will know what I mean. To hate someone is a heart issue. We don't hate them with our mind but we actually hate them with our heart. "But whoever hates his brother is in the darkness and walks around in the darkness; he does not know where he is going, because the darkness has blinded him" (1 John 2:11 NIV). God does not hate, He is love. I was discipled to hate the sin not the sinner. Tough to do and easier said than done I know but it is Bible.

Adultery, it is the act of betrayal, it is disloyalty, and it is unfaithfulness. It is also running rampant in our culture. "'You shall not commit adultery'" (Exodus 20:14 NIV). Marriage is sacred to God. He defines marriage as being between one man and one woman, nothing else.

Many people define adultery as being when you are married and you have an affair. Jesus said it is a lot more than that. "'You have heard that it was said, 'Do not commit adultery.' But I tell you that anyone who looks at a woman lustfully has already committed adultery with her in his heart'" (Matthew 5:27-28 NIV).

If we are staring or dreaming of a man or woman in a lustful way it is adultery. Jesus tells us it is better if we gauge our eyes out because it is better if we go through life with no eyes than to have our whole body thrown into hell.

I realize there are some catchy clichés that attempt to refute this truth but God doesn't have much of a humor on the subject of adultery. How many times have we heard these old clichés? Does this mean we cannot look at the menu even if we are not going to order? I am only married I am not dead! I got a marriage certificate not a death certificate. There is no harm in looking. Really!

The opposite of sacred is secular. Secular is the opposite of everything God stands for and what He asks us to stand for. We are not to be secular. We are to transform the world that is secular not conform to it.

Jesus said anybody who divorces a spouse must give her a certificate of divorce. Jesus also said, "But I tell you that anyone who divorces his wife, except for marital unfaithfulness, causes her to become an adulteress, and anyone who marries the divorced woman commits adultery" (Matthew 5:32 NIV). The Bible also says there are a couple other reasons we may divorce our spouse.

Jesus wants us to understand marriage is sacred and is not to be taken lightly. Cheating on a spouse has consequences and it cannot go unpunished. This act of unfaithfulness shows God we are not faithful to His ways. Our heart is not in the right place. We cannot say we are believers of His son Jesus Christ while living sinful lives. Does this have you thinking of scenario number two?

The Bible is very specific we are not to take anything that does not belong to us or that we do not have permission to take. Maybe out of all the commandments this is one we all understand or we think we understand. I said understand not obey. "'You shall not steal'" (Exodus 20:15 NIV). Stealing is not just taking items. It can be clocking incorrect hours where we work or signing our name to something we know is incorrect or a number of other scenarios.

If we are to be children of the light we cannot steal. Stealing is done by those who live in the dark. God's children are not thieves we are to be righteous and holy. Our enemy is the one who steals, he is a thief. "He who has been stealing must steal no longer, but must work, doing something useful with his own hands, that he may have something to share with those in need" (Ephesians 4:28 NIV).

"'You shall not give false testimony against your neighbor'" (Exodus 20:16 NIV). Lying is when we do not tell the truth. Who is Jesus? He is the Way and the Truth. We are to emulate Jesus which means we should not lie.

If we have transferred the word from our brain to our heart the guilt that we feel when we lie is unbearable. Lying is so dangerous because it can become a habit. Have you ever heard someone called a habitual liar or have you ever heard someone say, "He couldn't tell the truth if his life depended on it?" Reality is his life does depend on it, his eternal life!

It is hard to tell the truth all the time in every situation. This may be the hardest commandment to keep. Lying in many situations seems easier then telling the truth but that does not make it right.

We have convinced ourselves a white lie, small lie, or fib is acceptable. A lie is a lie. "Do not lie to each other, since you have taken off your old self with its practices and have put on the new self, which is being renewed in knowledge in the image of its Creator" (Colossians 3:9-10 NIV).

"I do not write to you because you do not know the truth, but because you do know it and because no lie comes from the truth" (1 John 2:21 NIV). We know lying is wrong and in the words of Bob Newhart, 'Stop it'. Lying is a choice we make and we must live with the consequence of the lie when it blows up.

We often lie because it is convenient and temporarily prevents us from dealing with the truth. It initially allows us to avoid stress and anxiety because we are avoiding or hiding something we do not want to face up to. Guess what? Sooner or later those lies catch up to us and they have a way of flooring us.

A few summers ago Rebekah made an All-Star baseball team. She was the only girl in the whole tournament and she was not having a lot of fun for numerous reasons. She would have quit if I would have let her. But she knew she had to finish if she started. The coach was a yeller and on the negative side. One practice after doing some yelling he asked all the kids to raise their hands if they were not having fun and didn't want to be there?

I would bet almost all of them would have raised their hands but they knew the coach didn't really want them to respond to the question. Rebekah told me later she wanted to raise her hand but she was too afraid. I told her I didn't blame her for not raising her hand and it was okay she remained silent even though she didn't speak up and answer his question truthfully. I don't believe God is going to hold that against her.

God is very serious when He describes the worst liar. Remember we touched on this in chapter three. God wants us to get this. "Who is a liar? It is the man who denies that Jesus is the Christ. Such a man is the antichrist—he denies the Father and the Son (1 John 2:22 NIV). Really! The antichrist!

Remember our enemy, the one we want to have nothing in common with is a liar. Jesus said if we lie we belong to Satan who from the very beginning has been lying giving him the dubious honor of being the father of lying.

If we lie we have not been renewed. If we are filled with the Holy Spirit lying should be difficult. Our conscience should eat away at us if we lie. The Holy Spirit will not stop us from lying this is a decision we make with our freedom of free will. One of the best examples we have from the Bible is the story of Ananias and Sapphira.

"Now a man named Ananias, together with his wife Sapphira, also sold a piece of property. With his wife's full knowledge he kept back part of the money for himself, but brought the rest and put it at the Apostles' feet" (Acts 5:1-2 NIV).

"Then Peter said, 'Ananias, how is it that Satan has so filled your heart that you have lied to the Holy Spirit and have kept for yourself some of the money you received for the land? Didn't it belong to you before it was sold? And after it was sold, wasn't the money at your disposal? What made you think of doing such a thing? You have not lied to men but to God'" (Acts 5:3-4 NIV).

"When Ananias heard this, he fell down and died. And great fear seized all who heard what had happened. Then the young men came forward, wrapped up his body, and carried him out and buried him" (Acts 5:5-6 NIV). Ananias lied because of his pride. There was no reason to lie the money was his. He was prideful and wanted to look good in the eyes of the Apostles. Pride is rebellion and the Lord hates rebellion.

"About three hours later his wife came in, not knowing what had happened. Peter asked her, "Tell me is this the price you and Ananias got for the land?"

"Yes," she said, "that is the price."

Peter said to her, "How could you agree to test the Spirit of the Lord? Look! The feet of the men who buried your husband are at the door, and they will carry you out also."

"At that moment she fell down at his feet and died. Then the young men came in and, finding her dead, carried her out and buried her by her husband" (Acts 5:7-10 NIV).

You are probably wondering why death came to Ananias and Sapphira. After all people lie all the time. In this case the Holy Spirit revealed to Peter that the two of them held back some of the money. They did not lie to Peter but to the Holy Spirit.

Ananias and Sapphira's story was put in the Bible so future generations would know lying is a serious offense in God's eyes. If God operated like that today we would be burying somebody every few seconds. Lying can be addictive and before we know it, it becomes second nature to lie for no reason at all. We will lie to make stories more interesting or to substantiate what we are saying. We have to be careful not to fall into the realm of lying because we could become 'habitual liars'.

"'You shall not covet your neighbor's house. You shall not covet your neighbor's wife, or his manservant, his ox or donkey, or anything that belongs to your neighbor'" (Exodus 20:17 NIV). Covet means we desire or yearn for something.

Coveting takes our focus away from what God is providing. If we are always trying to keep up with the Jones then we are not appreciating the things we do have. We should be a thankful people. We should be happy with what God provides. He is Jehovah-Jireh which is another Hebrew name for the LORD that means the LORD is my Provider or the LORD will provide.

Is it bad to want something? Yes, if it belongs to someone else. Yes, if it consumes your actions and thoughts. Yes, if it goes against the word of God. Yes, if the desire or want is out of jealousy. But it is perfectly fine to pray for something as long as you have a humble heart and if it's God's will you can trust He will provide it.

If we fail to obey the Ten Commandments does that really cost us our salvation? Well is God a liar? Hopefully, you said no. God takes obedience very seriously and that is why He says we can enjoy a long life if we obey His commandments. Obedience comes with faith. God is not capable of lying. Therefore God has to honor what He says and His word says if we do not follow and obey His commandments we do not have eternal life.

Jesus does not ask us to do anything he did not do himself. Jesus suffered for his obedience and his suffering allowed us the opportunity to have eternal salvation. "Although he was a son, he learned obedience from what he suffered and, once made perfect, he became the source of eternal salvation for all who obey him and was designated by God to be the high priest in the order of Melchizedek" (Hebrews 5:8-9 NIV).

Do you recall what love was? John the disciple who Jesus loved said, "And this is love: that we walk in obedience to his commands. As you have heard from the beginning, his command is that you walk in love" (2 John 6 NIV).

We must know who God and Jesus are to receive eternal life. God will punish those who do not know His son and those who disobey the gospel. "They will be punished by everlasting destruction and shut out from the presence of the Lord and from the majesty of his power on the day he comes to be glorified in his holy people and to be marveled at among all those who have believed" (2 Thessalonians 1:9-10 NIV).

If we deny Jesus with false prophecies or false teachings, we will face quick destruction. If we know the son, we have life. "Those who are far from you will perish; you destroy all who are unfaithful to you" (Psalm 73:27 NIV). Does it sound like we cannot make a half-hearted effort to get to know Jesus but we better get to know him wholeheartedly?

Notice that God adds to the gospel He doesn't take anything away. For example in the previous paragraph it says those who don't know God and disobey the gospel will be punished. We just got done talking about obeying His commandments and then God says do that and you better get to know me.

So many people believe that if they are just good, "I am a good person; I mind my own business and don't bother anyone" or if they give some charitable food or other items around the Holidays that ensures them eternal life even though they have no idea who Jesus is. That is a good deed but does not secure you eternal life, after all atheists give to the needy as well.

Jesus says, "Every tree that does not bear good fruit is cut down and thrown into the fire. Thus, by their fruit you will recognize them."

"Not everyone who says to me, 'Lord, Lord,' will enter the kingdom of heaven, but only he who does the will of my

Father who is in heaven. Many will say to me on that day, 'Lord, Lord, did we not prophesy in your name, and in your name drive out demons and perform many miracles?' Then I will tell them plainly, 'I never knew you. Away from me, you evildoers'" (Matthew 7:19-23 NIV)!

Luke writes the same story just slightly different but it is still Jesus who is speaking. Luke attempts to illustrate it in a way we will understand. "Once the owner of the house gets up and closes the door, you will stand outside knocking and pleading, 'Sir, open the door for us.'

"But he will answer, 'I don't know you or where you come from.' "Then you will say, 'We ate and drank with you, and you taught in our streets.'

"But he will reply, 'I don't know you or where you come from. Away from me, all you evildoers'" (Luke 13:25-27 NIV)!

Jesus is the homeowner and the door to his kingdom closes when we die. If we have not already entered into his kingdom the best defense lawyer who ever lived will not be successful in pleading our case, we lose. No catchy phrase like "glove don't fit must acquit" is going to work in front of this judge. Hell is the next stop.

How many of us open up our doors for complete strangers and allow them to hang out in our homes? Well, God does not allow complete strangers into heaven either. But He does invite each one of us to get to know His son while we are on this earth.

The cry of Jesus' heart is that we would all get to know him. Sometimes he must feel like shouting "what must I do for you people to get it?"

"I am the good shepherd; I know my sheep and my sheep know me—just as the Father knows me and I know the Father—and I lay down my life for the sheep" (John 10:14-15 NIV).

Jesus either gives us eternal life or if we deny him he denies us eternal life. "For you granted him authority over all people that he might give eternal life to all those you have given him. Now this is eternal life: that they may know you, the only true God, and Jesus Christ, whom you have sent" (John 17:2-3 NIV).

If we fail to exalt him as our king-it is likely we do not know him the way we should. He is worthy, we should live a life that is worthy of Jesus. When we hold true to Jesus' teaching we will know the truth. And the truth will set us free.

If we know Jesus we will be set free. Free from what? Free from our sins. Our bail is paid and we are no longer on probation. Our death sentence has been expunged, erased, eliminated. Our debts are paid in full when we spend the time to get to know the one who paid our bill, our redeemer.

Is there something we can do to earn eternal salvation? Some scriptures make us think yes and other scriptures make us think no. Salvation isn't something we earn, so there is nothing we can brag about (Ephesians 2:9).

Okay we can't earn it. But Paul wrote, "God 'will give to each person according to what he has done.' To those who by persistence in doing good seek glory, honor and immortality, he will give eternal life" (Romans 2:6-7 NIV).

"The ax is already at the root of the trees, and every tree that does not produce good fruit will be cut down and thrown into a fire" (Luke 3:9 NIV). Okay our good work can help us receive eternal life. Which is it?

James the servant of Jesus Christ sheds some good light into this confusing topic. "What good is it, my brothers, if a man claims to have faith but has no deeds? Can such faith save him? Suppose a brother or sister is without clothes and daily food.

If one of you says to him, 'Go I wish you well; keep warm and well fed,' but does nothing about his physical needs, what good is it? In the same way, faith by itself, if it is not accompanied by action, is dead" (James 2:14-17 NIV). Action! Wow! Does that substantiate our whole premise that if we really believe we will carry out an action?

"But someone will say, 'You have faith; I have deeds.' Show me your faith without deeds, and I will show you my faith by what I do" (James 2:18 NIV).

James even says, "You believe that there is one God." Big deal! Demons believe that as well. Faith plus actions work together. True faith cannot help but produce good deeds. Here it is: Good deeds without faith is useless and does not get us into heaven. But faith with good deeds is quantifiable. We won't have one without the other. Faith and action are partners. Deeds complete our faith. A person with faith is supposed to produce good fruit.

Rahab the prostitute was a sinner but by helping Godly men, God's spies, she was considered as one who had faith. "As the body without the spirit is dead, so faith without deeds is dead" (James 2:26 NIV).

We are not saved by works but we must produce fruit. We have to enlist in God's army and fight the war. Numbers matter in God's army. It is by the word of mouth that we recruit people to help spread God's word to all nations.

Faith + Action=Salvation

Just like we did with the earlier subjects let's look at what Jesus said about works and deeds. Jesus speaks a great deal about this subject. The NT records twenty-three scriptures where Jesus speaks about our works and deeds.

Jesus starts off by telling us if we are not for him, then we are against him. There is no middle ground or being on the fence. "'He who is not with me is against me, and he who does not gather with me scatters'" (Matthew 12:30 NIV). If we are not witnessing, we are scattering, we are being lukewarm at best.

Jesus is coming back in his splendor and majesty. Our hope should be that we have been worthy. Jesus will render a decision to every man according to his deeds (Matthew 16:27).

"Do not be amazed at this, for a time is coming when all who are in their graves will hear his voice and come out—those who have done good will rise to live, and those who have done evil will rise to be condemned" (John 5:28-29 NIV). Jesus is coming back to judge us and we should not be surprised at this. He is going to judge us on the good things we have done and the evil we have done.

"'Again, it will be like a man going on a journey, who called his servants, and entrusted his property to them. To one he gave five talents of money, to another two talents, and to another one talent, each according to his ability. Then he went on his journey. The man who had received the five talents went at once and put his money to work and gained five more talents. So also, the one with the two talents gained two more. But the man who had received the one talent went off, dug a hole in the ground, and hid his master's money.

"After a long time the master of those servants returned and settled accounts with them. The man who had received the five talents brought the other five. 'Master,' he said, 'you entrusted me with five talents. See, I have gained five more.'"

"His master replied, 'Well done, good and faithful servant! You have been faithful with a few things; I will put you in charge of many things. Come and share your master's happiness!'"

"The man with the two talents also came. 'Master,' he said, 'you entrusted me with two talents; see, I have gained two more.'

"His master replied, 'Well done, good and faithful servant! You have been faithful with a few things; I will put you in charge of many things. Come and share your master's happiness!'"

"Then the man who received the one talent came, 'Master,' he said, 'I knew that you are a hard man, harvesting where you have not sown and gathering where you have not scattered seed. So I was afraid and went out and hid your talent in the ground. See, here is what belongs to you.'"

"His master replied, 'You wicked, lazy servant! So you knew that I harvest where I have not sown and gather where I have not scattered seed? Well then, you should have put my money on deposit with the bankers, so that when I returned I would have received it back with interest.'"

"'Take the talent from him and give it to the one who has the ten talents. For everyone who has will be given more, and he will have abundance. Whoever does not have, even what he has will be taken from him. And throw that worthless servant outside, into the darkness, where there will be weeping and the gnashing of teeth'" (Matthew 25:14-30 NIV).

We know the master is Jesus and the translation of the parable of the talents is two-fold. First it instructs us not to be idle. We, all of humanity are the servants. Jesus wants his word spread (scattered). The harvest is all the people who have not heard about the Good News of Jesus Christ.

Jesus is relaying the message that the gospel needs to be preached. We cannot stand idly by and do nothing to help advance His kingdom. We have to get in the game! "Then he will say to those on his left (those who gave no help and were selfish), 'Depart from me, you who are cursed, into the eternal fire which is prepared for the devil and his angels'" (Matthew 25:41 NIV).

Jesus has entrusted us with the word. We need to be obedient and share the word. If we are not willing to carry out this action hell is where we could end up. "He who is not with me is against me, and he who does not gather with me scatters" (Luke 11:23 NIV). There is no middle of the road in his kingdom. We either stand for his way or by default we are in the camp of our enemy.

Secondly, Jesus is saying you need to get to know me. The guy who buried the one talent said I know you are a hard man. Jesus repeats that back to him with a question mark, "I know you are a hard man?" Jesus is firm in his word if that is what the guy was talking about. If he was saying Jesus was unfair or unjust then this shows he did not know Jesus.

Jesus is compassionate and proved it by dying for the forgiveness of our sins. Jesus is the epitome of generosity. I get the impression these types of people really offend Jesus. He knew these people would not take the time to really get to know him. Jesus knew they would fail to understand that his message is all about preaching the Good News.

Jesus also spoke about hearing the word. "I tell you the truth, whoever hears my word and believes him who sent me has eternal life and will not be condemned; he has crossed over from death to life."

"I tell you the truth, a time is coming, and has now come when the dead will hear the voice of the Son of God, and those who hear will live" (John 5:24-25 NIV).

We are all going to mess up but not all of us will be forgiven. Do you recall the two guys where one went to heaven and the other hell? The one who went to heaven was humble and Jesus told him to head on in. He had accepted Jesus and was justified so everything he did was not replayed back to him.

Jesus says, "My sheep listen to my voice; I know them, and they follow me. I give them eternal life, and they shall never perish; no one can snatch them out of my hand" (John 10:27-28 NIV).

What is Jesus saying when he says, "My sheep hear my voice?" He is saying the people who trust, put their hope in him, and are committed to him know what his word says. When situations arise whether they are good or bad these people know they can share everything with Jesus. They know that nothing or no circumstance can pull them away from him. He will not only standby us but he will carry us.

Several times I have said faith comes from hearing the word. If faith and believe are interchangeable can I say if we believe we will take the time to hear the word of God? How will our faith grow if we don't hear the word? It can't! The more we hear the word the greater our faith. Pretty simple!

The Bible says we must hear, pay attention, and heed the word. Does that mean we show up on Sunday and listen to what the pastor preaches and not apply it to our lives? No, it means we listen and apply it to our lives. If we fail to apply what we have heard then we might as well have stayed home and watched television.

If we don't make the word applicable then we are making the statement: "I heard what you said but I do not believe it."

"For we also have had the gospel preached to us, just as they did; but the message they heard was of no value to them, because those who heard did not combine it with faith" and the message did not do them any good" (Hebrews 4:2 NIV).

If what we hear (gospel) from the beginning remains in us we will remain in the son and in the Father. Then we will receive the promise of eternal life. We need to live out our lives what we hear preached. This will help us grow spiritually.

This fast paced world we have come accustomed to living in is not going to slow down. If anything it is going to speed up even faster. Multi-tasking has become a necessity in our lives. We need to adjust our way of thinking to fit the times we live in.

I am faithful when it comes to going to the gym. I know I am going to go to the gym so I have made a commitment to make the gym one of the areas where I multi-task. I can listen to sermons, music, or the Bible that I have downloaded on my iPod as I work out.

I am getting in shape and I am also hearing the word. I may read a book for the first thirty minutes when I am doing cardio and then switch to my music or sermons. When I am done working out the iPod plugs right back into my car and whenever I am driving I am listening to something pertaining to God. I have learned to create opportunities to hear the word throughout the week.

It is nice to just sit down, relax and watch a good movie. There are some awesome Christian movies available today. Are you thinking I am a little excessive? I don't think so but then again my eternal life depends on how I respond to God's word.

I challenge you to break down your week and see where your time is going. I did this awhile back and I was shocked to see how little time I was spending with Jesus. We have all said, "I am just too busy or I don't have the time." How much of our time should we devote to Jesus?

Figure 2

168	hours in a week
-56	sleep
-40	work
-16	Jesus, the word, church
-11	watching television
-10	eating
-10	driving
-10	working out
-15	miscellaneous

Figure 2 closely reflects how I spend my hours in a week. It reflects that I give about ten-percent of my time every week to Jesus. Is that enough? You can see if we don't learn to multi-task our whole week can be gone before we know it and we are left saying, "What happen to the time?"

I can easily increase my percentage by bringing Jesus into the conversation during meal time or like I mentioned earlier listening to my iPod. I likely fill some of that miscellaneous time up with Jesus as well. Try writing down where you are spending your time. You will probably be surprised to see where all your time is going.

We talked about repentance in chapter two and born again in chapter three so we will not spend much time on either of these in this chapter but we need to know that both are pertinent and have to take place for us to have eternal life.

We need to repent of our sins and then turn to God. When we turn to God we need to start producing some fruit. The Apostle Matthew wrote that we have to produce fruit in keeping with our repentance (Matthew 3:8).

Paul said we can have it one of two ways. We can turn to God and be saved which will allow us to feel good or we can allow the world to beat us up and feel sorry for ourselves and this can cause death (2 Corinthians 7:10).

Jesus put it bluntly when he said, "'I tell you the truth, unless you change and become like little children (innocent and obedient), you will never enter the kingdom of heaven'" (Matthew 18:3).

"I tell you, no! But unless you repent, you too will all perish" (Luke 13:3 NIV). That should be clear enough.

Jesus also said there would be rejoicing in the heavens over one sinner who repents. I imagine repenting must be serious if heaven is going to celebrate and rejoice when one person truly repents. Do you think they rejoice so much because it is so infrequent or because they are that excited? They probably rejoice in heaven for both reasons.

I witnessed this "lack of repentance" first hand growing up. My oldest sister was in her second marriage and she was married to an abusive man. It was guaranteed that they would start fighting on Thursday and continue through Saturday. Sunday would roll around and he would be sober. He would apologize and promise her a new washer and dryer or some other material item. Things would be good for a couple of days then Thursday which was payday (play day) would come around and the cycle would start all over again.

He would "repent" which meant he was sorry she didn't want to be around him for a few days while he was sober. He didn't quit hitting her because he didn't do anything to really change. He didn't ever commit to a lifestyle change and he certainly never turned to God. He spoke useless words and did worldly acts but he never had biblical sorrow.

Biblical sorrow is when our heart truly aches because of our worldly act that caused God to be disappointed. An act that grieved God so much He wished He would have never created us. "The LORD was grieved that he had made man on the earth, and his heart was filled with pain" (Genesis 6:6 NIV). We should all memorize that scripture. It is unfortunate that we do not seem to think twice about disappointing or causing our heavenly Father to grieve.

Peter and Jesus both talk about being born again. Peter said, "For you have been born again, not of perishable seed, but of imperishable, through the living and enduring word of God" (1 Peter 1:23 NIV). When we are born into God's kingdom, our salvation is settled and our journey from being an infant to being a spiritual parent has begun.

Nicodemus asked Jesus how he could have eternal life and Jesus said he had to be born again. Jesus was stressing that we are born into a kingdom of darkness and we need to be born into God's kingdom.

We are born of flesh and we need to be born again in the Spirit. That is what Jesus was talking about in the following scriptures. "Flesh gives birth to flesh, but the Spirit gives birth to spirit. You should not be surprised at my saying, 'You must be born again.'

The wind blows where it pleases. You hear its sound, but you cannot tell where it comes from or where it is going. So it is with everyone born of the Spirit" (John 3:6-8 NIV).

Jesus goes pretty deep when he is talking about salvation in Revelation. He tells us we need to overcome. "He who has an ear, let him hear what the Spirit says to the churches. To him that overcomes, I will give the right to eat from the tree of life, which is in the paradise of God" (Revelation 2:7 NIV). Overcome what?

First we need to overcome the fact that we are born into Satan's worldly system. We need to overcome darkness, our lack of faith, our self-indulgence, and our immorality. We need to overcome death by accepting Jesus as our savior.

This world we live in wants to beat us up. Remember it is controlled by Satan and his band of believers. Satan does not want us to know there is hope and that we can overcome all his obstacles if we keep our focus on Jesus Christ.

Jesus is rooting for us to overcome. He has something special for those of us who make it, an all expense trip already paid for. Jesus tells us he will go to bat for us again. Overcome the world and I will go to my Father and tell Him you won, you overcame the world. You defeated the works of the enemy. "He who overcomes will like them, be dressed in white. I will never blot out his name from the book of life, but will acknowledge his name before my Father and his angels" (Revelation 3:5 NIV). Jesus is the ultimate encourager. He says I did it and you can do it to. Many people have overcome; the reward is worth it.

"To him who overcomes, I will give the right to sit with me on my throne, just as I overcame and sat down with my Father on His throne" (Revelation 3:21 NIV).

We need to overcome and collect our inheritance. When we are born into God's kingdom it is our birthright to sit at his throne. Jesus said to John: "It is done. I am the Alpha and the Omega, the Beginning and the End. To him who is thirsty I will give to drink without cost from the spring of the water of life. He who overcomes will inherit all this, and I will be his God and he will be my son. But the cowardly, the unbelieving, the vile, the murders, the sexually immoral, those who practice magic arts, the idolaters and all liars—their place will be in the fiery lake of burning sulfur. This is the second death" (Revelation 21:6-8 NIV). I know since the choice is mine I am going for door number one and taking the throne. What about you?

Eventually the things of this earth are going to disappear. All that stuff we accumulate will go to someone else and it will not matter. All those things we spent our energy on needing and craving will be gone. What is left? A book! The book that either has our name written in it or our name is nowhere to be found.

The Book of Life will not have a record of what we have done, it will simply have our name written in it providing we have eternal life. "If anyone's name was not found written in the Book of Life, he was thrown into the lake of fire" (Revelation 20:15 NIV).

"The world and its desires pass away, but the man who does the will of God lives forever" (1 John 2:17 NIV).

Those who do what is right and obey God's will, which includes believing what Jesus taught, will enter the kingdom of God.

If I go to my oldest daughter Rebekah and tell her to clean her room today and she complains but still cleans her room she did what I asked. If I go to my second oldest daughter Olivia, and ask her to clean her room and she says okay Dad but she never cleans her room she did not obey what I asked her to do.

Rebekah's actions obeyed my will. Olivia's actions disobeyed my will. God's kingdom operates under the same principle. Knowing what God's word says is not enough. We have to know it and apply it in our daily living.

Are you beginning to get a clear picture of how we inherit eternal life? Can it be clearer?

God has His winnowing fork and whoever is not doing what is right according to His word will be picked up from the threshing room floor and discarded like chaff. God says they will be burned in an unquenchable fire (hell).

God says, "I am who I am! My word is right and you should be thirsty for my word." God's word covers everything for all time.

"The Spirit and the bride say, "Come!" And let him who hears say, "Come!" Whoever is thirsty, let him come; and whoever wishes, let him take the free gift of the water of life.

I warn everyone who hears the words of the prophecy of this book: If anyone adds anything to them, God will add to him the plaques described in this book. And if anyone takes words away from this book of prophecy, God will take away from him his share in the tree of life, and in the holy city, which are described in this book" (Revelation 22:17-19 NIV)! God's word is His word and it could be fatal if we change it or add something to it.

God is a gardener this is why He created the Garden of Eden. He could have created anything He wanted but He chose to create a beautiful garden. Jesus is recorded in John as saying he is the vine and we are the branches. A branch cannot live if it doesn't stay attached to the vine. The vine is the life line. We have to be attached, emotionally involved with Jesus to have life. "'I am the true vine, and my Father is the gardener. He cuts off every branch in me that bears no fruit, while every branch that does bear fruit he prunes so that it will be even more fruitful'" (John 15:1-2 NIV). Good fruit is the product of a Godly life.

Jesus tells us we cannot; it is not possible to live a godly life without making him the center of it. We need contact with him to survive. In fact, he says if we do not remain in him we will be thrown away like a branch and burned.

Every spring and fall on the district where I work we go out and burn debris left over from logging operations. We burn the limbs and logs that were not worth anything. The debris has become a fire hazard to the healthy trees that were left to thrive. Jesus does the same thing. He disinherits those who fail to live a godly life and throws them into the fiery furnace.

"The Son of Man will send out his angels, and they will weed out of his kingdom everything that causes sin and all who do evil. They will throw them into the fiery furnace, where there will be weeping and gnashing of teeth. Then the righteous will shine like the sun in the kingdom of their Father. He who has ears, let him hear" (Matthew 13:41-43 NIV).

The bad, immoral, and sinful who fail to repent will not have salvation. They will die in their wicked ways. When the angels come forth they will rid the wicked from the righteous. Regardless of our circumstances if we make the choice to be unbelievers Jesus will wash his hands of us.

Warning! Do not cause people to sin. Jesus says if we cause someone to sin it would be better for us if a great millstone were hanged about our neck, and we were cast into the sea.

We are just as guilty of sinning if we cause people to stumble and sin then if we sin ourselves. I think we have all heard those two famous sayings "I am not going down alone" and "We are partners in crime." The enemy is always going to try and bring darkness into our lives. We have to have wisdom and understanding to defeat him.

Salvation or eternal life is spelled out in God's Holy Scriptures. Salvation does not require us to just do one thing. There are thirteen criteria's that are all linked together, woven perfectly and how we respond to these thirteen criteria's will determine where we spend eternity. They are:

- We have receive Jesus as our Lord and Savior and believe-trust, commit, put our hope in him
- We have to Love the Lord our God with all of our heart, soul, mind and strength
- We have to know who Jesus is

  We have to know Jesus Christ was born to the Virgin Mary
  We have to know that he walked this earth for thirty-three years performing miracles and preaching the gospel
  We have to know he was beaten for our sins and he was hung on a cross
  We have to know he died and on the third day he was raised from the grave
  We have to know one Lamb was sacrificed for all the sins of the world

- We have to love our fellow man
- We have to obey the Ten Commandments
- We have to have Faith + Actions (good deeds)
- We have to hear the word
- We must repent and turn to God
- We have to be born again
- We have to overcome our fleshly desires and become spiritual
- We must do the will of God-believe in the one He sent
- We cannot add or take away from His word
- We cannot cause people to sin

At the beginning of this chapter there were two scenarios of two individuals and I said we would answer the question if they had salvation or not after we learned how we inherit eternal life.

The first individual says he believes in God but he does nothing to show he has anything to do with God. No church, no Bible, never prays, and does not fellowship with anybody who does those things but he is a good person and does what is right according to man's law. Is this person going to receive eternal life according to scripture? Yes or no! What do you think?

The second individual is a pastor who believes in Jesus and it seems like he has accepted Jesus as his Lord and Savior but he lives a sinful life. Supposedly, he is happily married but he is having an affair. One day after meeting with his mistress, he gets in a wreck and dies before he had the chance to repent or ask for forgiveness. He is a pastor and he believes there is a God and Jesus died on the cross for him. Does he get to go to heaven? What do you think?

Blessed are the poor in spirit, for their inheritance is the kingdom of heaven. Seek to have a pure heart because they are the ones who get to see His face. Blessed are those who suffer and endure for the sake of His kingdom. It is not always going to be easy but do not give up God rewards those who are faithful and love Him.

"If we deliberately keep on sinning after we have received the knowledge of the truth, no sacrifice for sins is left, but only a fearful expectation of judgment and of raging fire that will consume the enemies of God" (Hebrews 10:26-27 NIV).

Yesterday is history. Tomorrow is a mystery. Today is a gift that's why it's called the present! Live and savor every moment . . . this is not a dress rehearsal! God wants all men to be saved and to come to know the truth. For those who refuse to follow God's living breathing word destruction and hell is their destination. "There is a judge for the one who rejects me and does not except my words; that very word which I spoke will condemn him at the last day" (John 12:48 NIV). Receive Jesus Christ today. Nobody knows what tomorrows plans are except God.

CHAPTER 6

Life's Purpose

Do you ever ponder what life is all about? Life sort of reminds me of the game SORRY. If you have ever played the game you can probably see the comparisons between the two. If we look at the game SORRY and relate it to our journeys, it provides a good analogy for the different routes our journeys, our lives, can take.

There are many rules to the game of SORRY that makes it so applicable to our own lives. The goal of the game is to get all four *pawns* around the board and safely tucked away in their home. Individually we would be the pawns, the path around the board would be our journey, and home would be reflective of heaven.

If we play the game SORRY and at the end of the game our four *pawns* are still scattered in various places on the board we lose. This could be reflective of never receiving Jesus Christ as our Lord and Savior, we lose.

If we draw a one or a two we get off base and begin our journey. Depending on the cards we draw and the moves we make our journey can be slow or it can be fast. If we draw the number eleven and somebody is closer to our home we can exchange places with them which will get us to our home quicker. These moves reflect the level of commitment that we have to make Jesus Lord of our lives.

We can be knocked off by another player and sent back to base. This move illustrates that Satan is always going to attempt to insert people in our path who will cause us to stumble. When we are in base we have to wait until we draw a one, two, or a SORRY card.

SORRY! These cards send us back to the beginning. We have been knocked off and we are not even engaged in the game. Our journey ended and now we need to start all over. Satan is happy! We are back where he wants us, his prison. His goal is to keep setting us back so we will give up and he will win.

We can slide, go backwards, and get so close to home (heaven) only to be sent right back to the beginning (hell). This is exactly what can happen in our lives. We get so close to starting that wonderful journey or we may be way down the road well on our way and we let someone or some circumstance knock us back to the beginning.

Life is not a game. We need to discover why we were created. What is our purpose? Why do we exist? Do we have a purpose?

From the time we are old enough to ask questions until we die we should all ask ourselves what our purpose is while we are on this earth. Then we should ask ourselves am I fulfilling my purpose?

I often ask people what they think their purpose is in life. The most common answer I receive: To have fun! Would God really create us for the sole reason that we would just have fun? If that were the case why are there so much sadness, hardship, and pain in this world? Having fun is a direct benefit of life but it is not our purpose.

I believe we focus too much of our time on how we were created verses why we were created. Basically there are two ideologies on how we came into existence. One is evolution, we evolved somehow, and there can be many ideas from this basic theory including humans evolved from this single cell anemia, and we spent some time as monkeys etc . . . The other of course is creation which means we were created by God. This is often referred to as Intelligent Design.

Evolutionists and creationists will continue to battle back and forth but neither is likely to convince the other on their position. The theory of evolution has so many holes and requires assumptions to be made. Creationism is based on faith. Yet, many people need concrete evidence. They need Jesus to come down and speak to them directly before they are going to believe in God.

There was an article in National Geographic News that reported; [2]"In the U.S., only 14 percent of adults thought that evolution was "definitely true," while about a third firmly rejected the idea."

[3]"More than 9 in 10 Americans continue to believe in God." Ninety-percent is an awesome percentage although God would love it if it were one hundred-percent.

This should make us question why evolution is taught in our public schools system but creation cannot be taught. The mention of Creationism in our public schools almost incites riots and threats of lawsuits by a loud minority.

I don't put a lot of time into how I was created because I can't match wits with God. God is omnipresent, omnipotent, and omniscient. The Bible tells us God made everything in six days and I am a strict creationists so that is good enough for me.

God sets things straight in Job when he says, "Who is it that darkens my counsel with words without knowledge? Brace yourself like a man; I will question you, and you shall answer me.

'Where were you when I laid the earth's foundation? Tell me, if you understand.

Who marked off its dimensions? Surely you know! Who stretched a measuring line across it? On what were its footings set, or who laid its cornerstone—while the morning stars sang together and all the angels shouted for joy'" (Job 38:2-7 NIV). God firmly says we should not question what He has created because we do not have the knowledge.

If that wasn't enough He later says, "Do you know the laws of the heavens? Can you set up God's dominion over the earth" (Job 38:33 NIV). God goes on with twelve straight questions in the passage in chapter thirty-eight asking us if we can do what He did when He created everything and laid the foundation of the earth. The answer to all twelve questions are no. We need to take God for His word and believe He created us. We are not the product of something that evolved.

I know there is an earth, I know there is a heaven, I know there is a hell, and I know I was created in His image. We were made in His image and likeness but we were not given His power. I have yet to be able to create a single man with some dirt and a little air. I know God created man and I accept it.

Our energy and time should be focused on discovering why God created us. After we discover why He created us we should fulfill or act on this discovery. If we figure out why God created us, we will discover our purpose in life.

Personally, I do not believe our purpose in life is to work Monday through Friday and after work sit around watching television until bedtime. There has to be more to life then work, television, computers, and recreation.

Let's think about Creationism from the perspective of a trial. Creationism is based on hundreds of eye witness accounts, sixty-six books written by forty different authors who were ordained by God, extending over a period of fifteen hundred years all compiled in one book each testifying to the truth of Jesus. The evidence supporting Creationism is overwhelming.

So why did God create us? Argument one: He just did. He was bored and since He has the intelligence and power He thought He would create man by blowing on some dust. After creating man God would kick back and watch us from heaven as we run around aimlessly doing whatever we want as long as it benefits us.

Are we to believe God was bored so he decided He would create the human race so He could watch us grow old and die? Does that sound like the reasoning of an intelligent God? Please, we shouldn't insult His intelligence. This is a really bad argument. We could enter in tons of evidence from Genesis to Revelation to disprove argument number one.

Why did God create us? Argument two: To have fun. If we look at the beginning we will see Adam and Eve had fun right? Life was most assuredly fun until the fall of man. Adam and Eve were separated from God shortly after being created.

God said to Adam, "Because you listened to your wife and ate from the tree about which I commanded you, 'You must not eat of it,'"

"Cursed is the ground because of you; through painful toil you will eat of it all the days of your life. It will produce thorns and thistles for you, and you will eat the plants of the field. By the sweat of your brow you will eat your food until you return to the ground, since from it you were taken; for dust you are and to dust you will return" (Genesis 3:17-19 NIV).

Have you ever walked through a field of thorns and thistles? Certainly not fun. Adam's skin was no different from yours and mine. I am certain God did not provide him with gloves and pants made of kevlar.

Toil means hard labor. Adam's job, farming was going to be hard work. For Adam to provide food for himself and his family he was going to have to grow food in a thorn and thistle field. By the way he still had the memories of the garden. He remembered how beautiful it was. I am sure he longed for the food that was provided for him in the garden.

Oh ya and God said to Eve, "Eve I am going to increase your pain during childbearing. In fact, I am going to greatly increase the pain just to make it a little more fun and memorable for you." Finally, the one feminist and most ladies really don't like God said he was going to make it women's desire to have their husbands rule over them. Good times!

As if that wasn't enough fun how about living with the fact that Adam and Eve's oldest son Cain killed their youngest son Abel that must have been fun for them. Adam and Eve started off in a beautiful garden fellowshipping with God and having all their needs provided but they ended up kicked out of the garden, no fellowship with God, working in thistles and thorns, great pain during childbearing, and losing their first two sons.

Do you think the Israelites enjoyed being suppressed by the Egyptians for four hundred years? I don't believe anybody likes being a slave and being treated as a lower class person. I don't think that was fun.

What about wondering the desert for forty years? Desert's are hot, offer little shade, water and food are limited although God provided manna (bread from heaven) for them. There were two occasions when God provided quail for them but their main meal for breakfast, lunch, and dinner was bread without butter. The only way it was going to get toasted was if they laid it on a rock and let the hot sun toast it.

It was rumored the prophet Isaiah was sawed in half. They did not have anesthesia he felt every bit of that process.

Those are OT examples to teach us life is not just about having fun. There were no hard times in the NT were there?

History tells us many of Jesus' disciples died horrific brutal deaths. John for example was boiled in hot oil and then stuck on an island. Paul was ship wrecked and believed to have been crucified. Matthew died from a sword wound. The Apostle James was beheaded.

James (author of the book James and brother of Jesus) was thrown one hundred feet from a Temple which he survived so he literally had his brains smashed out by an angry mob. Let us not forget that John the Baptist was beheaded. These men were martyred because they would not denounce Jesus Christ and his kingdom.

Finally, Jesus Christ, God in the flesh, was always asked to move on because people didn't want him in their region. These people believed he brought too much trouble wherever he was. Not many people believed his message and called him a liar and claimed he spoke blasphemy. Jesus was beaten, made to carry his own cross, and crucified among common thieves. I can't even be facetious about that I know being crucified could not have been fun.

Yes, I am sure all these people had some fun. There were probably times of laughter and joking around but their purpose while on earth was not explicitly to have fun. They likely enjoyed some of the same recreational activities we do. We know they liked to fish. There were plenty of lakes so swimming was probably something they enjoyed.

Obviously, if we were in a real trial I could present much more testimony and a lot more evidence. I really don't know what the cross examination or rebuttal would look like.

I cannot recall any sentences in the Bible stating our purpose is to "just have fun." I do not know of any stories where anyone who is living in the twenty-first century has claimed Jesus spoke to them and told them to pass on to everyone our purpose is to have fun end of story.

Recreating and enjoying ourselves is fine. Seriously it is awesome! There is a reason we enjoy lakes, rivers, mountains, deserts, prairies, and trees. Most of us enjoy the great outdoors and visiting our National Parks (NP). We like to get away from the man made *stuff*. We take advantage of these amenities when we get a chance.

Each year our fifty-eight National Parks are visited by two hundred and seventy million people. Wow! What is the attraction? I believe the reason we enjoy these amenities is because it brings us closer to our Creator. The great outdoors brings us closer to the things God created. We don't have to go to these places to be close or hear from God but it is sure refreshing when we witness His work that has not been touched or changed by man.

Man has made some lakes, rechanneled some rivers, and even grown and planted trees but we have never created any of these things we find in nature. Nature is our direct line to God. We can have that direct line anywhere but the ambiance of God's nature seems to make the experience a little more special. We seem to be able to focus a little better. It seems like we are closer to God, maybe because there are fewer distractions. We get to capture that intimacy with something God created that man has not polluted.

Have you ever had a conversation where somebody asks you if you could travel back in time where and what time period would you want to travel back to? Obviously, I would go back to the time Jesus was preaching, teaching, performing miracles, and doing all kinds of wonders. But my second choice would be to experience the west during the Lewis and Clark expedition. Can you imagine what the west looked like before man settled in it? Huge trees, open meadows, no roads, spectacular waterfalls, and wildlife everywhere. It would look like it did when God created it. We would be able to see His awesomeness and His creativity. These places still exist but they are becoming fewer and fewer.

My work has led me to travel to some of the most serial, beautiful places imaginable. Think of those places you have seen that have taken your breath away! I have been in the Poseidon Wilderness, Yellowstone NP, Zion NP, Cave Ruins of NM, Mogollon Rim, Glacier NP, Yosemite NP, Kenai Peninsula and the northern parts of Alaska and Canada too mention just a few areas. The vastness of these places is so amazing. When I am in these vast lands I am reminded how God is so big.

When I look up at the stars I begin to wonder why He created me. I begin to ponder what life is all about. There has to be more to life than merely surviving for eighty or so years and then dying and going back into the ground.

Man has added a space station and launched satellites into space but we have not altered the moon, sun, stars, or galaxies God spoke into existence. I have never met or spoken to a person who is not fascinated by our vast universe.

Our universe is amazing! It is nothing short of a miracle. When we gaze up into the immense sky we get a glimpse of God's power and creativity. He created all of this for us. He thought of everything. "Lift your eyes and look to the heavens: Who created all these? He who brings out the starry host one by one, and calls them each by name. Because of his great power and mighty strength, not one of them is missing" (Isaiah 40:26 NIV).

Life is precious, it is fun, and it is perfectly fine to enjoy this life. God created us to enjoy all of what He created. For some it is skiing, for others it is cooking, or motorcycle riding, looking at art, visiting museums, shopping, painting, back packing, fishing, hunting, traveling, carving, the list is endless but we must make fulfilling our purpose our number one priority. I am convinced with proper planning we can do the things we enjoy while still pleasing God.

The problem is two-fold. We often enjoy this life so much we forget it is very short and not permanent. We are foreigners in this world. If we never learn or forget why we were created it could lead to destruction, hell. Secondly, if we get so wrapped up in life that we believe it is all about fun and games, we forget or don't make time to discover why God created us.

If we discover and fulfill our purpose our reward is life with our heavenly Father. God doesn't say love life and lose Him. God tells us to choose life by loving Him. Our reward is we get to enjoy both lives, the one on this earth and our life in heaven which is eternal.

Sooner or later we will all come to the realization that there is a void in our heart and mind that can only be filled with the *things* of Jesus. For many this realization will come too late and there will not be anything that can be done for them. We can look for something or someone to fill this void but it will not fit. It is not possible to fill the void with anything except the love of Jesus.

That second, third, fourth, or fifth wife or husband will not fill that void. That new car, boat, truck, trailer, or vacation in the Bahamas is not going to take that feeling away from us. Many of us realize there is something missing in our lives but we do not know what is causing the emptiness. We struggle to comprehend our inability to fulfill what is missing. We keep trying to replace one material thing with another but materialistic items are never the answer.

Just as one key is designed to fit one lock we our created so one thing can fit into our hearts and minds, Jesus. There is only one thing that can give us a feeling of completeness. It is a five letter combination: JESUS.

When we are standing in the checkout line in the grocery store we can read all about the Hollywood couples who were so in love and now they are getting divorced. Six months ago they were in the same magazine claiming they had finally found Mr. or Mrs. Right after three other marriages.

If we look in the records section of our local newspaper we will discover who is getting a divorce. At one time these individuals claimed to be madly in love with each other and that may have been the case. It still may be the case. They were going to be together forever. They were the apple of each other's eye. Now one or maybe both of them think the other is a jerk. What happen?

They all have one thing in common: their life is missing something, they are not happy otherwise they wouldn't be getting a divorce. It has to be the dummy they married. One day they woke up and realized their spouse is not able to fulfill the marital vows they took. You know the one where we promise to make our partner complete. The only time I can ever recall hearing "You complete me" was when Tom Cruise told Renee Zellweger she completed him in the movie "Jerry Maguire" of course that was after he cheated on her.

Don't go beating yourself up if you have been through a divorce or two or even three that is not going to do you any good. The point is we often feel we aren't getting the most out of our relationship because that void is still present. We blame the void on our partner's inability to fill what we need. There has to be a reason the void is there so by default we have to blame it on our spouse.

We need to realize this void is there because of the way we were wired by our Creator. Material things cannot mask or fill that void. Marriages, dogs, cats, nice homes, money these things will not get the job done. The completeness we desire and yearn for can only be filled when we figure out our purpose for being created and then act on that purpose.

A large segment of our population dreams about living a lifestyle like movie stars and professional sports athletes. At one point there was a show on television that was called the Lifestyle of the Rich and Famous. All that money, fame, and glory we desire it. We believe all our troubles and the emptiness we feel will be over if we can buy whatever we desire. From what I hear, read, and see on television the rich and famous don't appear any happier than those of us who are not rich and famous.

Material things do not matter in God's kingdom. Our reward is awaiting us in heaven. "Rejoice in that day and leap for joy, because great is your reward in heaven" (Luke 6:23 NIV). There are millions of people who are lost and they do not even know it. They are unhappy and they keep searching for happiness according to the standards of the world, material things that cannot replace or fill what they really need.

We have a tendency to live in this pattern of unhappiness and discontent so we keep changing something in our lives. We keep trying new things hoping, thinking, maybe this time it will work out. But it won't we need Jesus. This is the revelation we must discover in order to reclaim the life God has planned for us.

We are willing to try everything but Jesus. Have you ever heard or maybe even said yourself, "I have tried everything. I don't know what else to do. Maybe I'll try this religion thing and see if it can help. I guess it can't hurt." We try everything we can imagine and finally when nothing has worked, we have hit rock bottom and we have become desperate we may finally check out Jesus.

The good news is that is okay. We could save ourselves a lot of mishap if we would turn to Jesus sooner but as long as we turn to him that is what he cares about. The sooner we discover the word of God the sooner we can get on the road to discovering why we were created.

I pray some day it would be possible to make every kid take a course in school that would explain to them the only way they will ever feel complete and truly understand and fulfill their purpose in life is to understand what Jesus Christ did for them. The heartache they could be spared would be worth the effort. Not everyone would turn but some would realize Jesus is the only way.

What I really pray for is a miracle. Right now Christian students are the minority in our public school system. The pressure from secular students is tremendous. Since Rebekah was born I have been praying the opposite would become the norm in our public schools. I pray the secular students would be in the minority.

I have witnessed so many good kids be torn by the pressure of staying faithful to the ways of Jesus or being accepted by the popular majority. The majority wants them to make a choice. The pressure is immense. But Jesus said, "Do not suppose that I have come to bring peace to the earth. I did not come to bring peace, but a sword. For I have come to turn 'a man against his father, a daughter against her mother, a daughter-in-law against her mother-in-law—a man's enemies will be the members of his own household'" (Matthew 10:34-36 NIV). Jesus did not come to bring peace in to our school that is our job as his ambassadors.

It is all part of the war. Our kids must know that one of the battle fields where fierce fighting occurs is in the halls of our schools. There is an all out assault by Satan taking place in our schools. Unfortunately, we have very few soldiers engaged on the battlefield. We have to learn how to recruit more soldiers and take back what the enemy has stolen. We cannot afford to surrender the halls of our public schools and run to private Christian schools. We have to stand and fight for what is right, the Way. We have to teach our kids to persevere and stand for Jesus!

We were created to seek, find, and act on a purpose. The crazy thing is discovering our purpose is not hidden, it is not a secret. God wrote it all down in a manual called the Bible. The Bible is the instructional manual on how to do everything. It is the number one bestselling book in history. They don't even count it on the New York Best Selling list any more.

The problem is so few people discover we have a greater purpose. Until we discover our purpose we will remain unhappy, bored, and lost. We will continue to search for the newest and greatest thing that we believe will fill that void. We will keep searching for that right job that right spouse or those hobbies we believe will satisfy that internal craving we desperately want to feel. Sadly, until we discover that elusive *thing* that is missing in our lives we will keep driving down the road in the wrong direction until we crash. Unfortunately, it won't be long before we are back on another road still attempting to do things our own way until we crash again. It is a vicious cycle that most people will never escape.

A large number of people turn to drugs and alcohol to fill the void that is present. They try to fill that emptiness with a substance that is short term and very damaging to their mental and physical health. Others use drugs to masquerade the pain and suffering they feel. Their life is basically in the sewer. They cannot find a way out. If they can avoid reality while they are on that high they feel they have escaped their dark world for awhile. They use drugs as a coping mechanism until the drugs begin to use them. The only thing they have accomplished by turning to drugs is to go deeper into enemy territory. Our enemy doesn't need to spend time with these folks because they are destroying themselves.

It does not have to be drugs. It could be gambling or having adulterous affairs. We are finding out that an alarming number of men are turning to pornography. Pornography addiction is hitting epidemic proportions in our society. Looking at pornography is immoral whether you are married or single. Don't fool yourself into believing it isn't. Yes, you are human if you don't look at women lustfully.

Any or all of these can be very addicting. Addictions don't just happen. There are reasons people become addicted to their addiction of choice. They are running from something or looking for something. They are looking for something to fill the void that is eluding them. Reality is these *band aides* or more appropriately bad aides can only put a temporary patch over the wound. They cannot take the pain away. The drug, hobby, or addiction of choice does not matter none of them can take the place of Jesus.

I am not one of those guys that say drinking is either bad or good. I am not going to claim you are a sinner and you're going to hell because you drink. I don't drink alcohol because it affects who I am. Alcohol used me for a long time.

My morals would always become compromised. I would become a different person when I drank.

I have witnessed what drinking has done to too many of my family members. Alcohol ruled their lives. Drinking and getting drunk became a way of life. We need to understand there is a huge disparity between a glass of wine with your dinner or a couple of casual beers and getting flat inebriated.

The Apostle Paul wrote we should live wisely. He says, "Therefore do not be foolish, but understand what the Lord's will is. Do not get drunk on wine, which leads to debauchery. Instead be filled with the Spirit" (Ephesians 5:17-18 NIV). It is not the Lord's will that we would get drunk.

Paul associates drunkards with the people of this world who are immoral, greedy, swindlers, slanderers, and idolaters. Paul tells us it is God's will for us to be filled with the Holy Spirit, be drunk with the Spirit not alcohol.

There are many great books written about the Holy Spirit so I am going to give an elementary perspective on the Holy Spirit. I like to describe the Holy Spirit as our conscience that tells us to do what is right. The Holy Spirit is linked with Jesus and God and baptized with them to make the trinity. The Holy Spirit is God living inside of believers. One of the ministries of the Holy Spirit is to bear witness to all believers our sins and to show us the righteousness of Christ. The Holy Spirit imparts divine revelation from God.

The Holy Spirit will not operate in a body that is intoxicated. Being in a drunken state is where our flesh can feel comfortable. Paul asks us the question, "Do you not know that your body is a temple of the Holy Spirit, who is in you, whom you have received from God" (1 Corinthians 6:19 NIV)? We need to know and understand that God dwells in us (believers). I believe the Apostle Paul was probably shouting when he said, "Do you not know that your body is a temple of the Holy Spirit." I strongly believe the Holy Spirit does not like being inundated with toxic waste.

When our cup is full with God's word the Holy Spirit is helping us make the right decisions. But when we add substances that are toxic to our body the Holy Spirit refuses to operate. When we are under the influence of drugs or alcohol we are suppressing the comforter who God put inside each one of us who believe in His son to encourage and help us on our journey.

The problem is alcohol becomes a stumbling block for too many people. There are times due to our lack of knowledge and understanding of people's situations we put a stumbling block right in their path even though that was not our intention.

Give the following scenario some thought. It is Super Bowl Sunday and someone from church is throwing a Super Bowl party. The perception would be since you mainly invited people from church most of those invited would believe there is not going to be any alcohol. What if there was a new believer "spiritual infant" who just started attending church. This person turned to church after years of battling alcohol. This individual attends your Super Bowl party.

You have no idea this person has been battling alcoholism for years. You have no idea alcohol nearly destroyed this person's life. You offer this individual a drink. The individual is not ready to share he has a problem with alcohol. He doesn't want anyone to find out he is an alcoholic so he accepts the drink.

One drink leads to another and then another by the time the party is over this individual is drunk. Nobody sees him in church for a couple weeks and eventually someone finds out he has spiraled downhill and alcohol has regained control of his life. Unfortunately, the guy would have been better off if he would have never been invited to the party.

I don't know if there is any adult who can claim they have never known or heard of someone whose life was not ruined because of drugs or alcohol. Personally, I have seen way too many lives destroyed because of alcohol.

Somebody always wants to throughout there, "Wasn't Jesus' first miracle turning water into wine when Mary his mother asked Him to do something because they had ran out of wine at the wedding banquet? If so what is the problem?" Some say Jesus drank others say there is confusion or a misuse of the Greek word because it could also mean grape juice. Either way I am not saying it is forbidden unless you were to take the Nazirite Vow.

A Nazirite Vow means you take a special vow to the Lord and you abstain from wine and other fermented drink. You cannot drink vinegar made from wine or from other fermented drink. You cannot drink grape juice or eat grapes and raisins. You cannot eat anything that comes from the grapevine (Numbers 6:2-4).

Regardless, wine was never a stumbling block for Jesus. The Bible records no accounts to make us believe otherwise. The Bible shares no stories about how he was a different person when he was drinking. Jesus definitely never lost his morals or got drunk because the Bible says he was perfect.

I have alluded to the idea that our purpose for being created is to fill our lives with the *things* of Jesus. I have stated the only thing that can fill the void and make us feel complete is to find, seek, and act on the purpose we were created. If we go deeper and look specifically at what that means we will discover the key to our purpose and completeness is to nourish a relationship with our Lord and Savior Jesus Christ.

God designed us to need a relationship with Jesus Christ. This need is directly correlated with our understanding and fulfilling our purpose. That is it! It is nothing to do with materialistic things and has everything to do with a relationship with the King of Kings and Lord of Lords.

Every relationship needs to be kept fresh and new. A relationship with Jesus is no different. We cannot let it be business as usual. We need to make His word new every day and applicable in our lives. We can accomplish this by reading his word. We can read the Bible every year for fifty years and the Lord may turn a new light on. We may see a scripture in a new or different way and get a better understanding of how that scripture is applicable for our present situation. It is amazing!

The church preached religion: do this don't do that for so many years it basically turned many people away from Jesus. This type of preaching made people believe it was *religionism.* Religionism is an excessiveness of too much Thou Shall Not's in the eyes of millions of people.

Religion by definition is a good thing but our culture now views it as a dirty word. Religion is defined as the expression of man's belief in and reverence for a super human power recognized as the creator and governor of the universe. Religion is recognizing God as creator and governor of all that exists. That is a good thing!

James says, "Religion that God our Father accepts as pure and faultless is this: to look after orphans and widows in their distress and to keep oneself from being polluted by the world" (James 1:27 NIV). Again, I don't believe that definition would make religion something bad.

There are so many wrong perceptions about God, Jesus, Holy Spirit, church, and religion. The vast majority of our population really does not have a good understanding about any of the five of them.

Some of the perceptions about the church are legitimate but other perceptions are way off base. Some perceptions are created by man, some by Satan. But we need to get it straight it is not about religionism it is all about relationship!

Relationships are natural but they do not come naturally. Fruitful relationships require all those involved to work hard at making the relationship work. Relationships cannot be successful if we do not learn to contain our selfishness.

We have to make what we consider sacrifices in order for the relationship to work. Too often we don't want to make sacrifices because it doesn't benefit us. We have to work hard at changing our ways so we can focus on God.

We are raised to be selfish and that selfishness often follows us into our relationships. When we were babies we got all the attention. We believed life was really all about us. We thought everything belonged to us. Most of our mom's and dad wanted to provide for our every need which reinforced our selfishness in most cases.

The sound of an unhappy baby is not always a welcomed or pleasant sound. We do whatever it takes within reason to comfort the baby so we can get the baby to quit crying. Am I right?

Is there anybody who hasn't witnessed the kid in the store throw the temper tantrum until he gets the toy he wanted? Life is so centered on him it really does seem like the world is coming to an end if he does not get the toy.

Relationship derives from the root word relation which means to be connected by blood. Relation is defined as a logical or natural association between two or more people with relevance one to another. It is the meaningful bonding of people.

Interesting, religion and relationship are only separated by a few words in the dictionary. If we put the two definitions together it would read: a logical and natural connection that occurs and becomes significant when we acknowledge that God is our creator and governor of all that exists in our universe and our personal lives. Hey that is pretty neat. Looks like those two words were made to go hand and hand.

First, understand if we have a relationship with Jesus then we have a relationship with God. If we break down the definition of religion with the idea of having a relationship with Jesus it is logical because his Father is our Father so we are blood of His blood and God created us to have a natural connection with His son.

Do we have relationships with our earthly mother and father? Yes, the majority of us anyway. We were designed to experience relationships. God's original intent was for it to be more natural to have a relationship with Jesus than with anybody else. Jesus knows everything about us and everything that makes us who we are. Jesus understands the fiber of our DNA. It is God's desire that we will have a personal relationship with Jesus Christ so we can reach the completeness we were created to feel.

Many people do not know what a healthy relationship looks like because it has never been modeled to them.

Parents are supposed to model a healthy relationship for their children but that cannot happen in homes where mom and dad live separately. We know fifty-percent of all marriages end in divorce.

We do not need to be a psychiatrist to know that a broken marriage affects the children who are involved. Divorce likely affects children's understanding of how a healthy relationship functions. Often at least one parent will start looking for love in all the wrong places and with too many faces. It is confusing to children when mom or dad shows up with a new boyfriend or girlfriend every weekend.

Think of a good relationship you have with someone or think of a couple you know who have a good relationship. What does it look like? What is it that defines their relationship as good?

We were created with the raw qualities and attributes that are required for us to have a healthy relationship but often we lack the fortitude to tap into these qualities and put them to good use. We should learn and put into practice all the foundational qualities we can so we can enjoy vibrant, healthy relationships. The following is not a conclusive list and I won't spend time talking about all of them but the list is certainly a good starting point if it is our desire to have a healthy good relationship.

- Commitment
- Communication
- Celebrate
- Time
- Love-understanding-intimacy-compassion
- Contribute

Pat Riley long time NBA basketball coach said, "There are only two options regarding commitment. You're either in or out. There's no such thing as a life in-between." How true! God is quoted as saying, "You are either hot or cold there is no lukewarm."

Commitment is not a spectator sport we are either engaged or disengaged. Commitment ignites action. Commitment is a foundational stone of a good relationship. Commitment requires us to practice our beliefs consistently. The Bible says, "Commit your way to the Lord; trust in him and he will do this: He will make your righteousness shine like the dawn" (Psalm 37:5-6 NIV).

Commitment means we have a sound set of beliefs and our behavior or actions will give testimony to our beliefs. Have you heard the saying, "Stand for something or you'll fall for anything?"

Successful relationships are built on trust and faith. When we trust someone we are more committed to that person. The paradox is the more commitment we have the more trust develops, and our relationship blossoms. Our relationship becomes stronger and more fruitful. If we trust God we are committed to knowing more about Him and devoted to obeying His principles.

Complacency has no role in commitment and it does not have a place in God's kingdom. If we are committed to something it is not business as usual. If we are committed to Jesus we will possess the ability to be optimistic about the future and our eternal life. If we are committed to Jesus we will not get stuck and weighted down from regrets we have from our past. We will press on committed to his way because we know he went to the cross for us.

Commitment is strengthened by communication. Most of us would agree a good relationship consists of frequent and direct communication with that person we desire to have a relationship with. Communication is a fundamental foundation for a healthy relationship.

Communicate means we express ourselves in such a way that one is readily and clearly understood. Communication is the exchange of thoughts and messages. Communication has to be occurring if we are to have a relationship with Jesus Christ. If we are not communicating with our Savior then we cannot legitimately claim to have a relationship with him. We need to make time to have intimate conversations with

Jesus. He will become the most important person in our lives because he is perfect and he will never let us down. Jesus is not capable of being imperfect. I cannot make that any clearer.

There cannot be a day that goes by where we do not talk with him. We need to tell Jesus how we feel and what is going on in our lives. We need to share the good things as well as our struggles. We will feel his presence when we begin to trust him.

The success of any relationship is dependent on its quality and quantity of communication. Communication is not just talking it is a process of exchanging information between two or more people. Have you ever had those conversations where they are one-way and you did all the listening? Communication is two-way. We need to be heard and we need to listen.

When the divorce proceedings begin in those fifty-percent of marriages that end in divorce usually at least one partner will be totally blindsided by all the problems the other partner had with him or her because there was no communication. The divorce is final and now he or she learns that working all those extra hours so the family could enjoy all those material items was not what was important. Spending time as a family was important.

Communication is one of the essential skills a firefighter must possess. Lack of communication or improper communication is one of the common denominators on tragedy fires eighty-six percent of the time. There have been one thousand forty-four men and women killed in the line of duty in the profession of wildland firefighting since 1910.

To be successful during my twenty-two seasons as a professional wildland firefighter and remain alive I have had to develop and work hard on my communication skills in order to remain safe and keep others safe.

One of our standard fire orders says, "Remain in communication with crew supervisor, crew members, and adjoining forces." We have acronyms like:

- LCES-Lookouts, Communications, Escape Routes, Safety Zones
- CASTLE-Communications, Anchor Points, Safety Zones, Trigger Points, Lookouts, Escape Routes (CASTLE was my creative thinking)

The beginning of every fire season starts with our crew leaders drilling our firefighters with these concepts. We educate them on all facets of communication. We tell them what, how, why, and when they need to communicate and who they need to communicate with. Every day they are reminded of this in a briefing. A briefing to the crew would sound like:

- Here's what I think we will face today.
- Here is what, why, when, where, who, and how we are going to do things today.
- Questions?

We all need to show a little more patience, compassion, and understanding when it comes to communication. None of us are mind readers. We need to be willing to cut each other a little slack and to not be over sensitive all the time. We can call this grace. I try to stay focused during every conversation I have with Kelli but occasionally I will lack the discipline and my mind will race a head. I have to say, "I am sorry my mind wondered to something else when you said . . . . could you please say it again?" This is really true when she is asking a question and is waiting for an answer and I have no idea what the question was.

I find it so interesting that Jesus showed us so much grace and mercy yet grace and mercy are the two things we struggle with when it comes to our fellow man. We had to have his grace and mercy, no way around it. Why do we struggle with those two so much when we received an abundant of God's grace and mercy?

Rebekah and Olivia had a track meet where their performance was subpar. I had been gone on a fire assignment for two weeks which requires Kelli to be a single mom who has to manage getting the girls to piano lessons, soccer, basketball, softball along with working and feeding them and all the other stuff that comes with parenthood. Not an easy feat to accomplish when both of us are home.

We were talking about how the girls didn't perform to their previous standards when I said, "You should have made them run more." What Kelli heard me saying was it was her fault that they didn't do well because she didn't take the time to make them run. That was the way I projected it but in my mind I was trying to communicate that Kelli should be able to tell the girls to go run and they should run. This would put the responsibility on them. I said I was sorry that was not what I intended to communicate. Kelli afforded me some grace and that was the end of the story.

A healthy relationship will never go for long periods without communicating. A relationship with Jesus is no different. We need to trust God is listening because He gives us His word that He is listening. God listens and then He acts. He either says no, yes, or later but God always answers. It is a deeper exchange of experiences that brings understanding between the Creator and the one He created.

The more we communicate with Jesus the closer the relationship becomes. If we are looking for direction, answers, and decisions then we need to spend time with God seeking Him and His will for us. Remember He is a God of action. We need to listen and recognize when He is speaking to us.

He speaks to us we either chose not to listen or we ignore Him because we don't like what He may have said. This can be illustrated by a story of a lady who got stuck on the roof of her house during a flood. The water had come up so high the roof was the only safe place to be. She kept praying for God to come and save her. She had not been on the roof very long when a helicopter came by and dropped a ladder down but she said no thanks I am waiting for God to save me. A boat came by after a short while and the driver shouted to her to get in. Again she said no thanks I am waiting for God to save me.

The water finally rose so high that the roof was no longer safe and she drowned. She was a believer and went to heaven. When she got to heaven she demanded to see God. She asked Him why He didn't rescue her from the flood when she prayed earnestly for Him to come and save her. God looked at her and said, "I sent you a helicopter but you said no thanks. Then I sent a boat to pick you up but you would not climb in." If this story were true I imagine the lady would have probably felt a bit silly at this point. She failed to recognize God was listening and He had acted on her prayers.

When we are seeking answers, looking for direction, or solutions we should always go to God first. There are numerous stories in the OT when kings would seek the counsel of the Lord. Before going to war kings would ask the prophets to ask God if they should go to war. The kings would either go to war or not depending on what the Lord said to them.

There is a danger if we are not being honest and earnestly seeking and listening to His wisdom. *We can get God to say anything we want if we want.* But God is never going to tell us to leave our wife and flee with our mistress. He is never going to tell us to blow up an abortion clinic. His words will be wise and edifying.

If we don't understand what God is saying or we don't believe we have heard from God we should seek the advice of Godly people. If we would like to confirm what we believe God is saying then seeking the counsel of others is wise. The Bible says a wise man seeks the counsel of many advisors. We need to confirm things through the word of God, the Bible.

God allowed Kelli and I to be parents and we believe He will give us wisdom on how to raise our kids. It is not an exclusive club. Not every method works for everybody.

Kelli and I were asked to teach a parenting class at CLC and we said yes. We quickly realized that we did not agree with all the content or strategies that were being presented in the curriculum. Some of the methods and philosophies were out there a little too far for us as parents.

We prayed to God for wisdom as parents and as teachers of the curriculum. We believe we heard from God so we adopted and applied the techniques in our parenting that we liked but we did not apply the techniques we disagreed with.

We made a decision to teach the whole curriculum and there were no problems. If someone asked us our opinion we were honest with them. We would share with them what worked for us and what didn't work. Not everything works for everybody except Jesus. God has a unique special plan for all of our lives and He will communicate it directly to us. If we will listen we will know what His plan is for us. "For I know the plans I have for you," declares the LORD,

"plans to prosper you and not to harm you, plans to give you hope and a future" (Jeremiah 29:11 NIV).

I am all for getting advice from Godly people who have a wealth of knowledge especially for those who are infants and children in their spiritual walk. However, I am stating we all have a direct line to God and Jesus and it is free because Jesus paid the bill. If we have an open line of communication with Jesus we can travel anywhere we want and ask, "Can you hear me now," and the answer will be yes. The important thing is we consult God. If we don't consult God then we insult God.

One of the greatest lessons I have learned in my walk with the Lord is that His word is alive to everyone who is truly searching for Him and His wisdom. You don't need to be a Theologian or Pastor. You don't need to be a person who has gone to church your whole life and has always lived a biblical life. We need to understand God wants to communicate with us directly.

There are many examples in the OT when God communicates directly with His people. He was the main communicator with His people during the time of the OT. The following are a few examples:

- "And the LORD God commanded the man, 'You are free to eat from any tree in the garden; but you must not eat from the tree of the knowledge of good and evil, for when you eat of it you will surely die" (Genesis 2:16-17 NIV).
- "Then the LORD God said to the woman, 'What is this you have done'" (Genesis 3:13 NIV)?
- "Then the LORD said to Cain, 'Why are you angry? Why is your face downcast'" (Genesis 4:6 NIV)?
- "So God said to Noah, 'I am going to put an end to all people, for the earth is filled with violence because of them. I am surely going to destroy both them and the earth'" (Genesis 6:13 NIV).
- "Then the LORD said to Moses, 'Go, tell Pharaoh king of Egypt to let the Israelites go out of his country'" (Exodus 6:10-11 NIV).
- "But you have forsaken me and served other gods, so I will no longer save you. Go and cry out to the gods you have chosen. Let them save you when you are in trouble" (Judges 10:13-14 NIV)!
- "The word of the LORD came to Jonah son of Amittai: 'Go to the great city of Nineveh and preach against it, because its wickedness has come up before me'" (Jonah 1:1-2 NIV).

God does not speak directly to us as much in the NT. When Jesus came God became a direct communicator with us in the flesh. Jesus was fully man and fully God. Jesus said to Philip, "If you have seen me you have seen the Father" (John 14:9).

The Bible says, "In the past God spoke to our forefathers through the prophets at many times and in various ways, but in these days he has spoken to us by his Son, whom he appointed heir of all things, and through whom he made the universe" (Hebrews 1:1-2 NIV).

Throughout the NT we see examples of angels' speaking as messengers of God but Jesus was the main communicator.

The following are two examples of when God spoke in the NT.

- "And a voice from heaven said, 'This is my Son, whom I love; with him I am well pleased'" (Matthew 3:17 NIV).
- "While he was still speaking, a bright cloud enveloped them, and a voice from the cloud said, 'This is my Son, whom I love; with him I am well pleased. Listen to him'" (Matthew 17:5 NIV)!

Before Jesus ascended into heaven he said, "Unless I go away, the Counselor will not come to you; but if I go, I will send him to you" (John 16:6).

Jesus continued, "But when he, the Spirit of truth, comes, he will guide you into all the truth. He will not speak on his own; he will speak only what he hears, and he will tell you what is yet to come" (John 16:13 NIV). God sent Jesus then Jesus sent the Holy Spirit who lives inside believers with the purpose of being our communicator directly to God.

When we begin our journey with Jesus we need to learn to celebrate with him. We should celebrate the fact that Jesus conquered the grave! We have the celebrating down. We plan some of the biggest most elaborate celebrations that anybody has ever experienced. In fact, many of our celebrations leave us in awe and awful shape the next morning!

I have never been there but I have watched New Year's Eve celebration from Time Square on television. It is a no holds bar extravaganza. New Year's Day parades are anticipated by millions waiting to see all the fancy floats. Mardi Gras in New Orleans is another celebration where they pull out all the stops and you can collect all kinds of necklaces. How creative is that!

It would be awesome if every time a person accepted Jesus Christ as their Lord and Savior we made a commercial that said, "Hey you just accepted Jesus Christ what are you going to do now?" "I am going to Disney Land."

Jesus says, "Rejoice with me; I have found my lost sheep. I tell you that in the same way there will be more rejoicing in heaven over one sinner who repents than over ninety-nine righteous persons who do not need to repent" (Luke 15:6-7 NIV).

To celebrate means to announce publicly or proclaim. One of the biggest ways we can celebrate is to preach the Good News. The word preach in Greek is kay-roos-so which means of certain affinity or likeness. To herald a person who proclaims important news. We want to make the Good News public, it needs to be published. We have a responsibility to preach, publish, and proclaim the Good News! We need to communicate why we celebrate the resurrection of Jesus Christ.

Too often we get stuck on the idea that Jesus died for us but we forget he rose on the third day. His resurrection was a victory for all of us. "For everyone born of God overcomes the world. This is the victory that has overcome the world, even our faith" (1 John 5:4 NIV). This gave us authority to defeat the works of our enemy. If God is for us, who can be against us? No one! Victory is ours. God will trample our enemies.

Jesus' victory is ours to celebrate because no matter what gets thrown our way we can be victorious, receive that. Overcoming and winning is in our blood! We all have a little Rocky Balboa, Rudy, or Peter in us. We have the blood of Royal Priesthood, we are crowned with glory and honor, we have seeds of greatness, and we are heirs to His thrown. Ready, we are children of the Most High God, Amen! We need to be proud (glory to God) children and boast about our Father!

Jesus commanded us to preach the gospel to the people and to testify that he is the one whom God has appointed judge of the living and the dead. Jesus said, "I (anybody who is a servant of God) must preach the good news about the kingdom of God in other towns also, because that is what God sent me to do" (Luke 4:43 NIV).

What is this Good News? Certainly the concept of never dying and having eternal life is Good News. The Good News is that Jesus Christ the Son of God, was born of a Virgin, walked this earth, was crucified on the cross, and rose from the dead.

It was Good News when the angel delivered the news that a savior was being born in Bethlehem. "But the angel said to them, 'Do not be afraid. I bring you good news of great joy that will be for all the people. Today in the town of David a Savior has been born to you; he is Christ the Lord. This will be a sign to you: You will find a baby wrapped in clothes and lying in a manger'" (Luke 2:10-12 NIV).

Where does the Good News need to be preached? Our hope needs to be that as our faith continues to grow, our area of activity will continue to expand and God's word will go throughout the world.

We were commanded as Jesus' disciples to go into the entire world and preach the Good News. "Therefore go and make disciples of all nations, baptizing them in the name of the Father and of the Son and of the Holy Spirit, and teaching them to obey everything I have commanded you. And surely I am with you always, to the very end of the age" (Matthew 28:19-20 NIV). Amen.

We are to represent Jesus, to present ourselves in a worthy manner as ambassadors of Christ! If we have a relationship with Jesus Christ we will celebrate and tell people about the Good News! Everywhere our feet tread the gospel needs to be preached. If we deny Jesus he will deny us.

The Great Commission!! We should all be disciples of Jesus. We have been commissioned by Jesus to teach people about God's living word. We need to share our testimonies and our journey's with others telling them our Redeemer lives. Wow! Think of that 'Our Redeemer'!

Look at the word Gospel. If we break it down it reads GO-SPEL. Go preach the message to the people. Go and spell it out to them. It is not a suggestion but a commission.

When does the Bible tell us to preach the Good News? "Day after day, in the temple courts and from house to house, they (apostles) never stopped teaching and proclaiming the good news that Jesus is the Christ" (Acts 5:42 NIV).

They were having a celebration every day. They knew how to party. We need to speak the word daily to the people. The word must be spread throughout the world. Who will proclaim Jesus Christ is the way, the truth, and the source of life if not those who believe?

Who do we preach the gospel to? The word was first meant for Jews and had to be spoken to them first. But after they rejected Jesus as the Messiah the word was open to the Gentiles, all of us. "Then Paul and Barnabas answered them boldly: 'We had to speak the word of God to you first. Since you reject it and do not consider yourselves worthy of eternal life, we now turn to the Gentiles'" (Acts 13:46 NIV).

People who believe and celebrate the Good News are supposed to preach it eagerly. "That is why I am so eager to preach the gospel also to you who are at Rome" (Romans 1:15 NIV).

Why preach the Good News? "How, then, can they call on the one they have not believed in? And how can they believe in the one of whom they have not heard? And how can they hear without someone preaching to them? And how can they preach unless they are sent?"

"As it is written, 'How beautiful are the feet of those who bring good news'" (Romans 10:14-15 NIV).

We should preach the Good News because we might reach someone who was headed to hell. If we will be bold and proclaim the Good News and share it with others there is the possibility they will accept Christ as their Lord and Savior and their names will be written in the Book of Life. We also need to preach the gospel to glorify God. God is pleased with us when we tell people about His son, Jesus Christ.

People are dying every day who do not know Jesus. Some of these people are relatives of ours, neighbor's, coworkers, friends, or maybe just acquaintances. Are they not worthy to know Jesus? Do we not love them enough to tell them Good News?

I wonder what would have happened if the shepherds who went to see the baby Jesus in the manger would have kept the news to themselves? No doubt God had another plan but their obedience to spread what they had been told and what they had seen were the first eye witness testimonies that the savior of the world had been born. "When they had seen him, they spread the word concerning what had been told them about this child, and all who heard it were amazed at what the shepherds said to them" (Luke 2:17 NIV).

The people who heard this news and knew what the prophets from long ago had written had to start wondering if this was truly the Messiah. They had to be asking themselves if this really was the savior that the Prophet Isaiah had written about seven hundred years earlier. Isaiah told us that the virgin would have a child and his name would be Immanuel. Immanuel means God with us.

I encourage you to hang in there and don't give up. It will be rewarding if you will let the relationship develop. A good healthy relationship requires that people spend time together. How do we spend time with God? We pray, read the Bible, and worship Him. It really is that simple. We can't just communicate when we need something and expect Him to answer us. We need to spend time with Him every single day.

If we develop a healthy relationship with Jesus we will want to line our hearts up with his will. We will want to be obedient and follow the desires of our heavenly Father. Once we align ourselves with Jesus we will have that void filled that we have desperately been trying to fill with everything the world offers. We will experience what it feels like to have that feeling of completeness.

What do God and Jesus get out of the deal? They rejoice because they now get to fellowship with us. They also know that another person has signed up in their army. They have a recruit who is willing to go out and reach the world for them one person at a time.

We can only begin to appreciate and understand what God did for us by building a relationship with the Son of man, Jesus Christ. There is more to life than simply being born and satisfying our flesh with the things of this world. There is but one mediator between man and the Creator who we must foster a relationship with.

Jesus bore the cross so we could live forever. The journey that takes place when we begin to seek that relationship with Jesus is one that is different for all of us. It is uniquely formed and knitted together with love, laughter, tears, joy, sorrow, and all the other emotions we experience in relationships because it is real.

The difference between a relationship with Jesus compared to someone in the flesh is that Jesus understands and knows what makes each one of us who we are. He knows what makes each one of us uniquely special. We are all special in the eyes of Jesus. Jesus knows our deepest thoughts before we ever speak them. He has the inside scoop. To say we would take a bullet for someone we love is one thing but to be crucified for the sins of the whole world is the ultimate sacrifice.

Let us imagine the conversation between God and Jesus in heaven when God filled Jesus in on the redemptive plan. I wonder if Jesus looked at his Father and asked God if having a relationship with us was that important to Him. Jesus didn't ask God that question but if he would have God certainly would have looked His son whom He loved in the eyes and said, "It is worth you dying for son."

Jesus freely gave it all for us. A life was sacrificed for each one of us with a hope that we would walk side by side in a healthy relationship with our Father and our Redeemer. All of humanity is given the opportunity to fellowship with God forever because of the act of one man who was God in the flesh.

Are we going to be a people who will rise up and serve our purpose for existing? Come on! We need to be fighters. We have to fight for Jesus Christ, our Savior! Every person regardless of who they are or what they have done needs to be told they face an ultimatum. In fact, they need to be told they were born facing the Ultimate Ultimatum!

CHAPTER 7

A Case for Church

"He who has an ear, let him hear what the Spirit says to the churches. To him who overcomes, I will give the right to eat from the tree of life, which is in the paradise of God" (Revelation 2:7 NIV). Local churches as well as the universal church are intricate in God's plan, yet so undervalued by man-kind. The church has overcome and survived for thousands of years although not always thriving. The church takes a one two punch on the steeple from man and Satan.

For generations a large segment of our population has contributed in the battle to convince people that the church is not necessary. At the same time they have totally distorted the purpose of the church. Man has down played the role the church can play in our lives, communities, states, nations, and the world. Obviously, not everyone falls into this category but a large percentage of people do not speak well of the church for various reasons.

A lot of people see the church as a place that wants to judge them and tell them how to live, neither of which sits well with them. Many people perceive the church as an inconvenience so if they can devalue the church and make it insignificant to the majority they will not feel any conviction for not attending church.

Satan has invested countless hours trying to make humanity believe the church has no purpose. The enemy comes to steal, kill, and destroy. We looked earlier at what he likes to destroy but we didn't include the church. We need to understand the church is a primary focal point of our adversary.

Church is a safe-haven where Satan's paroles should run to after escaping his prison. Satan wants to revoke our parole before we can get help. If he can get us to mess up while on probation and before we become "entrenched" in the ways of God he knows he still has a fighting chance to lock us back up in his prison. Satan clings to the notion that the odds are in his favor.

Satan is not scared to chase us right through the doors of the church. He desires to have us back living in his dark world. He knows we could see the light if we begin to hear the word of God. He also knows just because we enter through the doors of church that does not mean we are actually sold on Jesus. Satan welcomes the challenge to get those of us who attend church back and serving him. He welcomes the challenge and turns up the heat.

Unfortunately, he laughs at some people knowing he will take them captive again. Satan knows and manipulates scripture. He attempts to use scripture against us. A perfect example is when Satan attempts to tempt Jesus. "'If you are the Son of God,' he said, 'throw yourself down. For it is written:'" 'He will command his angels concerning you, and they will lift you up in their hands, that you will not strike your foot against a stone'" (Matthew 4:6 NIV).

Satan knew that was scripture from the Psalms. "For he will command his angels concerning you to guard you in all your ways; they will lift you up in their hands, so that you will not strike your foot against a stone" (Psalm 91:11-12 NIV).

Satan knows the church is good so he spews lies about what the church is and what it can do for us. Satan realizes the power of God's church. If we make a commitment to the Bride of Christ he knows he has lost a member who was serving in his army of darkness and that causes him great anguish.

Once we get in church we can start hearing the word of God that is written in the Holy Bible, we can begin to make the Bible applicable in our lives. I struggle comprehending how someone says they believe in God but they do not believe what is written in the Bible. "See to it, brothers, that none of you has a sinful, unbelieving heart that turns away from the living God" (Hebrews 3:12 NIV). Believing in God means we have to believe His word. It is God's word that is written in the Bible. We cannot believe one without believing the other.

When Kelli and I came to the realization we needed to be involved in church we knew there was one principle that was nonnegotiable. If we were going to commit to a church it had to teach straight from God's living word, the Bible. Teaching from the Bible had to be a core value of the church we were going to attend.

If the church doesn't teach God's word then there is no need attending. Church is there to help the body understand what the word means and how we are to apply it in our daily lives. I wanted to know what God said. I had heard enough from men who never stepped foot in a church. I wanted to know for myself.

When the NT talks about the church, it speaks of an assembly of people. In the Bible the Greek word for church is translated from the word ekklesia, which means "a calling out." Church by definition is any where a congregation of people gathers who have been called out of Satan's dark world.

I believe the Holy Spirit can move powerfully in church if the congregation is in unity. Acts says, "They devoted themselves to the apostles' teaching and to the fellowship, to the breaking of bread and to prayer. Everyone was filled with awe, and many wonders and miraculous signs were done by the apostles. All the believers were together and had everything in common" (Acts 2:42-44 NIV).

Proverbs 13:20 says, "He who walks with the wise grows wise" (NIV).

God chose the Israelites and He called them out of Egypt to a land of their own that He would give them. "So I have come down to rescue them from the hand of the Egyptians and to bring them up out of that land into a good and spacious land, a land flowing with milk and honey" (Exodus 3:8 NIV). God led the Israelites by a pillar of cloud in the day time and a pillar of fire by night. God chose them and called them out of Egypt to gather together and follow Him.

I didn't say church is where a body of believers who all love God meets, that is not necessarily the case. Just because an individual or a group of people are attending church this does not allow us to assume they are believers and are committed to a relationship with Jesus.

We can find people attending church who are unbelievers, skeptics, and uncommitted. Obviously, there are those attending church who do believe in Jesus Christ and they realize they need God to survive.

We are all amazingly complicated. Only God knows what makes each one of us tick. There are many reasons why unbelievers and skeptics might go to church. They could be trying to get their wives off their back and by attending church they may be appeasing her. Maybe they are lonely and are looking for something to do. Some may be looking for a meal or some financial assistance. Others attend just to see if they can find mistakes in the sermon. Some attend so they can see who the hypocrites are who go to church. We cannot know for certain why they go to church but we can say with certainty that they are in church.

It just might be that God, regardless of why they might be attending just wants them in church. I initially attended church to make myself feel good while hoping for a divorce from Kelli. Regardless why they might be in church we need to pray that their hearts will be changed and that through prayer and hearing the message a relationship with Jesus will begin to develop.

So let's look at the role of the church. What is the role of the church? Does God have a plan for the church? What should the church teach, preach, and proclaim? In the last chapter we covered that we are to proclaim the Good News that Jesus Christ died and rose; he conquered the grave so all of us sinners who believe in him will have eternal life.

Without Jesus' sacrifice eternal life in heaven would not even be a possibility. We were destined for hell. It was death to us all. I cannot stress that enough.

There are two questions church leadership should ask when discussing the role of the church. First, what is God's purpose for the church? Secondly, is the church fulfilling this purpose?

God tells us His purpose multiple times but we can look at what the Apostle Paul wrote to the church at Ephesus in order to understand God's desire for the church. "His intent was that now, through the church, the manifold wisdom of God should be made known to the rulers and authorities in the heavenly realms, according to his eternal purpose which he accomplished and carried out in Jesus Christ our Lord" (Ephesians 3:10-11 NIV).

When Jesus established the church on earth God used this as a testimony of His wisdom to all those in heaven. By uniting Jews and Gentiles on earth this showed those in the heavenly realm God's perfect plan of redemption. God's redemptive plan is the ultimate example of wisdom. Think about it. He knew man would sin and be separated from Him forever but God comes up with this plan to come to earth in the flesh and die for all sinners who receive him as their savior. What a plan!

Jesus redeemed all of us who truly believe in him. This means the church's purpose is to share the news of great joy, a savior has come. This was God's purpose for the church from the beginning of time and Jesus made it all possible. The church is important and is always going to be a part of God's eternal plan. The church is serving its purpose if it is teaching and living out what is in the Holy Bible.

The church is the reconciliation place for believers. Church is where we learn to live our lives out through discipleship. It is the place where our reunion with Jesus Christ can take place. The church belongs to Jesus. "And God placed all things under his feet and appointed him to be head over everything for the church, which is his body, the fullness of him who fills everything in every way" (Ephesians 1:22-23 NIV).

God is saying that we cannot be complete without the church. We can fool ourselves into believing the church serves no purpose but it is a lie from the pit of hell. The church exists to carry out Jesus' mission.

The church has a responsibility to proclaim a message that says God has a plan for each and every one of us because He loves us and He gave His only son that whosoever believes in him shall not perish but have everlasting life. People who go to church need to hear that we all have sinned and fall short of the glory of God which separates us from Him but God being almighty provided a way for us to be reunited with Him and that way is Jesus Christ, he is the only one who can redeem us into fellowship with God. If the church has a message that proclaims something similar to that it will be lined up with God's will and serving its purpose.

We can say for certain that the unbelievers, skeptics, and uncommitted do not understand the purpose of the church. They do not know Jesus is the Great Physician. Some of these people believe many of us go to church because we live a lie all week and want to make ourselves feel good. The naysayers' don't care, never knew, or forgot that church is a hospital for people who need help.

As I began to attend church more frequently I realized that there were other sinners in church who were like me. In fact, many had done things worse than I had. Let's dispel any myths that people who go to church are perfect. Many of them are still struggling. They realize they are sick and could be dying so they check into a hospital to receive some love and care from the Great Physician!

I find it a bit ironic that the only perfect person to walk this earth, Jesus Christ was born in a stable. Most of us have heard of the baby who was born in a stable and placed in a manger but we don't realize a manger is actually a feeding trough for animals.

Jesus' hospital specializes in health related issues dealing with the brain and heart. Jesus has perfected his operating tools and has a one hundred percent success rate when it comes to surgeries involving the brain and heart. He knows exactly how to get the two of them functioning correctly and together. As long as the patients follow his directions and keep their scheduled checkups they can live forever.

Jesus' hospital accepts any and all patients. He doesn't care if you have been sick to the point of death most of your life he will take you as a patient. Nothing is too small or too large he will see any patient. If you just need a prescription refilled come on in Jesus will take care of you. All of his prescriptions say the same thing: take this as many times a day as you can and live forever. You will not be turned away for not having health insurance. In fact, there are no bills and there is not any paperwork. He works for free. The only thing he requires of his patients is they trust him. Everything else has been taken care of and completed by Jesus.

Maybe you are thinking you are not sick and you feel fine. How would you like to stay that way? Jesus' hospital offers preventive medicine. Our chance of surviving something that is fatal is greater if we catch it sooner. All of Jesus' churches come with health clubs so you can stay fit and in shape.

The purpose of the church is to feed the saints, protect us, and equip us for service so that we may come to maturity. The church which is the Bride of Christ is there to disciple us on how to walk in fullness. Is it one hundred percent? The word of God is one hundred percent but we receive what we put into it like everything else in life.

If we make a commitment to a local church we are becoming a piece (member) of Jesus' body. We are surrendering our desire to be selfish and always make ourselves number one. We are beginning to see the light. We are putting Jesus in his rightful place.

I mentioned earlier I enjoy working out. I have been pretty committed to lifting weights and doing cardio exercises since I was fourteen years old. I loved playing football but I knew if I was going to be successful I had to add some muscle mass to my one-hundred and forty pound frame so I became pretty dedicated to the weight room. Those habits have stayed with me (not the muscle mass of my youth). I have a gym membership and I am pretty faithful with my attendance. I look forward to going to the gym Monday through Friday. I have done it for so long it has become a way of life for me.

Throughout the years I have noticed the first four to six weeks of every New Year the gym becomes packed with people who have made a commitment to get themselves in shape and lose weight. This really frustrated me in my younger years because I would have to spend a little extra time looking for a parking spot. I would have to wait for this new person to get done with my favorite piece of exercise equipment.

Unfortunately, year after year with a few exceptions many fell away from their commitment. These folks were unable to make the necessary lifestyle change that we talked about in the introduction to obtain their goal.

When February comes around it is back to business as usual. I can find a close parking place and jump right on my favorite machine. Unfortunately, church is the same; we fail to make a commitment to attend church because it requires a lifestyle change.

For those who do make a commitment to a local church there is a very good chance you will be shocked after you spend a little time getting to know your new family. If you stick around you will begin to realize there are people who have dealt with and who are still dealing with various sin in their life. You will be surprised when people begin to share the sin they have dealt with and how they overcame their sin.

God's word tells us testimonies are powerful and should be shared. The Bible says, "They (all believers) will overcome him (Satan) by the blood of the Lamb and the word of their testimony" (Revelation 12:11 NIV). God's word says we will overcome Satan because of the blood Jesus bled at Calvary and our testimony. One of the exciting things about church is we get to hear the real life stories or testimonies from people who have beat all kinds of odds. These people overcame and are living for Jesus.

Several times I have been at a church conference or visiting a church while traveling and heard the preacher give a testimony about how he use to sale and use drugs, get in bar fights, and admit to committing all kinds of sexual immoralities but because of God's grace he is now preaching the gospel to others.

I find it amazing when I hear stories from pastors who were running with the devil and how God turned their life around so much they are now teaching other people the greatness of Jesus. Through the grace of God they were able to overcome their situation.

Unfortunately, even pastors have fallen. I have learned to admire that pastors know they can get back up after they fall. They don't have to stay down. They suffer like the rest of us but the chances are they know God's word and at some point most of them will begin to stand on the word and bounce back. They may or may not ever shepherd a flock again but they know they can have forgiveness.

During the non fire months I do a lot of coordinating and teaching of fire suppression classes. When I start telling the war stories like the time we were doing a back firing operation (when firefighters start fire to change the direction or burn the fuels in front of the main fire) and the fire began to run down hill in a horizontal vortice faster then we could run the students become engaged and curious.

When I tell them the main fire became so active that it began to pull our back fire downhill they become wide eyed and attentive. When I tell them the smoke was so thick you couldn't see two inches in front of your face and the situation was becoming dire they anxiously wait to hear what happened next. These kinds of stories engage the students. They become interested and start becoming involved. I have them hooked. They are ready to hear more war stories.

God instilled something in us where we get excited when it is story time. Think back when you were in grade school. Story time was probably the most anticipated part of the day with the exception of that afternoon snack. Story time works and that is why it is still used after all these years.

Individual testimonies from people inside the church are the same way. We enjoy listening to successful stories. Testimonies have that same power to hold people's attention. Testimonies have a way of making people feel comfortable.

One of the most powerful testimonies I have ever heard was by our pastor's wife. When she shared her testimony one Sunday it was so powerful I was enthralled by her every word. No way on God's green earth did I believe a pastor could be married to a sinner?

She shared that she had rebelled in the latter part of her high school years and experimented in the areas of drugs, alcohol, and sexual immorality. I remember being blown away! It actually made me feel good. Think about it. If a person could go through all that and be forgiven and marry a pastor there is hope for me, there is hope for all of us.

People have all kinds of "dirty laundry." We have all committed acts we wish we could take back. It doesn't matter what we have done or how bad we think it is God is bigger. No sin is too dirty and no sin is too big that God cannot wash it away.

I recently let an individual vent on the phone while I just listened. Wow! This individual had issues that went back thirty years. He was angry at his family for past mistakes and his anger was compounded by the fact that nothing was going right in his life. There was nothing I could say he wanted to remain angry. If he would have been willing to listen all of his issues could have been surgically removed by the Greatest Physician who has ever been created. To this day he could experience healing if he would call on the name of Jesus.

I will say it again if you're looking for perfect people then church is not a place for you. Well it is but you will be surprised at all the different backgrounds of the people who attend church. Can you believe some of the worse gossipers can be found in church? People who aren't even liked by their own family members can be found in church.

You may even see people at church who you know frequent bars. You may recognize someone who you have seen at those establishments where ladies dance and their clothes somehow end up falling off. Why were you there? I know baby steps! It is unfortunate they are not being a light for Jesus but they are still in the right place, a hospital.

I remember hearing a story while listening to a Christian radio station, a lady had called the program and shared she recently started attending church to find out about God because she felt there was more to life then what she had been experiencing. She quit attending when she saw some of the church leaders come into the establishment where she worked. She was an exotic dancer and shared that this incident pretty much ruined church for her.

A finger could be pointed at both parties involved in this unfortunate situation. The church leaders should not have been going to places like that for obvious reasons and she should have focused more on her personal relationship with her Lord and Savior. She was spiritually immature and did not know better so she deserves a little more grace. The church leaders should have used better judgment. Hopefully they have repented of such acts. Hopefully, they have realized that their actions speak volumes to a lot of people about the church and those who attend church.

When we have no understanding of God's word and we begin to hear testimonies and "feel good" stories it begins to give us hope. Our curiosity begins to peak, we begin to believe that maybe our life can be better. Maybe this Jesus thing is real. We begin to wonder if our life really could be different.

Could this really become your testimony? The answer is a resounding yes. Begin to believe. Begin to dream of a new Way! If you think you are living the dream and life can't get any better you're wrong. It can get better. Step into the light and see how bright your life can become.

Yes, we are going to find imperfect people in church but let me share this with you. You are also going to find people who will not judge you or point a finger when you mess up.

They will genuinely want to get to know you. They can't help but love you and instantly they want good things to be bestowed upon you.

Regardless of your situation or what you have done you will find people in church who will want to see you get healed. Church attendees will be as diverse and unique group of people that you will ever encounter in one building. They are people from all walks of life each of them with their own story. They will eagerly be waiting to share their journey while anticipating the beginning of yours. They will anxiously be wondering what the outcome will be. They are seeking help, they are looking for the cure, and they are searching for hope that the world cannot offer them. All who enter the church have a common bond but not everyone's eyes are open in the beginning. Remember it is a journey!

Church is where scripture is taught and its meaning explained. Scripture is a surgical tool that can be used to heal the cancer of false doctrine. Scripture is the pain reliever that can stop the hurting. It is scripture that can heal the blindness that doesn't allow us to see that hell and heaven are real places. Scripture can heal deafness (spiritual deafness) that keeps us from growing in faith. Scripture is the living bread and water of Christ Jesus.

Remember Satan doesn't want you going to church. It is likely he is going to attempt to move people right in to counter and discourage any thoughts you may have about going to church. Naysayers' may hit you from every angle but you have to ask yourself why aren't you deserving of eternal life. Why can't you have life? Nobody should discourage anyone from wanting to get better and do things according to God. Nobody should be discouraging rather encouraging people to get checked into the hospital.

People are the church but church is not about the people who go there. The people who fill it are special to God. But if we make church about the people we will be disappointed. We need to understand that the church is about each one of us and our relationship with Jesus. Church is relational. Church is where we can strengthen our relationship with

Jesus. The building and the people create the environment for us to worship the Creator of the universe who is our heavenly Father.

Worship means to love, to adore, and to pay reverence to. God told Moses to tell Pharaoh to let His people go so they could go and worship Him. We are to pay reverence to God and church is a place we can do that. Church is so special to God that He calls it the Bride of Christ. Christ is the head of the church. He is the head of the whole body because he is the savior.

Jesus said, "And I tell you that you are Peter, and on this rock I will build my church, and the gates of Hades will not overcome it" (Matthew 16:18 NIV). The rock to build on is Jesus Christ. He will build his church and hell will not prevail over his church. Churches are special to Jesus.

Jesus holds the keys to Hades. God's intent for the church is to be a place that is alive, warm, and filled with a caring body of believers striving to serve God, to do His work, and support each other.

Earlier I wrote that people make the church but the church is not about the people. I would like to clarify that statement. I cannot count the number of times I have come across people who want nothing to do with the church. These people got hurt, offended, or believe they were mistreated and in their eyes the church is bad and they want nothing to do with the church. Whatever their case there are a lot of them out there.

There are also a lot of people whose situation is similar to mine prior to me attending church. They have never gone to church and know nothing about its purpose or what even takes place at church.

I vividly remember one of the outreaches we did at CLC where our goal was to canvass the general vicinity located around our church building. We were going to canvas the neighborhood and see if any of our neighbors had a need we could help them with. We went in groups of two with some pamphlets to hand out.

It is very nerve racking to go up to someone's door and attempt to talk to them about a subject that is often not received very well by our culture. You never know what to say or what to expect and not too many of us enjoy that awkwardness that can occur when approaching complete strangers.

The outreach was going pretty well until about house number eight. Then our worst fears came true. After knocking on this door we were greeted with a voice from behind the door that said, "What do you want?" I managed to squeak out that we were from the church down the street and we were wondering if she had a need or if there was anything we could do for her.

She replied, "The church has hurt me enough. There is nothing you can do." She never did open the door or even look through a window. I don't recall what I said but somehow I got it out of her that she was once a Catholic. She said, "That should explain it all." We said sorry for the inconvenience and good bye. I was ready to call it quits after that encounter but we pressed on and some good things were accomplished because of our outreach.

There are many people in our communities who have the same attitude toward the church as this lady. She was had been hurt by someone in the church and she had not returned to the church nor was she able to forgive and forget.

This is where we have the problem. This lady and so many like her let somebody else affect her whole view of church and her relationship with Jesus. How do I know? Well we were bringing her Good News about the person who could give her life after death. She didn't want any part of it. Maybe you are thinking she just didn't want what I was offering and her relationship with Jesus was fine. Perhaps and let's pray that is the situation but her actions and words did not seem like they came from someone who applies the word of God in her life.

She took the time to tell us she had been hurt enough which demonstrates a lack of forgiveness. Jesus said,

"Forgive, and you will be forgiven." What do you think she is doing when she shares her story with unbelievers and skeptics? Exactly, she is substantiating their position that all people who go to church are mean, inconsiderate, hypocrites.

Have you ever said or heard someone else say, "I don't go to church because some of the most hypocritical people I know are those people who go to church every week." Unfortunately, that may be true to a minor degree. But it is not fair to say that all people who attend church should be classified into this category.

Remember we have all sinned and fall short of the glory of God. Only one man who walked this earth was perfect and never sinned, Jesus Christ. If someone is looking for an excuse to stay away from church they will find one.

We cannot make church about other people. We can find faults in every person but we have to make church about doing the will of Jesus. I am concerned that many people who claim they do not go to church because of the people who attend church may be using that as an excuse to justify why they lack the commitment they should have with a local church.

It is imperative we stay focused on Jesus Christ. It is all about him and us striving to be like him. Nothing should affect our relationship with Jesus. This is the one area it is okay to be selfish. We shouldn't let anyone or any situation keep us from growing spiritually.

Too many times people are looking for any excuse they can to avoid making a commitment to a church. They are afraid to face their situation so they look for excuses and a common excuse is the church offended them. Excuses give them the opportunity to flee from the church. We are supposed to flee from the devil not God.

We can't flee we were called out to tell the truth. We have to understand if the church doesn't tell the truth the world will tell lies and speak false doctrine. The church has to be in the rescue business. There is no one else who can or who is willing to tell the world about Jesus.

We cannot look to the government for help in matters that deal with Jesus. Government cannot bail us out. Government cannot play God and it cannot offer us eternal life. Our government cannot offer us the things we need so we can be happy and feel complete.

The government is not our savior. We should not look to the government but we should look to God. The state cannot help us, and a new one world global government will not work either. We keep looking for big brother to come and fix things. It is never going to happen only God can fix the problems we face in this world. He created us and He created the world. We should lean on Him not President's, not Wall Street, and not cable television.

The following email recently found its way into my email box. I believe it is a perfect biblical sermon that explains why we do not turn to man or government but to God. We were not created to lean on man's understanding; we were created to lean on God's understanding.

From: WAYNE PARK
STIMULUS SERMON
Genesis 47:13-27

I would love to give the Pastor of this predominantly black church in Virginia a hug and a high five. This guy is obviously a leader. Perhaps we should each decide who our real leader is . . . . It is amazing to see that very little has changed in 4,000 years.

Good morning, brothers and sisters; it's always a delight to see the pews crowded on Sunday morning, and so eager to get into God's Word. Turn with me in your Bibles, if you will to the 47th chapter of Genesis, we'll begin our reading at verse 13, and go through verse 27. Brother Ray, would you stand and read that great passage for us? . . . . (reading) . . .

Thank you for that fine reading, Brother Ray . . . . So we see that economic hard times fell upon Egypt, and the people turned to the government of Pharaoh to deal with this for them. And Pharaoh nationalized the grain harvest, and placed the grain in great storehouses that he had built. So the people brought their money to Pharaoh, like a great tax increase, and gave it all to him willingly in return for grain. And this went on until their money ran out, and they were hungry again. So when they went to Pharaoh after that, they brought their livestock—their cattle, their horses, their sheep, and their donkey—to barter for grain and verse 17 says that only took them through the end of that year.

But the famine wasn't over, was it? So the next year, the people came before Pharaoh and admitted they had nothing left, except their land and their own lives. "There is nothing left in the sight of my lord but our bodies and our land. Why should we die before your eyes, both we and our land? Buy us and our land for food, and we with our land will be servants to Pharaoh." So they surrendered their homes, their land, and their real estate to Pharaoh's government, and then sold themselves into slavery to him, in return for grain. What can we learn from this, brothers and sisters? That turning to the government instead of to God to be our provider in hard times only leads to slavery? Yes. That the only reason government wants to be our provider is to also become our master? Yes. But look how that passage ends, brothers, and sisters!

Thus Israel settled in the land of Egypt, in the land of Goshen. And they gained possessions in it, and were fruitful and multiplied greatly." God provided for His people, just as He always has! They didn't end up giving all their possessions to government, no, it says they gained possessions! But I also tell you a great truth today, and an ominous one. We see the same thing happening today—the government today wants to "share the wealth" once again, to take it from us, and redistribute it back to us. It wants to take control of healthcare, just as it has taken control of education, and ration it back to us, and when government rations it, then government decides who gets it, and how much, and what kind. And if we go along with it, and do it willingly, then we will wind up no differently than the people of Egypt did four thousand years ago—as slaves to the government, and as slaves to our leaders.

What Mr. Obama's government is doing now is no different from what Pharaoh's government did then, and it will end the same. And a lot of people like to call Mr. Obama a "Messiah," don't they? Is he a Messiah? A savior? Didn't the Egyptians say, after Pharaoh made them his slaves, "You have saved our lives; may it please my lord, we will be servants to Pharaoh"?

Well, I tell you this—I know the Messiah; the Messiah is a friend of mine; and Mr. Obama is no Messiah! No, brothers and sisters, if Mr. Obama is a character from the Bible, then he is Pharaoh! Bow with me in prayer, if you will. Lord, You alone are worthy to be served, and we rely on You, and You alone. We confess that the government is not our deliverer, and never rightly will be. We read in the eighth chapter of 1 Samuel, when Samuel warned the people of what a ruler would do, where it says "And in that day you will cry out because of your king, whom you have chosen for yourselves, but the Lord will not answer you in that day." And Lord, we acknowledge that day has come. We cry out to you because of the ruler that we have chosen for ourselves as a nation. Lord, we pray for this nation. We pray for revival, and we pray for deliverance from those who would be our masters. Give us hearts to seek You and hands to serve You, and protect Your people from the atrocities of Pharaoh's government.

In God We Trust . . .

We are told to trust God but we don't do a very good job of trusting Him. It is astonishing when you read 2 Kings and notice how many times it says the kings did not do good in the eyes of God. They did not trust God. Time and time again the kings would worship other idols and the Israelites would forsake God. A new king would come into power and history would be repeated.

Very few times the Bible says they did good in the eyes of the Lord. The result was always the same: They became captives and were carried off to serve a new king. God would rescue them then they would go right back to idolizing other things. God's chosen people repeatedly depended on man instead of turning to God. This was a mistake back then and it is a mistake now.

How are we doing as the church in fulfilling the Great Commission? Unfortunately, too many people in the church have developed what we can call the cocoon syndrome. Not all of us are in the cocoon but there are a vast number of people in the church who are stuck in the cocoon.

The cocoon syndrome is when people who are in church become sheltered and forget our purpose is to rescue lost souls for Jesus. We become so comfortable with our lives we cannot see the pain and problems that still exist in the world.

We cannot claim we know God but then deny Him with our actions. If we deny God He has a harsh word for us. He says we are detestable, disobedient, and unfit to do anything good.

We fail to understand that we are all one wrong choice away from being back in Satan's prison. We should not forget where we came from. We are not all that and a bag of chips. I know that sounds like condemnation but that is not my intent. But it is meant to wake us up.

Jesus said, "You are the salt of the earth. But if the salt loses its saltiness, how can it be made salty again? It is no longer good for anything, except to be thrown out and trampled by men" (Matthew 5:13 NIV). Those who trust and put their hope in God are the flavor this earth desperately needs. These are the people who help preserve the goodness of God's kingdom. If we forget we are to represent Jesus we cannot be used by him.

We are to let our light shine. People do not need to hear our condemnation. John the Baptist's came as a witness to the light. We are the light that can shine into darkness in our present day. We can be good witnesses and help lead people into the light or we can play a role in keeping people in the dark!

The nineteen individuals I supervised on the shot crew understood that they represented the Forest Service, the Idaho Panhandle National Forest, the Coeur d' Alene River Ranger District, and the Idaho Panhandle Interagency Hot Shot Crew. We could save hundreds of homes, stop fires before devastating towns but we would be forever remembered for one wrong choice.

Imagine if a bunch of fire fighters from outside the area got in a fight with some of the local citizens at a bar (never happened). It would be talked about forever. People do not have short memories when it comes to those types of incidents.

It could be as simple as going into town to grab something to eat and using foul language in a family restaurant (never happened). We can go from hero to zero pretty quick because of a bad choice.

One moment of weakness and a husband can ruin the lives of everyone in his family. A few too many emails or face-book entries to the wrong person and an affair can come to life. The Bible tells us that a great forest can be set on fire by a small spark.

I remember being reassigned from one division (section of the fire) to another division because a large smoke column had been spotted. There had been no hint of fire on this part of the fire for several weeks. One day it came back to life and by the time we got shuttled over by helicopter it was boiling through the forest. Due to the extreme fire behavior the only thing we could do was find a safe place and let the fire do what it was going to and we saved some equipment that belonged to another crew.

That section of the fire grew by seventy-thousand acres in a very short time; all that destruction came from a small spark that had been lying dormant for weeks prior to coming back to life. Something can start small and innocent and grow into something devastating with consequences we never imagined. If we are a bad witness we can have the same effect as a wildfire.

Those of us who are further along on our journey need to avoid looking down our noses at other people who are not as far down the road on their journey or those who have not begun their journey. God created all men equal. "Live in harmony with one another. Do not be proud, but be willing to associate with people of low position. Do not be conceited" (Romans 12:16 NIV). If we act prideful we are not being good witnesses.

We need to constantly remind ourselves that we are living blessed lives because we surrendered our will and our lives to Jesus. Jesus is the one who receives the glory. We need to have compassion and love for all those who have not received Jesus. This includes family, friends, co-workers, and people in our community. If we treat them as if they are not as good as us or as if they are second class citizens they will take heed and wonder why they would want to be a part of something so ugly. What it boils down to is we should not judge others.

I believe what can happen and become the root of our problem is we forget what it was like to live in hell. We lived so long without having Jesus in control and being in literal hell that we don't want to go back or be reminded what it was like. Sometimes this prevents us from going on our mission. It is a defense mechanism we put up so we don't have to be reminded of our dark days.

It is awesome we are blessed and that we have left that world behind but we must not forget what the world of Satan looks like. We cannot forget the torture that others are going through. We found Jesus and began our journey now we need to go as a body that belongs to Jesus into the entire world and share our testimony with others.

We must know that God crowned us with love and compassion. We are to be a people that when the world sees us they will recognize us as sons and daughters of God Almighty. They will know who we are and who we belong to by our acts of compassion and kindness.

Paul wrote, "If you have any encouragement from being united with Christ, if any comfort from his love, if any fellowship with the Spirit, if any tenderness and compassion, then make my joy complete by being like-minded, having the same love, being one in spirit and purpose" (Philippians 2:1-2 NIV). These are all characteristics of Jesus Christ whom we should attempt to emulate.

As followers of Christ we should be rooted in the word of Jesus. We know the truth and the truth will keep us free. He that is in us is greater than he that is in the world. We have a new foundation that cannot be shaken and certainly cannot be destroyed. Jesus tells us we can do everything through him. He is the one who gives us strength.

When we join and commit to a local church we come under a covering. Now, that does not mean bad things will not happen to us because we all know that people who go to church and love the Lord can get the same diseases and sicknesses as those who do not believe and never go to church. What it means is that there will be shepherds who will pray for the flock. They will pray for protection, they will do their best to inspect, see how things are going with you, and if you are submitted they will correct you in a loving biblical way.

I cannot claim to understand how or why God heals some and chooses not to heal others. I don't know why bad things happen to His faithful servants but they do. I read a story of a pastor who got electrocuted in his church while performing a baptism. Come on that makes no sense at all and sure doesn't seem like justice. But what I speak to are the things God has done for me and as I have said several times I am no more special than any of His other children.

Very early on I said firefighting is like war. Wars have casualties. Earlier I gave you some statistics on firefighting causalities. During my tenure (1999-2008) on the Hotshot Crew while spending five and a half months every year performing one of the toughest jobs in this world, we never had any personal accidents resulting in lost time or any vehicle accidents that were chargeable. That is an amazing statistic for our line of work. I contribute our accident free record solely to the fact that our crew was under the covering of our church. Every time we headed out I knew there were people praying for our safe return.

On July 10th, 2003 we were in Washington State. We were in a canyon where four firefighters had died on July 10th, 2001. Being aware of these unfortunate fatalities created eeriness about the fire. We had constructed fireline up a ridge with two other shot crews and we were preparing to burnout the line on the way back down.

I took the lead on the burnout and had five members of the crew with me to do the firing. Things were progressing as I had figured they would for about the first hour then things turned badly in a very short time. The fire that we were creating began to out run us down hill. It was running in a horizontal vortice faster than we could move (I mentioned earlier). This phenomenon is pretty rare for the steep terrain that we were in. Fires don't generally run horizontally like that except in areas like Alaska and Canada where the terrain is flat.

I realized the main fire that was down in the canyon had come alive. It was being pulled up the slope by our burnout and when it started generating intensity it began to pull our firing operations toward it. The two fires were feeding off each other and this was creating some very intense fire behavior. We were forced to move back up the hill to a predetermined safe area. Shortly after reaching the area we were over taken by smoke. The smoke was so thick we couldn't push our way through it. I instructed everyone to lie down and get their noses as far into the ground as possible.

After a few long minutes we were able to stand up and the fire had done what I feared it would. The fire was on both sides of the ridge which meant we were not safe yet and we would have to ride it out. Nervously, I did what I had been taught to do. I stood up and started praying to the One who I knew could intervene on our behalf. Instantly, the fire lay down and we were able to walk down to the road with ease. This is just one example of many where I know had

I not prayed and been under a covering things could have been much different. We all need the covering that comes from being a member of a local church.

Kelli recently went to court with an individual who had received an infraction for driving under the influence of alcohol. When she got home she explained to me the process and how horrific it was. This preliminary hearing explained to the defendant what she was accused of and what her punishment could be. Kelli estimated that there were about twenty individuals who went through this process. Kelli shared that it was horrible to witness how lost these people appeared.

These people were living in such darkness that you could see it on them. Their whole countenance was dark. Kelli explained that it was so hard to see all the lives that were affected by their actions. Their offense affected so many people. Twenty individuals all living in Satan's dark world and they didn't know how to escape. Who will speak light into their darkness? Who is going to tell them there is hope and that hope comes by knowing the greatest healer and the brightest light to ever exist?

God has recently brought a lady into Kelli and I lives that is living in utter darkness. Her state of mind is that God cannot love her. She does not know that God's love is unfailing and endures forever. The Bible tells us God abounds in love. "Are not two sparrows sold for a penny? Yet not one of them will fall to the ground apart from the will of your Father. And even the very hairs of your head are all numbered. So don't be afraid; you are worth more than any sparrows" (Matthew 10:29-31 NIV). God loves little birds that are sold for pennies and He loves each one of us even more. That is Bible!

"For the Son of man came to seek and to save what was lost" (Luke 19:10 NIV)!

Why is there so much darkness in this world? After all there are churches on every corner offering various doctrines and philosophies. These churches sponsor all kinds of different events but none of them are experiencing an abundant of new true believers, folks that are truly born again. None!

Why are we failing to see even low numbers of born again believers? Is it simply they are not buying what we are selling? Is it a doctrinal issue? What theology or doctrine should the church teach? Maybe that is the problem. Should the church tell us how to live according to the Bible?

Should theology be based on a doctrine that life becomes great and all our problems will be instantly gone when we come to Jesus? I whole heartedly believe life gets better when we accept Jesus Christ. The Bible says we can expect one blessing after another. I don't believe the part that all our problems will be gone. If we have Jesus we can overcome the problems this world will throw at us.

Life gets better when we allow Jesus to be in charge. I could give you testimony after testimony from people whose lives were so dark they might as well have been in outer space. Remember my marriage was horrible, we couldn't have children, and Kelli and I fought all the time. We didn't want to be around each other or even look at each other. Then I got the ultimatum; church or divorce and well I am writing the rest of the story.

The problem that can easily occur if we teach a "life gets great message" or "life enhancement" is that Jesus tells us trials and tribulations are still going to occur even after we accept him. History shows us time after time people turn and run from Jesus as soon as these trials and tribulations occur.

"Then Jesus told them many things in parables, saying: 'A farmer went out to sow his seed. As he was scattering the seed, some fell along the path, and the birds came and ate it up. Some fell on rocky places, where it did not have much soil. It sprang up quickly, because the soil was shallow. But when the sun came up, the plants were scorched, and they withered because they had no root. Other seed fell among thorns, which grew up and choked the plants. Still other seed fell on good soil, where it produced a crop—a hundred, sixty or thirty times what was sown. He who has ears, let him hear'" (Matthew 13:3-9 NIV).

Jesus said, "The one who received the seed that fell on rocky places is the man who hears the word and at once receives it with joy. But since he has no root, he lasts only a short time. When trouble or persecution comes because of the word, he quickly falls away" (Matthew 13:20-21 NIV).

If we preach a "life gets great" message and a trial or test comes up a new Christian may feel betrayed. It is likely if the person feels betrayed, cheated, or lied to he will take it out on Jesus. Instead of creating a disciple we have offended this person because what he was promised is not what he got. We have essentially created a bitter backslider who now preaches to others about how bad God and Jesus are.

I don't know why but bad, ugly, news sales. Our culture for whatever reason thrives on negative news. If we look at politics we will see that candidates no longer talk about the issues. We have all heard politicians say they wanted to keep their message about the issues but in the end they have to make it about their opponent. The way to get time in the press is to sling mud about your opponent. If a candidate gets behind in the polls they often bring in a new campaign manager and a strategy that is driven by an all out assault on the character of the individual he is trying to beat-up!

This phenomenon is no different when it comes to the church. Isn't another name for Satan Sower of Discord? News that reflects Satan's views spreads faster than the Good News of Jesus. Maybe it is a curse that came with the fall of man.

There are testimonies of people coming to the Lord after being promised a great life and it became reality. Kelli was told life could be better and that is why I received the ultimatum. I don't mind telling you my life is pretty awesome. It is not perfect but I feel fortunate to be blessed by God as much as I am.

Every spring on the shot crew we would go through two weeks of "Critical Training." The first two weeks of the season were dedicated to going over our Standard Operating Procedures and the safety issues pertinent to performing our job safely.

The very first day of critical training our firefighters would receive all of their gear they would need to perform their job. We always had the best line gear (back packs) that was on the market, customized to fit our needs. If we were on a fire these packs were always without exception strapped over our shoulders and fastened around our hips. Depending on your job your line gear could weigh between thirty-five and fifty-five pounds.

Our line gear had a pouch in the bottom that was home to our fire shelter. A fire shelter is a fire resistant aluminum shelter that looks like a tent. Our employees were drilled on how theses shelters function, how they get into them, and when they get in them.

Our firefighters knew if they ever became trapped by fire they could get inside their fire shelter increasing their chance of survival. The situation would be dire if they were getting in their fire shelter but it would likely be fatal if they failed to get in their shelter. Fire is very dynamic and very unpredictable. I thank God I have never had to deploy my shelter.

We constantly preached to our firefighters that these fire shelters may save their life in an emergency. By the time critical training was completed they understood the value of their fire shelter. They knew that their life may be saved because of their fire shelter.

If we would not have taken the time to share with our firefighters why it was important for them to always have their fire shelter with them they would not have wanted to wear their heavy packs hour after hour. But they did not forsake their pack because they knew their life may very well have depended on it. Regardless of the task being performed the crew never took their packs off unless they were getting something out of their pack.

The expectation of these firefighters was not that these top of the line, expensive, costume made packs was going to be comfortable and make everything seem weightless. The expectation was that they were going to wear them and trust them because their fire shelter was part of their pack and it could have saved their life at some point.

I have to wonder if the reason we have so many backsliders is because we preach an overload of "life enhancement" instead of a personal relationship with Jesus! We want them entering into a relationship with Jesus Christ because it is fulfilling not because they think their life is instantly going to be great and all their troubles will be gone.

We want people to understand that by developing a relationship with Jesus we receive the greatest gift and that is eternal life. He who comes to the savior knowing he has to face a Holy God on the Day of Judgment would never forsake the righteousness in Christ because his very life depends on it. If we preach a message of salvation they will not get angry with Jesus when the trials come, that is not why they came to Jesus. They came to Jesus to get saved on the Day of Judgment.

There are other churches that teach a doctrine of "anything goes" because God is gracious. This theology is totally misconstruing and snubbing God's word in my opinion. We talked about God's grace being sufficient but that does not mean He will like it if a church teaches false doctrine. It is false doctrine to teach we can do whatever we feel is right and God is good with whatever we decide.

For example, we are constantly seeing on the television where a church has split due to the association ruling that homosexuals can be pastors of churches. I have said I don't hate the person but I hate the sin. The church cannot teach that sin is okay or acceptable because God's love for us is so great He understands our disobedience. That is false doctrine.

These folks are changing the word to fit the world. They are allowing the culture to influence the church.

News flash! God's people are supposed to use the word to influence the world. The church should be battling to shape and direct the culture. Remember, Jesus is the way. We cannot idly stand back and let a Godless society define sin.

God has already defined what sin is. Understand, all sin is wrong but not all sin leads to eternal hell.

If we surrender to a small population that wants to have a "God Free Zone" we are also surrendering to Satan. If we do not stand for the Truth we will be another generation that has failed to advance God's kingdom. We will have to wait for the next generation and see if they can defeat our adversaries.

We no longer read the stories about Sodom and Gomorrah. Their whole culture had become so immoral God destroyed the two cities. If we read about Jonah's trip to Nineveh we usually only tell the part of Jonah getting swallowed up by a large fish. The story is about the city of Nineveh straying so far away from God that he sends Jonah to tell them to repent and straighten up. Both of these cultures had turned away from God and had to be dealt with.

Culture is the integrated pattern of human knowledge, belief, and behavior that depends upon the capacity for learning and transmitting knowledge to succeeding generations. Culture is the customary beliefs, social forms, and material traits of a racial, religious, or social group. Culture is also the characteristic features of everyday existence shared by people in a place or time (popular culture).

Did you notice the definition of culture said 'or'? Culture either follows the beliefs and traits of racial, religious, or social groups. It cannot be all three or two of the three. A culture will take the shape of one of these three.

Culture is what we do and what we believe. It is our way of life. Everything we say and do arises out of what we believe. We live what we believe. Who and what do we believe? Simply put culture is the belief of people living together in a specific geographical area.

Our culture is supposed to resemble God's value system not the other way around. How are we shaping the values in God's kingdom? We see the world the way we do because of what we have been exposed to in our lives. What are we being exposed to and what are we exposing people to?

We have started accepting the way of the world; we have accepted man's new renditions of traditions which do not include Jesus Christ. Believers of Jesus Christ have to rise up and the church has to take the lead and influence our culture in the ways of God. We, God's people need to start building in our communities.

If the church is going to wage a war we need to know Satan has an elite army called progressives. They are his Navy Seals. Their tactic is progressivism. Their strategy is to move every culture in this world away from what God stands for.

We are at war with progressivism because it is a strategy that comes straight from Satan. I am not saying everyone who is a progressive is working for Satan they may not realize the strategy comes from him. I am saying whether intentional or unintentional they are helping are adversary advance his anti-Christian, anti-God agenda.

We are fighting against a progressive movement in our culture that wants to rewrite history, proclaim there is no sin, and have no tolerance for religious beliefs or traditions. Progressives will stop at nothing and pull out all the stops to be successful.

Regardless of how you feel about the charismatic radio talk show host Glenn Beck I believe he has an eye wakening and educated understanding about progressives and their strategy. He understands the progressive movement is real and harmful to our nation.

The progressive movement was birthed in the early 1900's and it has been inserting itself in our culture every since. Progressives will never admit it but their movement is in direct opposition to the word of God. Christians and progressives are two different social groups and progressives are unwilling to let followers of Christ be a part of their culture. Our value systems are different. Our culture is either going to follow Jesus or it is going to follow a secular progressive group. Secular groups understand this concept and they want to win. The religious group has yet to really engage. We need to wake up and start fighting with Jesus.

Progressives want to move past the Constitution and get beyond the Christian ideology of our founding fathers. They detest the Constitution and the Declaration of Independence (We hold these truths to be self-evident, that all men are created equal, that they are endowed by their Creator (God) with certain unalienable Rights). Progressives believe both the Constitution and the Declaration of Independence put limits on the government and their progressive agenda.

Progressives want to make God obsolete and gone. Instead of indivisible they want God invisible. They don't want to see or hear from Him. They want the government to come up with all the solutions so we become dependent on them. Progressives cannot coexist with Christianity because they believe man is perfectible. They believe they can provide the solutions to make man perfect. Our founding fathers agreed with God that man is born with a sinful nature. Once you learn to recognize the strategy of progressives you can pick out a progressive rather easy.

Bill O'Reilly is another person who understands the progressive movement. I enjoy watching the O'Reilly Factor because I believe Bill O'Reilly and others like him are warriors. They are traditionalists like me. If you consider yourself a traditionalist then you are the opposite of a progressive. Traditionalists believe the majority of us who live in the United States are good people and our country is not perfect but it does not need a complete overhaul.

For years the minority (not talking ethnic) has proven time after time they can get things their way if they create wrinkles and scream loud enough. Mr. O'Reilly takes them on and stands up for the rest of us who don't have the same platform he does.

Mr. O'Reilly has a platform with a large audience. He is the most watched news cable show in all of cable television. He is not scared to take on the loud minority and I applaud him for that. In fact, I admire Fox News for their programming and the people they put on the air. I love the fact that Fox News celebrates the birth of Jesus Christ. Watching Fox's Christmas special is becoming a family tradition.

Progressives have an all out assault on the church. Progressives want the church confined and their strategy may be working. The church is being asked to be like a reservation-stay in your area, keep your beliefs and thoughts in your own four walls and way too often we are complying. It is ironic the church says we are not about these four walls but we find ourselves staying within our reservation more and more.

What happened to the Native Americans when they were required to go to reservations? They lost their pride and many lost their will to live. They were not free.

Chief Joseph (1840-1904) was a famous Nez Perce Chief. The Nez Perce tribe was a peaceful nation who spread from Idaho to Northern Washington. They had formed a good relationship with the white man from the Lewis and Clark expedition. Chief Joseph spent much of his early childhood at a mission maintained by Christian missionaries.

Chief Joseph was called In-mut-too-yah-lat-lat by his people. His name meant Thunder coming up over the land from the water. He is best remembered by his resistance to the U.S. Government's attempts to force his tribe onto reservations. He knew that if his people were captured and forced to be confined to a certain area it would be the same as a death sentence. He attempted to get his people to Canada to avoid being sent to a reservation but the U.S. Army circled in front of him right before he was about to enter Canada and forced his tribe to go to a reservation in what is now known as Oklahoma, where many died from malaria and starvation. When Chief Joseph was captured he said, "From where the sun now stands I will fight no more forever." According to the reservation doctor, he later died of a broken heart.

The proud free nation was no longer allowed to live the way they were accustomed. Being on a reservation broke their will to live. They lost their ability to move about freely and many of the Nez Perce people thought death would be better then living. The church can end up the same way if we do not realize our purpose and what we are fighting for.

The Apostle Paul told us to fight the good fight. We are in a battle to win souls for Jesus Christ. We cannot stay inside and wait for the people to come into the church they are lost and blind. How will they find the church? Instead of building a church where they will come we need to build a church that will go and seek the lost.

The church shines brightly but the lost can only see darkness. We have to travel into our communities and find them that God has chosen. We need to share a message of hope with the lost. All people need to see the love, kindness, and compassion that Jesus told us to have.

The word says believe, repent, confess, change, love, have compassion, go proclaim the Good News. Those we are battling say there is no place for Jesus, God, church, or those who like to believe there is. They tell us to stay inside the four walls of the church and do not attempt to push what we know the truth to be on them. They are trying to starve us. They want us to waste away.

We often use a confine, contain, and control strategy in suppressing fire. We start by defining a geographical area where we would like to stop the fire. Then we surround the fire with a fuel break and a line in the dirt about sixteen inches wide and eventually we gain command of the fire. Satan's strategy for the church is very similar. He wants to imprison or detain us and restrain us then he believes he will have power over us. It is an all out assault and he wants to win. Satan needs prisoners and he is not a respecter of people anybody will do. He only cares about numbers.

In worldly terms our enemies have an advantage because they can use whatever lowly, deceitful tactics they wish to engage but we have to play by the rule book, the Bible. They get to hate us but we have to love them. They can use dirty tricks and proclaim hate but we have to demonstrate kindness and understanding. They get to use horrible demeaning words and tear us down. We have to say kind words and build them up. They get to condemn and we have to commend. They use a club we use light. They get to judge and we have to accept them. We have to take the high road every time because that is what children of God do. We don't need lies, tricks, gimmicks, or anything deceitful we have the truth-Jesus Christ.

Satan knows half the battle is making sure the lost can't hear us. If we can't proclaim the Good News people's faith will not increase. If we shrink back into the walls Satan will take hundreds of thousands of prisoners.

Is the church leading the way so our culture will build on a solid foundation or are the lost steering and guiding our culture? We can either build on rock or we can build on sand. If the church leads biblically our culture will be on solid rock. If the lost takes the lead we will build on sand and sand cannot hold up under pressure or through storms.

If we have a strong foundation we can build on top of it and the foundation will remain strong and last. We need to start building using Jesus Christ as our foundation, floor, walls, ceiling, and roof. Jesus is the foundation that God intended us to build on.

Jesus said, "Therefore everyone who hears these words of mine and puts them into practice is like a wise man who built his house on the rock. The rain came down, the streams rose, and the winds blew and beat against that house; yet it did not fall, because it had its foundation on the rock. But everyone who hears these words of mine and does not put them into practice is like a foolish man who built his house on sand. The rain came down, the streams rose, and the winds blew and beat against that house, and it fell with a great crash" (Matthew 7:24-27 NIV). We are to be a nation built on the solid rock! The rock of course is symbolic for Jesus Christ.

Jesus is the foundation the United States was built on so when recessions, terrorists' attacks, hurricanes, and earthquakes come, when death to a love one comes, when unemployment comes, we will not fall or collapse. If we stand on the word of God and hold on to our faith we can trust that everything will work out, we have a foundation that will last. "For no one can lay any foundation other than the one already laid, which is Jesus Christ. If any man builds on this foundation using gold, silver, costly stones, wood, hay or straw, his work will be shown for what it is, because the Day will bring it to light (1 Corinthians 3:11-13 NIV).

The United States was founded on a beautiful principle and that principle is "In God We Trust." We were founded on Christian principles with the idea that we were a nation under God. The United States was founded on ideas and values that came directly from God's word.

Unfortunately, the older our country gets the further away we seem to venture (progress) from our Christian heritage. Progressive's took baby steps and tested the waters and now they seem to think they have momentum behind them. They are racing ahead with one goal and that goal is to get God out of our country. They know if they are going to win the war and obtain their goal of changing our country they have to break down our foundation and rewrite history. They know they must fight the battle aggressively to get God removed from all areas of our nation. This includes local, state, and federal governments, schools, colleges, and universities. They want God removed from our Holidays and public squares.

What makes the United States united? Our forefathers came here to escape religious persecution and to receive religious freedom. The one thing that unites the large majority of us is our trust in God. He looks down at us, cares for us, and protects us. My Bible which is written by God says, "Blessed is the nation whose God is the LORD, the people he chose for his inheritance" (Psalm 33:12 NIV). Do we believe that?

Over the last several decades our country has begun to believe we are special because of the people who live here and the resources we have. God set our country up so it would be great and be the model for the whole world so His name could be glorified. We have good, intelligent, and gifted people in this country but our country is great because God chose to bless a country that founded itself on His principles. If we keep kicking God out we will see a mighty fall and it will devastate us until we repent and ask for forgiveness.

The following is not meant to condemn or disrespect our president but to show how far our country has moved from our Christian foundation. It is a great example of people trying to rewrite history by shaping our culture away from our Creator.

April 6th, 2009 President Obama, the most influential man in the flesh on this earth while giving a speech in Turkey proclaimed the most damaging announcement to our Christian faith that has probably ever been spoken by a man in such a position. While the whole world was listening he proclaimed something but it was not the Good News.

President Obama proclaimed and delivered a blow directly to the heart of Jesus Christ. He may have did more during that minute to hurt the word of God than any other human who has walked this earth because of the sheer numbers who are listening when the President of the United States of America speaks.

President Obama said, "One of the great strengths" of the United States is that "we do not consider ourselves a Christian nation or a Jewish nation or a Muslim nation. We consider ourselves a nation of citizens who are bound by ideals and a set of values."

If that were not enough President Obama told the Turkish Parliament: "We will convey our deep appreciation for the Islamic faith, which has done so much over the centuries to shape the world—including in my own country." What!

Do you see what we are up against? Good thing we know how the war ends or we could get pretty discouraged when we hear things like that from the President of the United States. Personally, I do not believe a person who is saved and has a relationship with Jesus Christ could make that kind of statement. I don't believe someone who believes in Jesus Christ should want to go out of his way to proclaim that we are not a Christian nation.

It would be a good idea for President Obama and others who are like minded to go back and read some of our historic documents such as the Mayflower Compact.

The Mayflower Compact
by William Bradford
November 11, 1620

"In the name of God, Amen. We, whose names are underwritten, the Loyal Subjects of our dread Sovereign Lord, King James, by the Grace of God, of England, France and Ireland, King, Defender of the Faith, etc., Having undertaken for the Glory of God, and Advancement of the Christian Faith, and the Honour of our King and Country, a voyage to plant the first colony in the northern parts of Virginia; do by these presents, solemnly and mutually in the Presence of God and one of another, covenant and combine ourselves together into a civil Body Politick, for our better Ordering and Preservation, and Furtherance of the Ends aforesaid; And by Virtue hereof to enact, constitute, and frame, such just and equal Laws, Ordinances, Acts, Constitutions and Offices, from time to time, as shall be thought most meet and convenient for the General good of the Colony; unto which we promise all due submission and obedience. In Witness whereof we have hereunto subscribed our names at Cape Cod the eleventh of November, in the Reign of our Sovereign Lord, King James of England, France and Ireland, the eighteenth, and of Scotland the fifty-fourth. Anno Domini, 1620."

The first Pilgrims came to America to advance the Christian Faith. While the Pilgrims were still in the harbor, off Cape Cod in Massachusetts, before ever getting off the Mayflower they wrote this covenant. They proclaimed their Colony would get strength through God.

There are those who would argue that Article 11 in the Treaty of Tripoli which was ratified unanimously, by the Senate in 1797, ten years after the adoption of the U.S.

Constitution, directly challenges the claim that the United States is to be "a Christian Nation."

ARTICLE 11.

As the government of the United States of America is not in any sense founded on the Christian Religion,-as it has in itself no character of enmity against the laws, religion or tranquility of Musselmen, (Muslims)-and as the said States never have entered into any war or act of hostility against any Mehomitan (Muslim) nation, it is declared by the parties that no pretext arising from religious opinions shall ever produce an interruption of the harmony existing between the two countries.

Article 11 has created fierce debate between Christians, historians, and those of a secular mind. Christians are suspicious because Article 11 does not appear in the Arabic text of the treaty.

This is what we must understand. Christians are not asking for the government to declare Christianity as the official religion of the United States. But we are asking that those elected by the people not kick God out of our culture. We are perfectly fine with battling with the forces of evil. We know we win. But since government was created for the people by the people we ask that the government not hinder our preaching of the gospel.

It is generally accepted that the first congressional representatives intended to prevent future congress or presidents from declaring only one church could exist in the United States. Over time it was generally accepted that the First Amendment prohibited federal, state, or local governments in the United States from raising tax money for a church, or for a particular group of churches.

The Constitution says the government may not favor one religion over other religions, or favor religion over non-religion. There must be a wall of separation between church and state. The challenge for the Supreme Court has been to determine just how high that wall must be.

We should find it interesting that the Supreme Court opens every session with, "God save the United States and this Honorable Court." The Justices are sworn in by being asked, "Do you promise to uphold the Constitution so help you God." Our elected officials take their oaths upon a Bible, and use the words "so help me God" although we are seeing this less and less.

Our founding fathers were men who considered and leaned on God's view, the Bible to write our Constitution. As a general matter, the Constitution embodies the principles of Christianity. There are people who will deny that vehemently but it is reality.

Thomas Jefferson actually said that the wall of separation between Church and State is "one-directional." I believe that means Jefferson believed that the church was to be an influence in our entire culture but government is not to interfere with the church. Jefferson supported Bible reading in school; this is proven by his service as the first president of the Washington D. C. public schools, which used the Bible for their textbook for reading.

Further proof to illustrate how far we are getting away from our foundation the first president of the United States said, "It is impossible to rightly govern the world without God and the Bible" George Washington. Hundreds of books could be filled with quotes from our founding fathers in respect to God. We can be certain that our country was founded on Judea Christian beliefs.

The Star Spangled Banner was written in 1814 by Francis Scott Key but I would be willing to venture most of us are no longer taught the full rendition of his epic poem. The following is the fourth paragraph to Mr. Key's poem and it just happens to be the section with a lot of reference to God.

O thus be it ever when freemen shall stand
Between their loved homes and the war's desolation!
Blest with vict'ry and peace, may the Heaven-rescued land
Praise the Power that hath made and preserved us a nation.
Then conquer we must when our cause it is just

And this be our motto: "In God is our Trust."
And the Star-Spangled Banner in triumph shall wave
O'er the land of the free and the home of the brave!

The heaven rescued land. The United States is a country that is very blessed by the hand of God. God has rescued and preserved our country for over two hundred and thirty years. God blesses the United States of America. We are a blessed nation not because of our works but for the works of God al' mighty Himself. This is our countries motto: "In God we trust." We are in a war to hold on to our heritage as a nation that follows God.

Ben Stein is a lawyer and he served as a speech writer for President Nixon. He also writes editorials and columns for several publications. He wrote and shared the following on a CBS Sunday morning commentary:

A few confessions from my beating heart: I have no clue who Nick and Jessica are. I see them on the cover of People and Us constantly when I am buying my dog biscuits and kitty litter. I often ask the checkers at the grocery stores. They never know who Nick and Jessica are either. Who are they? Will it change my life if I know who they are and why they have broken up? Why are they so important? I don't know who Lindsay Lohan is either, and I do not care at all about Tom Cruise's wife.

Am I going to be called before a Senate committee and asked if I am a subversive? Maybe, but I just have no clue who Nick and Jessica are. If this is what it means to be no longer young. It's not so bad.

Next confession: I am a Jew, and every single one of my ancestors was Jewish. And it does not bother me even a little bit when people call those beautiful lit up, bejeweled trees Christmas trees. I don't feel threatened. I don't feel discriminated against. That's what they are: Christmas trees. It doesn't bother me a bit when people say, "Merry Christmas" to me. I don't think they are slighting me or getting ready to put me in a ghetto. In fact, I kind of like it. It shows that we are all brothers and sisters celebrating this happy time of year. It doesn't bother me at all that there is a manger on display at a key intersection near my beach house in Malibu. If people want a crèche, it's just as fine with me as is the menorah a few hundred yards away.

I don't like getting pushed around for being a Jew and I don't think Christians like getting pushed around for being Christians. I think people who believe in God are sick and tired of getting pushed around, period. I have no idea where the concept came from that America is an explicitly atheist country. I can't find it in the Constitution, and I don't like it being shoved down my throat.

Or maybe I can put it another way: where did the idea come from that we should worship Nick and Jessica and we aren't allowed to worship God as we understand Him?

I guess that's a sign that I'm getting old, too. But there are a lot of us who are wondering where Nick and Jessica came from and where the America we knew went to.

Mr. Stein is right on target. Where is the America we know going? Too often we are going in the wrong direction. Not being able to worship and talk about our God is not written in the Constitution. The old America has decided to remain silent. We have to ask ourselves if we have been confined to reservations. We decided that we were not going to listen to the Bible and fight the good fight. Our enemy launched an all out assault on our religious beliefs and we retreated back into our forts (churches) and have yet to counter attack.

Listen to Anne Graham's response when asked about God not being visible in our world and why He lets tragedies occur. She gave a response that could only come from having Godly wisdom.

Billy Graham's daughter was interviewed on the Early Show by Jane Clayson the Thursday after the terrorists' attacks on September 11. Clayson asked, "I've heard people say, those who are religious, those who are not, if God is good, how could God let this happen? To that, you say?"

I say God is also angry when he sees something like this. I would say also for several years now Americans in a sense have shaken their fist at God and said, God, we want you out of our schools, our government, our business, we want you out of our marketplace. And God, who is a gentleman, has just quietly backed out of our national and political life, our public life. Removing his hand of blessing and protection. We need to turn to God first of all and say, God, we're sorry we have treated you this way and we invite you now to come into our national life. We put our trust in you. We have our trust in God on our coins, we need to practice it.

The following is another email that circulated through the internet. I have chosen to not share the names written in the email but it is still a good read.

"I believe God is deeply saddened by this (9/11), just as we are, but for years we've been telling God to get out of our schools, to get out of our government and to get out of our lives. And being the gentleman He is, I believe He has calmly backed out. How can we expect God to give us His blessing and His protection if we demand He leave us alone?"

In light of recent events . . . terrorists attack, school shootings, etc. I think it started when a lady (she was murdered, her body found recently) complained she didn't want prayer in our schools, and we said OK.

Then someone said you better not read the Bible in school. The Bible says thou shalt not kill; thou shalt not steal, and love your neighbor as yourself. And we said OK.

Then a Doctor said we shouldn't spank our children when they misbehave because their little personalities would be warped and we might damage their self-esteem (This Doctor's son committed suicide). We said an expert should know what he's talking about and we said OK.

Now we're asking ourselves why our children have no conscience, why they don't know right from wrong, and why it doesn't bother them to kill strangers, their classmates, and themselves.

Probably, if we think about it long and hard enough, we can figure it out. I think it has a great deal to do with "WE REAP WHAT WE SOW."

Funny how simple it is for people to trash God and then wonder why the world's going to hell.

Funny how we believe what the newspapers say, but question what the Bible says.

Funny how you can send 'jokes' through e-mail and they spread like wildfire but when you start sending messages regarding the Lord, people think twice about sharing.

Funny how lewd, crude, vulgar, and obscene articles pass freely through cyberspace, but public discussion of God is suppressed in the school and workplace."

We reap what we sow what does that mean? Interesting that in the NT the Greek words for reap and sow can either be positive or negative. If you are sowing something good you will reap something good. For example, we read in Galatians where it says, "Do not be deceived: God cannot be mocked. A man reaps what he sows. The one who sows to please his sinful nature, from that nature will reap destruction; the one who sows to please the Spirit, from the Spirit will reap eternal life" (Galatians 6:7-8 NIV). If we do good we will reap good. If we do evil we will reap death.

The Hebrew meaning for reap is usually in the context of receiving something bad or discouraging. "He that sows wickedness reaps trouble, and the rod of his fury will be destroyed" (Proverbs 22:8 NIV).

If we plant a seed that is wicked or evil we will eventually pay for that seed we planted. A seed will germinate, and grow until eventually it comes to fruition, and then we will pay for the wrath inspired by what we have planted.

If we take God out of our culture we can expect to do a lot of grieving. If we continue to kick God out of our lives and the affairs of our nation we can expect to see more shootings, terrorist's attacks, earthquakes, floods, hurricanes, recessions, and many other sad incidents. God wants to be in charge.

We cannot take God out of our culture because He is intended to be our culture: our way of life and who we believe in. There are many things that are still entrenched in our culture that are from the Bible, the Ten Commandments probably being the most prevalent.

As a society we have laws and standards that tell us what is right and wrong and many of them get there root from the Bible. We cannot steal, we are taught lying is bad, marriage is suppose to be forever and sacred but this one is going south in a hurry, and for the most part Saturdays are rest days. We are to treat people justly. We cannot just walk up to someone and start wailing on them. There would be retribution according to the law if we were to do something like that.

During a sermon I taught I asked the congregation if someone would do me a favor and look up the scripture that says if you are being politically correct and not standing up for God's way, God understands. Amazingly, they could not find any scripture that referred to being politically correct.

Politically correct is nowhere in the Bible. It is fabricated by man and Satan. We live in a world that has become so tolerant and politically correct we are forgetting what really matters.

Political correctness is not the way of God. Compassion, honesty, love, and faithfulness to His word are His traits that we are to desire. We cannot separate God from any part of our lives end of story.

There cannot be politically correctness if it compromises the word of God. If God despises certain actions we should as well. If God doesn't tolerate certain actions then we shouldn't either. We have grown cold to His word and we have become more and more accepting to lifestyles that are sinful.

By accepting sin we are not doing sinners any favors because they could be facing everlasting hell. Sadly, we may be indirectly responsible for putting them there. We cannot continue to accept their sin when we know their sin leads to a death sentence. God wants us to love people but we have to dislike, despise, and hate sin. We should never give into anything that undermines God's living word.

Understand this can be done in a loving way. We don't just start preaching condemnation telling people they are sinners who are going to hell. We can build a relationship with people and explain our position on different subject matter. For example, we could share with people that we believe God defines marriage as being between one man and one woman and we cannot accept or promote anything else. Again, we share that we do not hate the sinner but we do hate the sin.

I have been asking this question the last several months whenever I get the opportunity. Here is the dilemma: I cannot accept the sinful life of a homosexual because I love them. The majority of our population believes that homosexuality is morally acceptable. They accept their lifestyle without ever considering the consequence.

This is the question. Who has their best interest in mind? I claim the majority are doing nothing to try and prevent these people from a life of hell. I cannot do that-I love them but hate the sin. I am not homophobic. I dislike that these guys are buying into Satan's lies and the majority of people don't care. I cannot stand idly by and allow them to believe their sin is acceptable in God's eyes.

Do we really believe our "Self Imposed" "Politically Correctness" is going to be a defensive strategy when we face judgment? No! Our words and our actions will be our defense. What have we said and done? Did we agree to put the billboard next to the Nativity scene that said, "There is no God, no Angels, no demons, it is all just lies?" Did we ride the bus that advertised for atheists that read, "There is no god, just be GOOD!" Did we have anything to do with pulling a banner across the sky with a plane that said, "There is no god!"

As we can imagine Christmas is a time of year when the battle really heats up and brings the worst out of the progressives. They attack Christmas relentlessly because it is a Christian holiday. Christmas is the celebration of the birth of our savior who is at the core of our foundation. There is a long list of acts that have taken place in the last several years that goes right to the core of our Christian beliefs. The following are a few examples:

- Removing nativity scenes from public property
- Banning Christian songs such as Silent Night from school concerts
- No wearing green or red colors around the Christmas Holiday
- Allowing a nativity scene but no Jesus, Mary, or Joseph
- Refusing to allow students to write about the Christian aspect of Christmas in school projects
- Renaming Christmas break winter break or winter solstice
- Refusing to allow a city sponsored Christmas parade to be called a Christmas parade
- Not allowing a Christmas tree in a public school
- Renaming a Christmas tree displayed on public property a Holiday tree

In addition to their war on Christmas, the following is a list of other situations that have been attacked by those who want all reference to God and what He stands for kicked out of our culture.

- Sue states to force them to legalize homosexual marriage
- Force libraries to remove porn filters from their computers

- Sue the Boy Scouts to force them to accept homosexuals as scout leaders
- Help legalize child pornography
- Legalize live sex acts in bars in Oregon
- Protection of the North American Man Boy Love Association whose motto is "sex by eight or it is too late"
- Censor student led prayer at graduation
- Remove "under God" from the Pledge of Allegiance it violates church/state
- A move to remove "In God we trust" from our currency
- Christian counselor fired for refusing to council a gay couple on intimacy
- Suspend a little girl from school for drawing Jesus
- Disciplining a ten year old boy for reading his Bible, on the playground, during recess
- School districts forbidding Christian music
- No longer required to swear to God to be sworn in to public office
- Crosses removed from along a highway in Utah for fallen officers
- No crosses on the headstones in Arlington National Cemetery

Does that sound like an all out assault on Christianity to you? This list is the tip of the iceberg and growing daily. If we remain silent and allow these assaults to go uncontested we are compromising the word and will of God. It is God's will that we would defend the Gospel with love. The church has a responsibility to stand up and defend the word of God.

A few years ago the progressives decided to test our culture and see how far they had progressed with their anti Jesus agenda and NBC introduced a show called The Book of Daniel. A Christian who decided to watch the show said, "I watched the Book of Daniel show on NBC tonight just so I could see if it was as bad as you said. Mr. Wildmon you have it wrong—it was worse than you described. The so called pastor takes drugs, smokes, drinks, takes the Lord's name in vain. He supports homosexuality and drug use. He broke the law by giving out prescription drugs to a Bishop. Two Bishops were committing adultery. They miss-quoted the Bible and the program portrayed our Savior in a joking way. There was a corrupt Catholic priest. The maid smokes pot. The Bishop drinks, the pastor's wife is a drunk and her sister is a lesbian and the son is a homosexual. One son sleeps around. I found this program very offensive to my Christian beliefs. They were poking fun at our Savior."

Thankfully, the show didn't even make it through a full season. But instead of dissuading the progressives it seems to have awakened them. They were not where they wanted to be as far as influencing our culture away from God. They realized they needed to do more to push their agenda and that is what they are doing.

Satan and his team realized they had a ways to go but they didn't get discouraged they were committed to their purpose: getting God out of our culture. They realized they had caught God's children snoozing and they had won some battles. Satan and his followers began to get same sex marriage legalized in some liberal progressive states. They also got Don't Ask Don't Tell repealed. They were riding pretty high after winning these battles and decided it was time to check their progress.

I think we all agree that the old cowboys were pretty rough and tough. They were no non-sense kind of guys and didn't know or care about political correctness. Well, where better to check their progress than to see what kind of a response they would receive by attacking the rough and tough lifestyle of our traditional cowboy. They attempted to strike a blow to the history of our country.

Hollywood came out with a movie called Brokeback Mountain that featured a couple of cowboys who were gay. If they could have success here it would mean they had made significant gains. The movie was pretty successful. We can be sure it has encouraged the progressives that their work is paying off.

We have to understand Hollywood does not have the answers. We need to trust the Holy word. I would like to see HOLY WORD stretched out across a hillside rather than HOLLYWOOD!

Subtle little moves go a long way in pushing the progressive agenda. It is odd how we can get caught up in Soap Operas as if they really reflect life. I am talking from experience. My mom got me hooked on Days of Our Lives from an early age. I was a faithful watcher until I was out of college. Have you ever heard any reference to church, God, or Jesus during a Soap Opera episode? Probably not very often if at all.

Soap Operas are all about romances that go sour. The average adult on a Soap Opera must get married and divorced three times. Nobody ever commits to one husband or one wife. They will all end up getting mixed up in affairs if their character stays on the show long enough. Soap Opera's treat marriage like an old shoe you throw in the garbage when you are done with it. They certainly do not portrait marriage as sacred to God.

There is a tremendous amount of pressure on the church to get things right because lives really do depend on it. The church has to lead the charge. We must be willing in the name of Jesus to take some lumps but we will be fine.

We must gather together in the name of Jesus Christ and become united for his kingdom. Church is where we can do this. Unfortunately, our culture has dismissed the idea of attending church. Forty-five percent of American adults attended church in a typical weekend according to a 2005 survey by Barna.org, not including a special event such as a wedding or a funeral.

From the mid-eighties to the mid-nineties, church attendance was on a roller coaster ride. In 1986, forty-two percent of adults attended a church service during a typical week in January. Attendance rose steadily, reaching a peak of forty-nine percent in 1991, before beginning a very slow but steady descent back to forty-three percent in January 2004.

In a 2006 and 2008 Gallop Poll it appeared the statistics for church attendance was running steady at forty-two percent. Sadly, that means fifty-eight percent of adults in the U.S. are not attending church. The other news that we gleam from these statistics is that we are not winning the war. Nearly a quarter of a century has passed and we are still at the same level of church attendance. We are not losing but we seem to be in a state of gridlock or so we thought.

Unfortunately, new research is indicating that those percentages are about half of what research originally reported. People actually are not being very honest at reporting how often they attend church.

The low attendance level goes back to man and Satan relentlessly proclaiming generation after generation that it is not necessary to attend church. The Bible spells out that we should go to church.

God's word clearly talks about the benefits, blessings, and the covering provided to those who grow roots in a local church. Hebrews says, "Let us not give up meeting together, as some are in the habit of doing, but let us encourage one another—and all the more as you see the Day approaching" (Hebrews 10:25 NIV).

Our decrease in moral standards is likely directly related to our low attendance levels in church. We are accepting moral issues that do not reflect God's point of view at an alarming rate. People who are committed to God do not believe in:

- Terminating life (Over 43 million abortions)
- Censoring the Bible
- Same sex marriage
- Christian pharmacists being forced to prescribe the morning after pill
- Christian doctors being forced to perform abortions
- The notion that it is a hate crime to teach the Bible
- Embryonic stem cell research or cloning
- Cities banning the procedure of circumcision

Earlier I mentioned the church is failing to see people be born again. One reason may be because we are failing at making true disciples. We are not being successful at converting people to a lifestyle change that starts and ends with Jesus Christ. In 2008 less than two percent of all churches in the United States were able to say they saw a single conversion take place in their church.

I believe true conversion comes by the work of the Holy Spirit. Individuals and the church are to create an environment and relationships to help facilitate the process of being born again. We can lead a horse to water but we cannot make the horse drink. We can encourage, disciple, and educate people about the word of God and testify to what He has done in our lives but we cannot make them commit to a lasting, life changing experience this is the job of the Holy Spirit. The Apostle Paul new this when he wrote, "I planted the seed, Apollos watered it, but God made it grow. So neither he who plants nor he who waters is anything, but only God, who makes things grow" (1 Corinthians 3:6-7 NIV).

A Barna Group survey examined the changes in worldview among Christians over the past thirteen years and they discovered some astonishing results. A biblical worldview was defined as believing that absolute moral truth exists. The following statements were used to determine if individuals held a biblical or worldly view.

- The Bible is absolutely true in everything it teaches
- Satan is real not symbolic
- No one can earn their way to heaven by being good or with good works
- Jesus Christ lived a sinless life
- God is all-knowing, all-powerful creator of the world who still rules the universe today

Anyone who held these beliefs was considered to have a biblical worldview. The research was not very encouraging. Only nine percent of all American adults have a biblical worldview. Ninety-one percent of people do not agree with the Bible.

Satan has been very successful. How did he convince ninety-one percent of our adult population that the Bible is not true? Undoubtedly, these adults will pass on this same belief to their children. We have our work cut out for us and we must become diligent with our focus on reclaiming what the enemy has stolen. Satan has managed to deceive us (Christians) with his trickery. We don't even know what is and what isn't biblical.

The church has a responsibility to get people focused more on the word and less on the world. We send missionary's out into the fields to change the world not to have the world change the Word!

According to statistics if we filled a room full of people on January 1st who said they wanted to change and allow Jesus to be Lord of their lives they would all be gone on December 31st of that same year. In one year they would all be gone.

Eleven thousand Evangelical churches got together a few years ago with the goal of recruiting as many people as they could with the hope they would be saved. This was going to be their focus. They were very successful at getting people to come to church but retention became the problem. They thought they had converted nearly two hundred and eighty-four thousand people. But at the end of one year when they got together again they discovered that as a group two hundred and seventy-thousand could not be accounted for. That means they were only successful at actually converting slightly less than five percent of those they had hoped to convert to disciples of Jesus Christ. Statistics show that eighty to ninety percent of people backslide and unfortunately this was no exception.

Why the low conversion? Why are husbands still leaving their wives and children for other women and vice versa? Why are grown men molesting children? Why are gunmen entering theatres and schools killing complete strangers? Why? Why are we loosing so many battles? Maybe it is because we don't understand our role and the role of the Holy Spirit.

What is it that makes converting nearly impossible? What makes a person so determined to live in darkness that they will not commit to a life style change regardless how minor or major the change?

I have witnessed hundreds of people come through the church doors but the doors are made to swing both ways and many who come in leave at some point and chances are they will never come back.

Many churches fail to teach about the Holy Spirit. He is the forgotten God. It is considered taboo to let the Spirit be in control during church services. "You, however, are controlled not by the sinful nature but by the Spirit, if the Spirit of God lives in you. And if anyone does not have the Spirit of Christ, he does not belong to Christ" (Roman 8:9 NIV). I prefer to surrender my will and let the Holy Spirit be in charge.

I really get frustrated every time I run across the statistic that one out of every three adults in the United States have read the book Da Vinci Code. The root of this book is to raise questions of Jesus' deity. If those who oppose God can convince people that Jesus is not divine then we really do not have to worry about our sins because there is no such thing as sin and we do not need forgiveness.

If Jesus does not exist as the son of God then, we all just die and never face judgment. That would mean there is no heaven or hell and this whole concept of creation is absurd. This would essentially allow the door to be opened for paganism.

Paganism is an expression that has been used to describe a belief that is not Christianity. Pagans do not believe in heaven or hell rather they believe in reincarnation. Paganism can be traced back to the middle ages when it was flourishing until Christianity caught fire and became popular. Christianity became so powerful that it essentially wiped out the whole idea of paganism (a victory).

Paganism is a religion which is founded under the concept of worshipping nature. Paganism worships many

Gods and that is why it is at conflict with our God the one and only true God. Paganism cannot survive if people believe in the Bible. This is why paganism must attack Christianity.

The Da Vinci Code is written as a fictional story but the problem is it can cast a little doubt. It allows a little justification for people not to commit to Jesus Christ. It takes time away from people who could read the Bible. I witnessed this one summer on the crew when the book was being passed around. I offered up my Bible for people to read and got zero takers but they were lining up to get the Da Vinci Code.

Again, intentional or not the book and movie plants doubt. It has the capability to weaken the foundation of Christianity. It is a tool for those who want Jesus Christ out of our culture. It is ammunition for the powers of darkness who wish to attack the core of our foundation. What is that old saying? If we hear something enough times it must be reality.

It is not a bad idea to be informed on what these books say. The problem is the majority of the people who are reading these books are uninformed on what the Bible teaches. These books and movies are counterproductive and at some point Christians will get asked questions about what makes the Bible more accurate then the claim that is made in the Da Vinci Code.

We need to be prepared to answer such questions. We can get answers to these questions and other questions if we read our Bible and attend church. Can you imagine how sad it will be on the Day of Judgment when Jesus says to someone, "I see you read the Da Vince Code but you never bothered to read the Book my Father wrote that could have given you eternal life" or "I see you were the first in line to see Brokeback Mountain but you never did see Passions for the Christ." I wonder where their eternal destiny will be.

I am not going to say taking that first step is going to be easy if you decide to attend church and begin a relationship with Jesus. It was a big step for me and many others, a life changing step, and it will be a big step for anybody who has never attended church or who has been away for a long time. But it is a necessary step so we can gather the tools necessary to fulfill our purpose while on this earth.

It is a life changing step when you sign up in God's army. Many people living in the world believe if they start living a life that leads to salvation they are forfeiting their right to have fun. The world believes Christians live a boring life and we are not allowed to have fun. I remember the stereotype. I am certain I said the same thing. I was wrong when I said it and they are wrong. I live an enjoyable, fulfilling life.

It should be encouraging to know God will not give us more than we can handle. He will be with us every step of our journey. His word says, "I will not leave you or forsake you." This means He will not give up on us; He will not abandon us or turn His back on us. Listen to His words. Jesus is saying I am here for you. Lean on me.

God is the one with the big shoulders. He is the one who created the universe. Put your trust in Him. For those who go to church but are not committed get committed! Get off the fence. You signed up for God's army to fight. Come beside the other sisters and brothers and take up your weapon and get engaged.

How do we reengage and start our counter attack? We have read it several times already and the strategy has never changed: "He said to them, Go into all the world and preach the good news to them. Whoever believes and is baptized will be saved, but whoever does not believe will be condemned" (Mark 16:15-16 NIV). This is our mission. We are to reach the world for Jesus Christ.

There are an estimated one hundred million lost souls in the United States alone. These souls are either going to be rescued by God's people or remain imprisoned by Satan. They are living a life that only functions in darkness.

Why are these people afraid to come out of the dark and into the light? We have to be doing something wrong when we have this great news and have no takers. Something is not right.

"Then he (Jesus) said to his disciples, 'The harvest is plentiful, but the workers are few. Ask the Lord of the harvest, therefore, to send out workers into his harvest field" (Matthew 9:37-38 NIV). Thousands of people are investing countless hours, resources, and finances but we are coming up empty.

If there is a harvest and it is ready that means the break down has to be occurring with the workers. Among other things the church does not have the numbers to reach all those who are lost. We need better trained recruiters who can get people to enlist in God's army.

We have been at war in two different countries for over a decade and our military recruiters are turning potential recruits away because the branches of our military are full. They are only looking for a few quality recruits. What do these recruiters know that keeps people wanting to re-enlist? The military is offering a chance to go to war and potentially get killed while Jesus is offering eternal life, yet the military are meeting their quota but God's church is struggling to get anybody who is interested.

It does not make any sense to me. Given the choice to get shot or maybe blown up, or save lives (I understand our military is saving lives) of lost souls one would think God's deal is the safer choice and the church would be enlisting all the recruits. I am very thankful for the men and women in our military. They make huge sacrifices when they enlist in the military and I am very thankful to Jesus because he was sacrificed so we could enlist in God's army.

We need to recruit people from every generation. We have to ground our young people in the way of Jesus. We need to be educated when it comes to our children and our youth.

By eleven children in focus groups say they no longer even think of themselves as children. Rebekah is thirteen and I have been hearing "Dad I am not a child" for two years. Yes, you are! Yesterday's twelve and fourteen year olds are today's ten and twelve year olds.

If we fail to get the word of God rooted in our young people by an early age we may never give them the foundation they need in order to survive in the "world." Studies have shown two-thirds of those who come to Christ do so before the age of eighteen and as many as seventy-five to ninety percent do so before the age of twenty. Think about that statistic. We will only reach ten to twenty-five percent of people after they graduate from high school. We have to work harder to get this pattern changed.

Maybe we can learn something from the Christians in China. China has a long way to go in regards to Christianity and human rights but they have made substantial gains over the last fifteen or so years. In the autumn of 1998 the Chinese church passed a resolution that they believed would help in their efforts to proclaim Jesus Christ. They wanted to develop a well defined role or guide for their theology in building the church. They adapted a "Strengthening Theological Construction" motto in their churches. They believed they could strengthen the church by adapting three-self principles.

They decided and adapted the idea that "Theology is the church in the act of thinking." Thankfully they made a decision to accept the wisdom that comes from the Bible. After accepting this extremely important message it gradually became the focus and attention of the church. They decided that they must ponder all their actions and responsibilities from the standpoint of the mission of the church.

The mission for the church became a theology of proclamation. They were going to spend their energy and resources on proclaiming Jesus Christ is the son of God and eternal life is received by believing in his name.

The Christian churches in China determined that biblical principles and the heritage of the historical church are related to the development and progress of their nation and culture. To me it sounds like they have figured out that they must influence their culture in the ways of the Bible by using the word of God instead of letting Satan influence their culture.

There were sixteen million Christians in China prior to 1998 and after defining a strategy and implementing this new strategy it is estimated there may be over one hundred million Christians in China today. It is hard to know the exact numbers because China is still a communist country and many of the churches are in private homes. Those numbers are pretty amazing considering we are talking about China. Remember this is a Buddhists entrenched culture.

If you recall Bereshith my whole journey began so I could be set free from my marriage. The true freedom I needed could only come from Jesus Christ. Whom the Son sets free is free indeed. We can make all the futile attempts we want to do things our way but in the end it will be wasted energy.

If we insist on traveling down the road without Jesus we will fail. The sooner we can get this revelation through our head and establish it in our hearts the sooner we can begin the journey God has marked out for us.

The biggest challenge we face as a church and as believers when it comes to directing our culture so it will represent God's value system is to get people to fear God. "Now all has been heard; here is the conclusion of the matter; Fear God and keep his commandments, for this is the whole duty of man" (Ecclesiastes 12:13 NIV). We need to fear God not man.

"Praise the Lord. Blessed is the man who fears the Lord, who finds great delight in his commands" (Psalm 112:1 NIV).

We are to revere God and hold Him in the highest honor. The Bible says to fear God is the beginning of wisdom.

The following is an exchange that took place on face book recently. We can gleam quite a bit out of this exchange. It is a reflection of where our culture is at the present time.

The religious bubble. Sorry if this offends any holy rollers but stay out of my bubble. No! I haven't been saved. I haven't found Jesus Christ. I don't want to pray with you. We DO NOT need to hold hands and sing. Yes I'm probably going to hell, I'm OK with that most of my friends will be there (according to you).

Love you!!

Tue at 10:13am

Ha! I love your humor. I'll be down there with ya, (name withheld)!

Tue at 10:36am oh jesus anyway.

Tue at 10:40am

And . . . . see you there (name withheld) LOL

Tue at 10:52am

My sister would want to Kick my A—for these comments too . . . but I say . . . If you can't live your life with humor . . . then you're already living in hell!

Tue at 10:54am

Exactly and shes a Bishop.

Tue at 10:56am

There is no way you are ever going to hell—whatever it may be. You are a wonderful young woman. Just keep on being the sweet, caring person you are. There is more than one way to believe in life. I have many friends that are from all different types of religions, beliefs, or don't necessarily believe in any . . . thing specific thing at all. But, they are good people, who are kind and loving just like you. I wouldn't trade them for anything. I would be missing out if I did. I miss you and you amazing family—tell you siblings and parents hello for me.

It is unfortunate that "religion" has become more about the traditions of man. I do understand how judgmental people come across when they use scripture to condemn rather than encourage. However, don't let that distract you from a relationship with Jesus. He is the way the truth and the life and without Him you will not go to Heaven. Hell is a real and horrible place where a person would be tortured for all eternity. Pursue Jesus and ignore the offensive people. You are so strong and beautiful and have such influence over people I know you will make the right choices and eventually show others how to choose Jesus without being offensive.

OK maybe I should clear this mess up. My religious feelings are private. I don't appreciate touchy, feely, religion, and I'm tired of everyone shoving it down my throat. If you think you have it all figured out then you most likely don't.

Tue at 12:44pm

God bless you . . . . Amen

My god is bigger than most people can grasp. I don't believe a book is going to decide who gets in or not. There are lots of religions in which people treat each other the way Jesus teaches, but they are not considered Christian religions. The people who walk to walk will be in heaven (last entry).

I wonder why there is no fear or reverence for God. If we break this exchange down from the beginning the individual states that she is going to hell and she is alright with that because most of her friends will also be there. I do not believe the devil is going to allow friends to be cell mates in his prison. Obviously, this person does not really know the word of God and she fails to comprehend hell is real.

If you love your friends why would you want to see them in hell? Unfortunately, she gets mostly positive feedback including a few "I'll see you there."

If we look at one of the lengthier responses we read where one person assures the individual she will not go to hell. Really! Is she sure about that? We cannot mock and have a total disregard for God's word and still think we receive His grace. We have fallen for Satan's great deception.

There is not more than one way to get to heaven. Why would you reassure somebody or make such a claim when it is not biblical. Jesus is the way the truth and he is the only one who can give us life. Unfortunately, this ideology echo's the sediment of sixty-four percent of Americans who believe there is more than one way to get to heaven. Jesus will say to these people, "Get away from me I don't know you."

Finally, we see someone makes the comment that he doesn't believe a book is going to decide who gets in or not. We have covered this lesson as well.

Our knowledge of the one and only true God comes from the book called the Bible. Failure to believe in His word gets us a one-way ticket to eternal torture. The Book of Life does matter because if our name is not written in it nothing but torment awaits us.

"Then those that feared the LORD talked with each other, and the LORD listened and heard. A scroll of remembrance was written in his presence concerning those who feared the LORD and honored his name. 'They will be mine," says the LORD Almighty, 'in the day when I make up my treasured possession. I will spare them, just as in compassion a man spares his son who serves him. And you will again see the distinction between the righteous and the wicked, between those who serve God and those who do not'" (Malachi 3:16-18 NIV).

Perseverance and determination must finish its work so we may be mature and complete, not lacking anything. We all need to share a common goal while we are on God's green earth; we are to become mature like Jesus-the Son of God!

If we will become faithful church attendees, and apply the five steps we have already discussed, reading our Bibles, praying to a mighty God, fellowshipping with like-minded believers, being open to changing some habits, and sharing the Good News we will reach unity with each other in faith.

These steps will help us develop the trust in Jesus that we need.

If we will do these few things we will become complete in the knowledge of the Son of God and at this time Satan will tremble and fear the people that God has created to defeat his work.

I have looked at life from both sides now: Life without Jesus and life with Jesus and I like what I found. I prefer to be a NESA (Nobody Everybody Somebody Anybody) not a Naysay! I am a Nobody telling Everybody that there is Somebody who can forgive and love Anybody! My mission is to help rescue those lost souls who are in captivity.

We must all do the work of the ministry of Jesus Christ so we may all be in unity of the faith, and of the knowledge of the Son of God, attaining to the fullness of Christ.

I have learned a great deal since I started writing this book. I believe the biggest lesson I have learned is we do not realize how big our God is. If we truly realized how awesome God is we would not turn to the world, instead we would seek His way.

If we fail to come to the realization how great God is and if we fail to fill the void we are experiencing with a trusting relationship with Jesus nothing else we do counts for anything.

The second thing I have come to realize is the church is more than just a hospital. It is a sanctuary, a training camp, and a war room where disciples of Jesus get together to discuss ways to defeat the works of our enemy. The church is where we make plans to rescue the captives.

Church is where we hear the word of God which gives us the strategy to "Go" conquer and rescue. We are supposed to get excited about doing God's work. He gives us armor and goes before us, our job is easy. All we have to do is speak to people about our savior.

We don't want to be a part of the next generation who disappoints and turns their back on God. We want to come beside an army of millions and rescue souls that are heading into a life of hell. Our desire should be to make God's heart feel good not broken like it was before He flooded and destroyed the whole earth.

Our prayers should be that we do not disappoint our heavenly Father. We need to honor God and exalt Him by standing for Truth. Let us have a greater compassion and take a stand and build on the foundation of Jesus Christ who is perfect in all his ways. Above all let's have a greater fear and reverence for our God.

If we continue to get further away from God: Another young man or young lady will commit suicide when they had their whole life to look forward to. Another couple will be found murdered in our forests because they got involved in drugs. Babies will continue to be born to high school girls or the babies will be aborted by these young teenagers.

If we continue to grow colder to the ways of God we will hear of stories where a teacher takes her first grade class to watch her marry her girlfriend without ever seeking permission from the parents of students and it will not be questioned because that would be politically incorrect.

Satan fights the war from more than one front. He has many strategies and a large army of dissidents including progressives and worshippers of other gods and worshippers of idols. We know who wins the war in the end but the number of casualties that Satan manages to take to hell is unacceptable. There is no treaty at the end of the war. God and Satan are not going to exchange prisoners. Satan keeps all those who never accepted Jesus Christ as their Commander and Chief for eternity.

God created us for no other reason except to fellowship with Him. He loves each and every one of us so much that He gave His only son as a ransom so we could again have an opportunity to fellowship with Him. "For there is one God and one mediator between God and men, the man Christ Jesus, who gave himself as a ransom for all men" (1 Timothy 2:5-6 NIV).

Jesus came to set the captives free. He became the way for all believers to have eternal life. One of the ways he provided for us is the church, his bride. Jesus said, "Come to me, all you who are weary and burdened, and I will give you rest. Take my yoke upon you and learn from me, for I am gentle and humble in heart, and you will find rest for your souls. For my yoke is easy and my burden is light" (Matthew 11:28-30 NIV).

His commands are not burdensome, for everyone born of God overcomes. We have a savior who wants to walk beside us who loves us very much. If he has to he will carry us after all he already died for us.

The greatest war that has ever taken place is occurring in our lifetime. It is a war that has been fought since the beginning of time. Every generation is a part of this war. Some of us have joined the fight, we have enlisted in God's army, and we are on the front lines fighting beside our brothers and sisters. There are others who are AWOL and refuse to fight for various reasons.

This is a war that we must all engage in; it is a war for souls. Our own souls and the souls of family members, friends, and countless unknowns are all at stake. Do not be a deserter you are vital in this war, every person counts. We all have a mission and we all have a journey. We were created for a greater purpose. We were created to stand for a kingdom of good that fights evil. Join and fight the good fight.

"Therefore, since we are surrounded by such a great cloud of witnesses, let us throw off everything that hinders and the sin that so easily entangles, and let us run with perseverance the race marked out for us. Let us fix our eyes on Jesus, the author and perfecter of our faith, who for the joy set before him endured the cross, scorning its shame, and sat down at the right hand of the throne of God. Consider him who endured such opposition from sinful men, so that you will not grow weary and lose heart" (Hebrews 12:1-3 NIV).

Truly Jesus gave it all for us. My journey is really just beginning. I know God has even greater things in store for me. I know He has great things for all of us who will obey and follow His word.

I pray you have chosen the correct ultimatum and light is shining in your lives. I hope you have started on the wonderful journey God has planned for you. Persevere and go on a Rescue Mission for Jesus. God Bless!

BIBLIOGRAPHY

NIV Scripture taken from the HOLY BIBLE, NEW INTERNATIONAL VERSION®. Copyright © 1973, 1978, 1984 by International Bible Society. Used by permission of Zondervan. All rights reserved.

Message Bible "Scripture taken from the Message. Copyright© 1993, 1994, 1995, 1996, 2000, 2001, 2002."

[1]Mark Twain (1835-1910), "Concerning the Jews, in Harper (New York, Sept. 1899; repr. in Complete Essays, 1963)."

[2] Evolution Less Accepted in U.S. Than Other Western Countries, Study Finds By James Owen for National Geographic News August 10, 2006; National Geographic News REPORTING YOURWORLD DAILEY, Thursday October, 2010.

[3] Professed belief is lower among younger Americans, Easterners, and liberals. More Than 9 in 10 Americans Continue to Believe in God by Frank Newport; PRINCETON, NJ—More than 9 in 10 Americans still say "yes" when asked the basic question "Do you believe in God?"; GALLUP January 3, 2011. (www.gallup.com/poll/147887/Americans-Continue-Believe-God.aspx).